Meet Me on Lake Erie, Dearie!

Cleveland's Great Lakes Exposition, 1936-1937

John
Vacha

The Kent State University Press
Kent, Ohio

For the aunts

    (Alice, Eleanor, Helen, Laura, Mary, Rose, Tess, Viola)

and uncles

    (Bill, Clarence, Ed, Elmer, George, Louie, Reg, Vic),

Who might have told me a lot,

    If I'd had the foresight to ask.

© 2011 by The Kent State University Press, Kent, Ohio 44242

ALL RIGHTS RESERVED

Library of Congress Catalog Card Number 2010020019

ISBN 978-1-60635-058-4

Manufactured in the United States of America

Library of Congress Cataloging-in-Publication Data

Vacha, John.

Meet me on Lake Erie, Dearie! : Cleveland's Great Lakes Exposition, 1936–1937 / John Vacha.

    p. cm. – (Cleveland theater series)

Includes bibliographical references and index.

ISBN 978-1-60635-058-4 (pbk. : alk. paper) ∞

1. Great Lakes Exposition (1936–1937 : Cleveland, Ohio)

I. Title.

t5211937.b1 v33 2011

907.4′77132—dc22

                 2010020019

British Library Cataloging-in-Publication data are available.

15 14 13 12 11   5 4 3 2 1

Meet Me on Lake Erie, Dearie!

Cleveland Theater Series

Showtime in Cleveland:
The Rise of a Regional Theater Center
John Vacha

The Music Went 'Round and Around:
The Story of Musicarnival
John Vacha

From Broadway to Cleveland:
A History of the Hanna Theatre
John Vacha

Meet Me on Lake Erie, Dearie!
Cleveland's Great Lakes Exposition, 1936–1937
John Vacha

Contents

Preface

To begin with, let's address any quibbles purists might raise over the inclusion of a volume about an exposition in a Cleveland Theater Series. Theater, as any student of the field will affirm, needn't be confined within the four walls of an auditorium or behind the "fourth wall" of a proscenium stage. Through the ages theater has appeared in such venues as hillsides, wagons, courtyards, town halls, barns, and even boats. A prior volume in this series, *The Music Went 'Round and Around,* told the story of a local tent theater named Musicarnival.

In essence, the theater is show business, and a theater is any place where a show is produced. In the 1930s the Federal Theatre Project provided a "big tent" covering not only "legitimate" theater but vaudeville, circuses, pageants, dance, puppet shows, and even radio. It was in that same period that the Great Lakes Exposition materialized on the southern shore of Lake Erie to put on the biggest show, far and away, that Cleveland had ever seen.

"But for once, at least, we had some big-time stuff flourishing along the lake front," *Cleveland Press* columnist Winsor French put it fifteen years later, largely from personal memory. Other anniversary articles would follow at fairly regular five-year intervals. Some of the earlier reminiscences, such as French's, came from writers who could remember for themselves. More recent observances have necessarily come from the hands—or keyboards—of writers born after the event. Something about the Great Lakes Exposition still fascinates those who were never there. It was, and remains, the biggest party Cleveland ever threw.

When this writer first tackled the subject for a sixtieth-anniversary article in 1996, it appeared in *Timeline,* the publication of the Ohio Historical Society, under the title "Biggest Bash." That left me free to save

Published at the end of the 1936 season, this Willard Combes cartoon from the *Cleveland Press* expresses the showmanship of the Great Lakes Exposition. Its attractions ran the theatrical gamut, encompassing circuses, vaudeville, pageants, water spectacles, industrial exhibits, horticultural displays, ethnic customs, and Shakespeare. *Cleveland Press*, October 13, 1936.

my original title, "Meet Me on Lake Erie, Dearie," for the cover of this far more extensive account. A paraphrase of the *Timeline* head now appears at the top of this introductory essay. I have also drawn upon two extensive interviews conducted for the earlier piece, those with Jean Skelly Garrity and the late Herman Pirchner.

For this volume, I conducted interviews with the dwindling ranks of eyewitnesses: Robert Andree, William Murtough, Dick Panek, Lois Powell Reulb, Cynthia Reese, John Straka, and Fred Schuld. Providing insight and perspective on the afterlife of the exposition were interviews with Matt Franko and Chris Ronayne. Others who were helpful in steering me toward sources of information include Judith Cetina, Scott Franz, Sheldon MacLeod, Cindy Spikowski, Erick Trickey, Evelyn Ward, John Winter, and Jeff Zgone.

I would also like to acknowledge the generous assistance of Dean Zimmerman, chief curator of the Western Reserve Historical Society; Ann Sindelar, Vicki Catozza, and Connie Hammond in the Western Reserve Historical Society Library; Bill Barrow, Bill Becker, and Lynn Bycko of Cleveland State University's Special Collections department; Deborah Hefling at the Cleveland Orchestra Archives; and the staffs of the Photographic Collections and the Science and Technology Department of the Cleveland Public Library.

Special thanks are due to Victoria Nash for transferring these words from paper to computer disc and, as always, to my wife, Ruta, for her constant company and encouragement. Sincere appreciation is also due to the Kent State University Press for its continued support of the Cleveland Theater Series.

Now it's time to put yourself back in 1936 or 1937 and come downtown to the main entrance of the Great Lakes Exposition on the Mall. There may be a Depression still lingering outside, but once inside you can forget about it for a day or two or even a summer or two. Cleveland is throwing a party—the party of its life! There will be exhibits, concerts, rides, shows, snacks, bistros, boats, floral displays, and exotic foreign scenes. Everything from Shakespeare to strippers, topped by a dazzling reclaimed lakefront, awaits your pleasure.

Lakefront Visions

Cleveland's downtown lakefront in the early 1930s was viewed primarily as a convenient dumping ground for refuse—"Tin Can Plaza," the wags dubbed it. Since this was the Great Depression, the refuse happened to be human as well as material. The former were the lowest and loneliest of the down-and-out, the bottom stratum of society even as they constituted the upper stratum of society's dumping ground. An inevitable element even in the best of times, their numbers multiplied exponentially in the hard times of the 1930s. Every city in America had at least one makeshift town of the homeless, located sometimes in parks but more commonly on the edges of railroad yards and garbage dumps.

Named sarcastically after the president popularly blamed for the Depression, Cleveland's lakefront "Hoover City" was described by Noel Francis in the *Cleveland News* in 1933: "Hundreds of homeless and unemployed men have built themselves tiny houses from old sheets of tin and wooden boxes and live in peaceful, if not lavish, contentment." Ramshackle as they were, the dwellings aped the amenities of the city's more comfortable homes, with radios, white-washed terraces, and even "front porches looking out over the water." The strictly male inhabitants raised the Stars and Stripes on a tall pole and even had their own mayor. "If you are curious, and willing to pay a little something, you can go inside many of the houses," confided Francis.

Three years later, the Hooverville residents were gone from the lakefront. In their place had come men with occupations and homes of their own. They were also men with plans. Big plans.

Making plans for the downtown lakefront has always been a popular civic pastime in Cleveland. Before the turn of the twentieth century there had been a park on top of the bluff overlooking the lake, appropriately if unimaginatively named Lakeview Park. It was located on the north side of Lake (later Lakeside) Avenue, stretching from Seneca (West 3rd) to Erie (East 9th) Streets. Walkways led gently down the bluff, past gurgling fountains, only to terminate ignominiously against an obstacle destined to be the bane of all future lakefront planners: the tracks of the Lake Shore & Michigan Southern Railway. Antedating the park, for more than a century they would lay across the path of Clevelanders seeking the recreational waters of Lake Erie.

It was a problem unsolved even by the celebrated Group Plan of 1903, prepared for the city by Chicago architect Daniel H. Burnham and two colleagues. The centerpiece of the plan was a broad civic mall, extending northward from the northeast corner of Public Square to the lakefront bluffs. It would be enclosed by impressive Beaux-Arts public buildings, from a federal building and main library on the south to a county courthouse and a city hall on the north side of Lakeside Avenue. Burnham and company proposed to make a virtue of necessity by anchoring the north end of the mall with a monumental union railroad terminal, set back between the courthouse and the city hall, on the cusp of the bluff and covering the tracks down below.

By 1931 the Federal Building, Cuyahoga County Courthouse, Cleveland City Hall, and Cleveland Public Library had risen as planned, joined on the eastern border of the Mall by the Public Auditorium and the Cleveland Board of Education Building.

The proposed Union Terminal, however, materialized not on the lakefront but on Public Square as a central component of the Van Sweringen Brothers' Terminal Tower Group. City Manager William R. Hopkins promoted a new plan to bridge the tracks with a landscaped plaza leading to a new stadium and exhibition building to be built on landfill north of the railroad. Municipal Stadium had actually opened, despite the Depression, in 1931. Billed at the time as the world's largest outdoor arena, with more than 78,000 seats, it had squeezed in a record-setting crowd of 125,000 in 1935 for the Seventh National Eucharistic Congress.

East of the stadium the lakefront remained vacant until early 1936, when surveyors and a gaggle of local officials appeared to herald the implementation of a new vision for Cleveland's lakefront: the Great Lakes Exposition.

■

"Imagine the possibilities!" urged a letter to the editor of the *Cleveland Press* on the first day of 1925: "An amusement city on the bank of Lake Erie to which would come representatives of all nations!" The figment of the writer's imagination was "a world's fair in Cleveland." Identified only by initials, "R. O. N." ticked off such local assets as geographical location, transportation facilities, research institutions, and the Hulett iron ore unloaders. "It seems to me that the one thing we need more than anything else is a leader—a man with vision; a man who is not afraid and who has ability to organize us into one great working body." A world's fair "would give us a place on the map as a first-rank city," he promised, finishing with a rhetorical challenge: "We have money. We have brains. Have we courage?" No one took him up on it.

In the long run, however, R. O. N. may simply have been a prophet before his time. Ten years later, the planets seemed aligned in a position more favorable for his vision. Yes, there was the Great Depression, but, paradoxically, perhaps that acted more as a stimulant than deterrent. Chicago had shown the way in 1933 with a major world's fair, the Century of Progress, launched in the very nadir of hard times. It was not only a huge success in itself but was regarded as a positive morale builder for the Windy City. Desperate times, desperate measures, perhaps. Three years later, the times weren't quite so desperate, but other cities were still waiting for a serendipitous breeze to waft them out of the economic doldrums. In Cleveland, the times appeared ripe for R. O. N.'s "vision thing."

The way Herman Pirchner remembered it, the idea was hatched in table talk between him and Lincoln Dickey, former manager of Cleveland's Public Auditorium, at Pirchner's Euclid Avenue nightclub, the Alpine Village. "He was a regular guest at the Alpine and often discussed what to do to stimulate commerce in Cleveland," said Pirchner. One night the talk revolved around the possibilities of a summer festival. "Dickey said . . . it would have to attract people from all around the Great Lakes. I said, how about a mini world's fair? Dickey took the ball and ran with it."

In a more official version, Cleveland historian William Ganson Rose wrote about informal discussions among various groups in 1935, culminating in a meeting of himself and Dickey with Frank J. Ryan, a Cleveland Electric Illuminating (CEI) Company vice president. They met at the latter's invitation to draft "comprehensive plans for an exposition representative of the commerce and industry, arts and science, and culture of the Great Lakes States and the bordering provinces of Canada." Writing at the time of the event for the *Cleveland Press*, John M. Johnston corroborated Rose's account and placed the meeting in a room at the Hotel Statler. He added that "the idea had been quietly nursing for some years in the vest pocket of Lincoln G. Dickey," which squares with Pirchner's version.

Obviously, the common denominator was Lincoln Dickey. A native Nebraskan, Dickey had honed his promotional skills as a manager of

It wasn't his idea, but Dudley Blossom, in the words of the *Cleveland Plain Dealer,* was "probably destined to be known in Cleveland history as the father of the expo." He was the civic leader who called the town's movers and shakers together to get their support—and seed money—behind the Great Lakes Exposition. "We've got some wonderful people pulling together for the first time since 1929," later observed the man who had made it possible. *Cleveland Press* Collection.

Chautauqua circuits in the Midwest. Following World War I, he came to Cleveland to manage the Cleveland Athletic Club; then in 1922 he was named first manager of the city's new Public Auditorium. He filled the huge hall with diverse attractions for six years, once simultaneously presenting the Polish pianist Ignace Paderewski upstairs, a poultry show below, and frantically rigging up soundproofing in between. In 1927 the Cleveland Industrial Exposition drew 650,000 to the hall to view the displays inside and a 221-foot illuminated "Tower of Jewels" outside on the Mall. "He was a very good promoter," said Pirchner; so good, in fact, that Atlantic City lured him away the following year to manage its new auditorium. From there he went to New York City as head of the Convention and Visitors Bureau, but he had kept his heart as well as his home in Cleveland.

In Lincoln Dickey, Cleveland had the "man of vision" called for in that 1925 letter to the *Press.* What was still needed was the man "who has the ability to organize us into one great working body"; in other words, one with clout. It wasn't Dickey, but "Linc" knew where to look for him. At the moment that happened to be Maine, where Dudley S. Blossom had gone to beat the midwestern summer heat. Dickey packed up his plans and headed Down East to do the biggest selling job of his life.

Blossom was an outstanding example of enlightened upper-class leadership—noblesse oblige, if you like. A director of many Cleveland corporations, he enjoyed financial independence through his marriage to one of the principal heirs of Standard Oil executive O. H. Payne. Thus enabled to devote his life to civic improvement, he served for ten years as Cleveland's welfare director. Under his tenure, the City (now Metro) Hospital and Cleveland Girls' Farm (renamed Blossom Hill School for Girls) were improved and expanded. "All his life," said the *Cleveland Plain Dealer,* "he has done worth-while things with an intensity and fury which refuse to admit any possibility of failure." Since 1934 he had been chairing the city's annual fall Community Fund drive. He had also chaired a fund-raising drive to complete Severance Hall, home of the Cleveland Orchestra, on whose board he also served. To that particular boardroom he brought not only the expected business acumen but the enthusiasm of a skilled amateur violinist.

In Maine, Blossom turned his trained ear to Lincoln Dickey's pitch and liked what he heard. Once that year's Community Fund campaign was out of the way, Blossom would see how much more the money tree could yield for Dickey's exposition. First he called a meeting of fifteen movers and shakers to get feedback on the project's feasibility. In attendance were a representative cross section of department store, bank, and corporate presidents; editors of the city's three dailies; and the president of the Chamber of Commerce. Ryan was there, along with his boss, CEI president Eben G. Crawford. Their main doubt centered on the city's ability to raise the estimated $1 million needed to launch the enterprise. Blossom personally underwrote the campaign to see if it could be done.

Promoting the cause was a prospectus that opened with a candid statement of the problem: "Cleveland has for several years been so depressed by adverse circumstances that a forward-looking enterprise is needed to revive the spirit of civic pride that formerly characterized the city." Among the remedies that the Great Lakes Exposition might provide, the most immediate was the attraction of hundreds of thousands of out-of-town visitors. Not only would they patronize local businesses for the duration, but many would become repeat customers and possibly even future residents. It would also demonstrate the city's ability to handle a truly big event, thus assuring the attraction of future expositions and conventions. By advertising Cleveland constructively, it would "overcome the destructive publicity that has worked serious harm." Finally, through the participation of community organizations and the development of local leadership, it would provide the desired booster shot to civic self-esteem.

■

At a luncheon at the Union Club on January 20, 1936, Blossom revealed the fruits of his tree-shaking: they had made their million with $37,043 to spare! Among the heaviest hitters, at $25,000 to $50,000 apiece, were such usual suspects as Standard Oil of Ohio (Sohio), Plain Dealer Publishing,

Scripps-Howard (*Cleveland Press*), Republic Steel, U.S. Steel, Ohio Bell Telephone, CEI, and Sherwin-Williams. In the $10,000 to $25,000 class were the larger banks, department stores, and hotels. Substantial contributions also came from such once-familiar local concerns as Telling-Belle Vernon dairy, Warner & Swasey, Richman Brothers, Leisy Brewing, Clark's Restaurants, Forum Cafeteria, and Fries & Schuele. Small businesses also wanted to do their bit, with $50 contributions coming from Cohen's Lunch and the Rockefeller Garage (no relation, presumably, to John D.).

Almost buried under the corporate weight of Blossom's donor roll was a lone individual contribution—a very impressive widow's mite of $2,500 from Josephine Kohler. "I thought it was the kind of thing my husband would have been interested in if he were alive," she explained to reporters. Her late husband Fred, if not Cleveland's best mayor, had certainly been its most colorful. First appointed chief of police by Mayor Tom L. Johnson and extolled by President Theodore Roosevelt as "the best chief of police in America," Kohler was nonetheless dismissed after being caught (framed, he said) in flagrante delicto at the west side home of another man's wife. Eventually he became a "comeback kid" by winning election as mayor in 1921, predicting that he would get the newly enfranchised women's vote: "When I got into that mess I protected the woman's name right from the start." Installed in office, he continued his confrontational style by dismissing several hundred workers to put the city in the black, even if services became noticeably slack. He left his mark visibly by ordering all city property—buildings, poles, park benches, fire hydrants—painted in his campaign colors, orange and black. After two years of Kohler, Cleveland decided to experiment with the city manager form of government for the next ten years. "You can just bet that Fred would have been active in it if he were alive," said his forgiving widow of the proposed expo. (Maybe it's just as well Fred Kohler wasn't around, or the Great Lakes Exposition might have ended up dressed for Halloween.)

With seed money in hand, the organizers proceeded to incorporate. Named general chairman was Blossom, with Mayor Harold H. Burton as honorary chairman. Crawford would serve as president; the four vice presidents included an industrialist (H. G. Dalton), an accountant (A. C. Ernst), and two bankers (I. F. Freiberger and L. B. Williams). An executive committee of eighteen included, besides all of the above, Frank Ryan and future U.S. secretary of the treasury George M. Humphrey. The list of 127 trustees read like a Who's Who of prominent Clevelanders. Among them were Newton D. Baker, former mayor and secretary of war; Congressman Chester C. Bolton; Alva Bradley, owner of the Cleveland Indians; Frederick C. Crawford, president of Thompson Products; Tom Girdler, president of Republic Steel; department store owner Samuel H.

Halle; Cleveland Safety Director Eliot Ness; Louis B. Seltzer, editor of the *Cleveland Press;* Rabbi Abba H. Silver of Temple-Tifereth Israel; restauranteur Vernon B. Stouffer; and, finally, Oris P. Van Sweringen, still a potent name in Cleveland despite the recent double loss of his brother Mantis and most of their fortune.

Day-to-day progress of the exposition would be under the direction of an operating staff headed by Lincoln Dickey as general manager. Dickey picked two former colleagues as his associate directors—his right and left hands. Almon R. Shaffer, associate director in charge of amusements and concessions, was a veteran showman who had worked for the Shuberts in St. Louis and for Chicago's American Exposition Palace before coming in 1927 to help Dickey with the Cleveland Industrial Exposition and remaining to work on other expos and festivals. He pledged to make the Great Lakes Exposition unobjectionable by blackballing any risqué acts. Associate director in charge of sales was the expo's only woman in a position of authority, Peg Willen Humphrey. Since serving as Dickey's secretary during his tenure at the Public Auditorium, she had assisted him in producing several shows in the East. Though she indulged chauvenistic questions by admitting "I bake a pretty fair angel's food cake," she cultivated a strictly business image on the job, eschewing cosmetics, favoring "smartly-tailored suits, with pleated backs and pointed lapels," and putting in sixteen-hour days at her new assignment. "But she doesn't go around flashing S. A. [sex appeal] to sell space," one reporter felt constrained to note, "And she won't hire anyone who depends on feminine charm to get by."

Dickey's staff began gathering expressions of support from the Greater Cleveland community. Pledging the cooperation of the Cleveland Building Trades Council was Albert Dalton, its business representative. Dalton was also president of the Cleveland Federation of Labor, which may have held even more significance. "Realizing the extreme necessity for speed in the exposition, I . . . can assure you that there will be no stoppage of work due to jurisdictional disputes," he wrote to Dickey. Cleveland's chapter of the American Institute of Architects (AIA) appointed a committee to work with exposition officials on architectural questions. Headed by Abram Garfield, son of President James A. Garfield, the committee included fellow architects Antonio Dinardo, J. Byers Hays, Frank Meade, and Frank Walker. Adding their endorsements to the undertaking were the Cleveland Chamber of Commerce and the United States Department of Commerce.

Cleveland's three daily newspapers promptly assumed cheerleading roles. "There is no reason why this 'world's fair' of ours should not be as great a success as Chicago's in 1933 and 1934, and San Diego's in

1935—expositions that were undertaken while the Depression was still going strong. Now the country is getting out of the depression, and Cleveland should show the whole United States in 1936 that it is leading the procession," concluded the *Cleveland News*. "We have had other expositions and shows emphasizing Cleveland's importance as a great industrial center, notably the one in 1927, but nothing comparable in magnitude, in variety, in beauty or in diversity to the proposed undertaking," observed the *Press,* afternoon rival of the *News*. "It is an enterprise which must command the continued support of every element of the community," commented the *Plain Dealer* on the morning after Blossom's Union Club luncheon. "The exposition is a go. Let's go with it!"

■

One more thing was needed besides vision, money, and enthusiasm: there had to be an official reason for the exposition. Merely lifting a city out of the Depression blues wouldn't do; it had to commemorate an anniversary of some sort. Chicago's Columbian Exposition of 1893 had marked, a bit belatedly, the four-hundredth anniversary (quadricentennial) of the discovery of America; Philadelphia had mounted expositions marking the centennial and sesquicentennial of the Declaration of Independence; Chicago's recent Century of Progress had celebrated the hundredth anniversary of that city's founding. That wouldn't do for Cleveland, which was founded in 1796—no one observed 140th anniversaries, and Lincoln Dickey wasn't about to wait another decade for a sesquicentennial. But Cleveland had remained a mere village until 1836, when it was finally incorporated as a city. So that was it: the Great Lakes Exposition would officially celebrate the centennial of Cleveland's cityhood! For good measure, the organizers also came up with an official theme more representative of the Great Lakes region: "The Romance of Iron and Steel."

Though the term "world's fair" was thrown around somewhat promiscuously at first, the Great Lakes Exposition, despite the aspirations of its vision, would fall short of world fair stature. Save for Canada, there would be no official participation on the part of foreign governments, one of the principal criteria of a world's fair. The best that could be looked for in this regard was the unofficial cooperation of numerous foreign consuls and attachés, who announced their intentions to visit the exposition themselves or publicize it in their home countries. Not even the U.S. government would erect an exclusive building, though the Federal Exposition Commission signed up for a generous amount of space in one of the principal exposition buildings.

Officials and trustees of the Great Lakes Exposition gathered on the lakefront on a chilly March Saturday to witness Mayor Harold Burton turn the first spadeful of earth for the Hall of Progress. Burton was using a 126-year-old shovel borrowed from the Western Reserve Historical Society for the occasion, although a modern steel model had actually broken ground. Only eighty working days remained before opening day. Cleveland Public Library.

Size, it seems, also matters in the realm of world's fairs. Focused originally on the lakefront area immediately east of the Stadium, local planners quickly expanded their vision in two directions. Further eastward, they set aside the former Tin Can Plaza on the other side of East 9th Street for an amusement area. Looking southward, they also incorporated the Mall on the bluff overlooking the railroad tracks in their vision, including the Public Auditorium and its underground exhibit halls. Including the Stadium as well as the Mall itself, the exposition would get the rent-free use of $40 million worth of in-place public facilities, in return for which it would assume operating costs for the duration and restoration costs afterward and leave the city with certain permanent improvements to the lakefront, including a horticultural building, gardens, and a 9th Street underpass. Together, the three main areas of the exposition added up to an impressive 125 acres—135, by some accounts. While that fell far short of Chicago's 400 acres or the two square miles of the 1939 New York World of Tomorrow, it at least approached the 185 acres of the future Disneyland. In the eyes of *The Highway Traveler,* organ of the Greyhound bus lines, the size of Cleveland's Great Lakes was a perfect fit: "Large enough to capture the imagination of the visitor with the strange, the bizarre, the magnificent, . . . the Exposition will still not be so immense as to defeat its own purpose by tiring out the visitor completely before he has covered the grounds."

On March 7, 1936, city, county, and expo officials gathered on a wind-swept lakefront to break ground for the first new exposition building, the Hall of Progress. It was only two days after the centennial of the official incorporation of the City of Cleveland. In Europe, it was the day that Hitler chose to formally break the Treaty of Versailles by sending German troops into the Rhineland. Mayor Burton and Exposition vice president A. C. Ernst were more concerned about the possible breakage of a pioneer shovel they had borrowed from the Western Reserve Historical Society to turn the first spadeful of frozen lakefront landfill. They wisely decided to substitute a modern shovel for the hard work, then symbolically transfer the first shovelful to their fragile relic for the cameras.

Time was now the main hurdle facing the Great Lakes Exposition. From groundbreaking to the scheduled June 27 opening remained only sixteen weeks. Back in 1891, Chicago had begun construction sixteen months in advance of the Columbian Exposition. For its 1933 Century of Progress, the same city let out its first building contract a full three years before opening day. Great Lakes officials tapped the man who built the Century of Progress, Albert N. Gonsior, as their construction chief. "My job is to see that a city to accommodate a population of 50,000 persons is built inside an area of 125 acres on the lake front in the next 110 days," Gonsior stated to the local press. "It's a big job, but it will be done on time." Headline writers promptly dubbed him the "miracle man."

A good example of the project's fast-tracking was evident in that first building, the Hall of Progress. With the benefit of research by students at Case School of Applied Science, engineer C. Merrill Barber erected a building made of plywood stressed coverings over rigid timber frames. Strong enough to withstand offshore Lake Erie gusts, it also met the requirements of economy and speed in construction. Next door, steel scissor trusses were soon raised for the expo's other major new structure, the Automotive Building. Designed by Antonio Dinardo of the AIA's architectural advisory committee, it too went up quickly but at 20 percent greater expense because of its steel framing. Both halls were ready for exhibitor setups by the beginning of June. Other structures were taking shape in the expo's skyline, including a horticultural building on the lake, a pageant stage along the railroad tracks, and a monumental band shell up on the Mall.

Alongside such structures, infrastructure had to be installed at the same time. Three miles of alternating corrugated iron and chain-link fencing

Checking on the progress of construction for the Great Lakes Exposition were Lincoln Dickey, Lenox R. Lohr, and Albert N. Gonsior. "Linc" Dickey was named general manager of the lakefront extravaganza he had promoted for years; Lohr, president of the National Broadcasting Company, had served as general manager of Chicago's Century of Progress; Gonsior was the construction chief appointed to keep the Cleveland show on schedule. *Cleveland Press* Collection.

was ordered to enclose the expo on its outside perimeter as well as along the stretch of East 9th intersecting the lower grounds. Its eight-foot height, "tastefully trimmed on the top with three strands of barbed wire" in the words of one reporter, was designed to discourage gate-crashers. Inside, fifteen miles of asphalt paving, twenty feet wide and six inches deep, would carry pedestrian and special bus traffic through the exposition. Connecting the upper and lower grounds, constructed at a cost of $100,000, would be a 350-foot bridge across the railroad tracks.

Some intramural scuffling broke out over the matter of where the show's electricity would come from. Original plans assumed power would be supplied by CEI, expo president Eben Crawford's company. Since the days of Tom Johnson, however, Cleveland had operated its own municipal power plant, designed partly to provide a check on the private company's rates. Early in March, the contract between the exposition and the city was challenged by members of Cleveland's City Council, who wanted some of the power business channeled to the city plant. Since the city's utilities director admitted that the expo's total needs were beyond the current capacity of the municipal plant, the council amended the contract to specify that the exposition would use city power to the limits of its facilities before switching to CEI.

High above the fray, the exposition staffers could view their plant shaping up on the lakefront from their offices in the Terminal Tower. From a nucleus of five at the start, they had multiplied to twenty-five at the beginning of February and eighty a month later. By the time of the event, they expected a workforce numbering around five thousand. Until then, their main job was to fill with exhibitors those buildings going up by the lake. Eleven thousand invitations to manufacturing and business concerns in the Great Lakes region had gone out in December. A field office had already been opened in the Grand Central Palace in New York City, and early in 1936 another was established in Detroit.

Peg Humphrey's sales staffers proved more than equal to their task and soon doubled their original goal of a hundred thousand square feet of exhibitors' space. Among their earliest big catches were the local firms of Standard Oil of Ohio, the Grasselli Chemical Company, and Cleveland-Cliffs Iron Company. U.S. Steel signed on for a large space early in March, followed shortly by Ford, with an even bigger deal. Not only would the automaker be taking a large part of the Automotive Building to show his latest models, Henry Ford also agreed to loan some early cars from his personal collection for the exposition's transportation pageant. Even that was topped four weeks later by Akron's Firestone Tire and Rubber Company, which contracted for 180,000 square feet of space. Too big for even the expo's largest buildings under construction, Firestone would put up the biggest independent exhibit on the grounds. "It's going to be a superior show," promised an exultant Lincoln Dickey.

■

While the exposition took care of its business, Cleveland looked to its own role as host for the big show. With a population of 900,429 in 1930, it was the nation's fifth largest city. (It was probably slightly under the 900,000 mark by 1936, as the 1940 Census would record 878,336 inhabitants.) Suburbanization was barely underway, as three out of every four residents of Cuyahoga County still resided within the central city limits. Exposition officials also touted the city's central location within the heavily populated Great Lakes region. Even before CEI coined its "best location in the nation" slogan, they pointed out that 5.4 million people lived within a hundred miles of Cleveland. Within three hundred miles, considered a comfortable day's drive in the thirties, the exposition could draw from a population pool of 26 million—compared to only 24 million for Chicago.

Cleveland's downtown hotels prepared to make the out-of-towners feel at home. Although, at half a century, the city's oldest hostelry, the ideally located Hollenden, a block and a half from the expo's main entrance, had something new to offer. On April 15 it opened the Vogue Room, dominated by a ten-foot-square blue mirror etched with "modernistic figures." There was dinner dancing nightly from 6:30 to 8:30 and supper dancing from 10:00 to 2:30—all to live music, of course. The Hollenden had one thousand rooms, as did the Hotel Cleveland on Public Square and the Statler on Euclid Avenue (rooms were undoubtedly smaller then). Other downtown hotels included the Carter on Prospect Avenue, Allerton on East 13th, and the Auditorium on St. Clair—the smallest, but closest to the exposition grounds. Best of the outlying inns were the Alcazar and Wade Park Manor to the east and the Lake Shore Hotel to the west. Anyone still needing a place to stay might apply to the housing service of the Cleveland Convention and Visitors Bureau, which had registered thousands of rooms in private homes.

Half a dozen downtown department stores prepared to relieve visitors of their dollars. On or near Public Square were Higbee's, Bailey's, and the May Company. A dozen blocks up Euclid Avenue, the Halle Brothers catered to the carriage trade on Playhouse Square. Filling in between the two squares were Taylor's and Sterling-Welch. Most of the larger stores had promotional tie-ins with the exposition. Specialty shops on Euclid included Cowell and Hubbard jewelers, Burrows' bookstore, and Richman Brothers men's furnishings. For those sated with expo fare, Euclid Avenue also offered several Clarks restaurants, two Stouffers operations, and a Mills cafeteria.

Visitors naturally would be encouraged to venture outside the exposition and see the rest of the town. A special Great Lakes rotogravure section, prepared by exposition headquarters, after four pages of expo

In an era when service stations provided free road maps for motorists, the Standard Oil Company of Ohio (Sohio) prepared a "Map of Cleveland and Guide to the Great Lakes Exposition." Included on the back was a special diagram illustrating how to negotiate a requisite "rotary left turn" on the city's streets. Author's Collection.

views, devoted its remaining dozen pages to a sepia-toned tour of the city's permanent attractions. Industrial scenes, among them ore boats and steel mills, faced such aesthetic destinations as Severance Hall and the Cleveland Museum of Art. The stately civic buildings of the Group Plan were pictured, as were views of Edgewater Park, Euclid Beach, League Park, Playhouse Square, and Brookside Zoo. Lake Erie's "Universal Thrills and Novel Diversions" included the Cleveland Yacht Club at Rocky River, Cedar Point, and the excursion boat *Goodtime*. Many of those sights might be seen on a Royal Blue Line city tour covering thirty-five miles in two-and-a-quarter hours, which left the Greyhound terminal three times a day. City Hall launched a "Clean Up: Company's Coming" campaign to put on a good civic face for sightseers. Sohio and Fisher Brothers promptly announced they would be repainting their gas stations and grocery stores, respectively.

For visitors who preferred to do the city on their own, the Cleveland Railway Company planned to offer five-cent fares in the downtown district. Colorful weekly passes featuring Great Lakes Exposition logos were issued that summer by the company, which was also introducing modern "trackless trolley" buses on some city streets. Powered by overhead electric trolley lines but not confined to the tracks in the middle of the street, the new vehicles could swing over to the curb to pick up or drop off passengers. Greyhound buses would also be much in evidence, both inside the expo and out. A special fleet of the company's minibuses, "the only motorized transportation system inside the grounds," offered complete tours of the exposition as well as shorter hops from one attraction to another. Many visitors, of course, would be coming to Cleveland via the regular Greyhound intercity lines, alighting at the company's local station at East 9th and Superior Avenue. (A package tour advertised in a Greyhound brochure offered three days and two nights in Cleveland, two admissions to the expo and to two inside concessions, a thirty-minute tour of the grounds, the two-hour "Grand Tour of Cleveland," and cab service from bus terminal to hotel—all for $8.25 a person, or $14.50 for five days and four nights.) Most train travelers would enter Cleveland through the subterranean depths of the Union Terminal, climbing the ramps to emerge on Public Square.

Probably a majority of expo visitors would be arriving by automobile. (According to exposition researchers, 10,690,470 of the 23,827,290 cars registered in the United States bore license plates from the Great Lakes states.) Those coming from Pennsylvania and New York along the heavily traveled U.S. 20 would encounter a new exposition information booth in Willoughby, ten miles out, where they would find material and answers about the expo and the city. Once in town, however, many motorists would learn the hard way about a unique feature of driving in Cleveland: the notorious rotary left turn. Cleveland was the only major American city retaining this somewhat eccentric procedure, Washington, D.C., having abandoned it a few years previously. A Sohio map of the city warned drivers about the turn and provided a diagram for their instruction. To make a left turn in Cleveland, cars had to first move to the *right*, make a partial right turn into the intersection but immediately execute what amounted to a shallow U-turn, wait for the light to turn green, and then proceed in the desired direction. Some thought the procedure, by making left turns wait until the light changed, made it safer for schoolchildren; but the main rationale evidently was to keep drivers waiting to turn left from blocking the streetcar tracks in the middle of the street.

With the coming influx of visitors in mind, the Cleveland Advertising Club's Come-to-Cleveland Committee lobbied in spring 1936 to abandon the rotary, or outside left turn, for the inside turn customary elsewhere. When the *Cleveland Press* asked readers for their opinions on the proposed change, it sparked a heated exchange. "Why continue to keep [an] obsolete traffic system to the amazement of your visitors who can't understand how your officials can be so dumb?" challenged a letter from Detroit. "Why should we change for a lot of visitors? They can learn all about that rotary turn on their arrival," responded a Cleveland woman, "and, for goodness sake, let's hope they know enough about handling a steering wheel so they can follow a simple rotary turn." A Cleveland man, in no-nonsense terms, demanded, "Let's discontinue the 'old ladies' favorite turn' for the inside turn." Another maintained, in the voice of reason, that "The one great contribution that Cleveland has to offer to the rest of the United States along safety lines, is the rotary turn. Please do not change it." By better than three to one, the numbers were in favor of keeping the outside turns—although more than a third of the ballots were cast by employees of the Cleveland Railway Company. "I'm here to give the people what they want," commented Safety Director Eliot Ness, keeping his own opinion to himself. In a token concession to visitors, the Cleveland Automobile Club would provide traffic cops with leaflets explaining the Cleveland system, to be distributed to drivers with out-of-town plates—in lieu of traffic tickets, one might hope.

So visitors would have to contend with Cleveland's "old ladies' favorite turn." In turn Clevelanders would have to put up with the closing of Lakeside Avenue between Ontario and East 6th Street, which would be enclosed within the upper exposition grounds. It was seen as "a thorough and unmitigated nuisance" by one east side woman, who filed a taxpayers' petition in Common Pleas Court for an injunction to keep the thoroughfare open. A letter to the *Plain Dealer* remonstrated that "a city is no greater than its 'enterprises,' and individuals intent upon thwarting the efforts of public spirited citizens seeking to enlarge the scope of Cleveland's influence in the marts of the world deserve no place in a progressive community." The court sided with the letter writer, and the exposition's eight-foot fence turned aside Lakeside traffic for the duration of the summer.

■

Meanwhile, back at expo headquarters, Dudley Blossom showed up in mid-April for an inspection. Three months earlier, the *Plain Dealer* had fancied him as having said, in effect, "Now I've got the money for you. I'm going to Florida. You better get busy." He wasn't disappointed in the progress made during his absence. "I'm positively amazed," he declared from the vantage of the Terminal Tower's eighteenth floor. "I had no idea the exposition was going to be so big." All water lines and sewers were laid, allowing work on the surface to continue unimpeded. Footings were completed for the Automotive Building and the bridge over the tracks. Frameworks were in place for the Hall of Progress and the Horticultural Building. On the far side of East 9th, the Italian section of the planned international village was nearing completion.

With his heavy-lidded eyes, flattened nose, and wide, thin slash of a mouth, Blossom looked more like a veteran pugilist than recreational violinist and civic do-gooder. To the *Plain Dealer,* he was the man "who is probably destined to be known in Cleveland history as the father of the expo," but Blossom wasn't loath to spread the credit. "We've got some wonderful people pulling together for the first time since 1929," observed the one who had brought them together. Thanks in large part to the demands of the Great Lakes Exposition, jobs in the building trades of Greater Cleveland would hit a six-year peak in June. "Naturally the public is chiefly concerned with the pleasure and educational attractions of this gigantic show," said Albert Dalton of the Cleveland Building Trades Council, "but we in the labor movement also would like the public to know we have done our bit to make this exposition possible."

Nearly three thousand workers were laboring on the lakefront by the end of June. Nineteen supervisors were directing the efforts of 866 electricians, 806 laborers, 757 carpenters, 135 painters, and 78 plumbers. Some of the more specialized callings represented on the site included 18 plasterers, 16 lathers, 12 surveyors, 8 awning workers, 7 masons, 3 linoleum layers, and 2 tile setters. Although some structural iron workers had briefly walked off the job when they spotted laborers applying welding equipment to some flagpoles, the unions by and large had honored their pledge to eschew jurisdictional disputes.

In addition to those enumerated above, hundreds of the New Deal's Works Progress Administration (WPA) workers had been assigned to specific tasks. Most of these were involved in planting and landscaping the Horticultural Gardens north of the Stadium. In another labor-intensive job, others were engaged in digging out the East 9th Street underpass, which would connect the lower exposition grounds to the amusement zone, allowing continued overhead access to the municipal piers at the foot of 9th Street. Some thirty WPA sculptors, artists, and laborers were working indoors on the upper level, fashioning a $12,000 scale model of the entire city in the basement of Public Hall. Slightly off-site, what was called the nation's largest single WPA project at that time was rushing to complete an eastern gateway to the exposition—Lake Shore Boulevard. Eventually, it would extend eastward to Gordon Park; some five thousand workers had completed the hundred-foot-wide section from East 9th to East 22nd Street. Before the opening of the expo they hoped to open the next stretch to East 49th Street, finally eliminating the trash heaps that had long disfigured the local lakefront.

Last-minute preparations were taking place on all levels during the final days of June. Tickets were on sale in various packages: for $10 one could buy a season pass, for general admission for all one hundred days of the exposition. A popular seller was a souvenir ticket book offering $4 worth of tickets for $2.50. It included five fifty-cent general admission tickets to the expo, plus five individual admissions to such pay concessions as the transportation pageant and the horticultural exhibit. They were very cunningly arranged: anyone wishing to use all five general admissions could take in only one special concession per visit.

On the grounds, a *Plain Dealer* reporter described construction chief Gonsior signing papers, listening on the telephone, and giving an interview all at the same time. "Oh, sure," he confidently responded to the question of whether the show would be ready for the opening on the twenty-seventh. "Incredible, to pass a dump one day and the next to find it a garden, complete with rolling lawns and flowering shrubs, but that's the way they do things," observed Winsor French in the *Press*. When the landscapers set down their tools each evening, another crew moved in to water their work by moonlight. Back in February, Lincoln Dickey had promised that "if nothing unexpected turns up," everything would be ready a week before opening. "The only thing unexpected that turned up was a great lack of difficulty," commented a *News* reporter in June.

About the nearest thing to an unforeseen snag involved the East 9th underpass or subway, necessary to allow unimpeded traffic between the

Several thousand workers labored through spring 1936 to get the Great Lakes Exposition ready for its opening in June. Shown under construction is the Horticultural Building, while men from the Works Progress Administration (WPA) toil to landscape the adjoining Horticultural Gardens. Other WPA crews were excavating a tunnel under East 9th Street and assembling a scale model of Cleveland for a display in Public Hall. *Cleveland Press* Collection.

exposition's lower exhibition and amusement areas. Blocking the way was the *Gerthel II,* a thirty-five-foot unfinished cabin cruiser, which doubled as home for William Chapman, a sixty-eight-year-old former Cuyahoga River dredge inspector. It was in no condition to be launched, and Chapman had no other dry dock to which to move her. When he made the tactical error of leaving the premises, a construction boss decided to simply move the craft to one side and deal with its skipper later, thereby clearing the path for the WPA to come in and excavate. The WPA employed similar methods to evade the potential impediment of governmental red tape. Before they could begin, all WPA projects were supposed to travel through bureaucratic channels, ending with the final approval of U.S. comptroller general John McCarl. By the time word trickled from Washington that McCarl had vetoed the underpass, it happened to be already virtually completed. County WPA director Joseph Alexander received news of the rejection looking like the cat who had just swallowed the canary. In the absence of any more serious obstacles than those, Gonsior's construction deadline was met with little sense of urgency.

The Come-to-Cleveland Committee urged downtown establishments to greet visitors with a "Spectacle of Light." After having been dimmed during the Depression, floodlights were turned back on the city's two tallest buildings, the Terminal Tower and the Ohio Bell Telephone Building on Huron Avenue. Huge illuminated arrows pointing toward the exposition were being affixed to the Higbee Company and the Hotel Cleveland. Other department stores and hotels were preparing expo-themed displays. More than a million bottles of Waldorf Special Great Lakes Exposition Lager, distributed by the Forest City Brewing Company, effectively spread the word over a three-hundred-mile radius. Even the Roxy Theater, Cleveland's burlesque house at 9th and Chester, got into the spirit of things, anticipating the unveiling down the street with its own unveiling in a new revue: "Expo Babies."

■

Cleveland would not be the only show on the road that summer, as comparable expositions were also scheduled for San Diego and Dallas. The California Pacific International Exposition, which had attracted a reported 5 million visitors to San Diego in 1935, was reopening for its second summer. It was arranged around an "Avenue of Palaces," with theme buildings devoted to electricity, housing, fine arts, science, and education. One might view the "world's largest mural" in the Palace of Transportation or a thirty-foot dinosaur skeleton in the Palace of Natural History. Other superlatives included the country's largest zoo area and the "largest pipe organ ever built." Special days were scheduled for every state in the Union, designed to draw not only tourists from out of state but transplanted locals to mingle with "old friends" from their home states. If that didn't pull 'em in, there was always the Nudist Colony in Zoro Gardens. "Here the members of the colony live under the open sky and . . . through their example encourage other persons to appreciate the joys and values of sunlight and natural living out of doors," touted the publicists. "The girls and young men live their outdoor life freely and openly, within sight of visitors for whom special paths and tiers of raised seats have been provided." Promoters were banking on the Nudist Colony as San Diego's answer to Sally Rand at Chicago's Century of Progress.

Dallas had been selected as host city for the Texas Centennial Exposition in 1936. Built around the nucleus of the Texas State Fair, it represented the expenditure of a reputed $15 million. A cool million of that went into the Texas Hall of State, naturally the largest building on the grounds with its Hall of Heroes and museum of Texas history. With typical swagger, Texas governor James V. Alfred led a delegation from Dallas right into Cleveland to pitch his state's expo on the home turf of the competition. The Cleveland team was more than a match for them. Mayor Burton insisted that the Lone Star governor try on a tricorn Mo-

Looks Pretty Good, Doesn't It?

After months of preopening ballyhoo, a million Clevelanders were as eager to catch a peep at the "magic city" rising on their lakefront as this figurative Moses Cleaveland drawn by Willard Combes. Thirty thousand of them showed up on the eve of opening day for a "sneak" preview of the grounds. *Cleveland Press*, June 25, 1936.

ses Cleaveland hat before he would don the ten-gallon hat brought by the visitor. The local Hotel Statler kitchen served what was described as "probably the slowest lunch on record," leaving the Texans little time to promote their show before their train left town. If they were planning any displays of undraped femininity, the Texans for once didn't brag about it. They stressed family values instead, with such attractions as fifty thousand schoolchildren singing "Home on the Range."

Both competing expositions had been off and running well before the Great Lakes—San Diego's since February 12 and Dallas since June 6. On the morning of June 27, however, the nation's eyes shifted northeastward to see what Cleveland had to offer.

Clevelanders were given a "sneak" preview on the eve of the official opening. It was intended for expo officials, workers, the press, and their families, but an estimated thirty thousand stretched the definitions of kinship. They poured in all evening, testing the concentration and forbearance of workmen still applying hammers, saws, and paintbrushes to some final touches. Concessionaires with food and drink in supply didn't mind the gate-crashers at all, as they took advantage of the opportunity to break in their cash registers. A good proportion of the crowd headed straight for the amusement area and some of the night spots they had been hearing about. They saw more electricians than chorines, although a few of the latter showed up later to polish their routines. A good number of previewers still roamed the grounds at midnight.

Back at exposition headquarters in the Terminal Tower, congratulatory telegrams were coming in from all parts of the country. One transmitted through U.S. senator Robert J. Bulkley apologized that "an engagement with which you are familiar and which will require my presence in Philadelphia, will prevent my personal participation in the opening exercises of the Great Lakes Exposition. But I cannot restrain the impulse to give you this assurance of my sincere wishes for the success of the undertaking." This from President Franklin D. Roosevelt, who was expected in Philadelphia the next night to accept the Democratic National Convention's presidential nomination. "Break a leg" messages also came in from Chicago's Mayor Edward J. Kelly and even from Frank Watson, promotion chief of the Texas Centennial Exposition. The one that undoubtedly caused the biggest stir, however, read, "Having spent my earlier years in Ohio, I take this opportunity to wish you and the city of Cleveland unbounded success with your Great Lakes Exposition." Pasted underneath was the name Clark Gable.

....

HARD TIMES ON THE CUYAHOGA

Commuters crossing the High Level (Detroit-Superior) Bridge on the morning of March 28, 1932, were arrested by the sight of a man mounting the railing on the side of the roadway. Two pedestrians, taking in the situation at a glance, ran toward the climber but were too late. The man, later identified as a forty-year-old father of two from the east side, evaded them by leaping ninety feet to the edge of the Cuyahoga River below. He died of multiple injuries an hour and a half later. A former insurance man, he had been jobless for two months.

The victim was a foot soldier in an army of unemployed in Cleveland. A year later, in the statistical pits of the Great Depression, their number was recorded at 219,000—more than 30 percent of the county's labor force. Industrial wages in Cuyahoga County, as reported in one study, dropped from a quarter of a billion dollars in 1929 to under $100 million in 1933. Even those lucky enough to still hold jobs felt the pinch of hard times. City workers sometimes waited weeks for overdue pay; when it came, it might be as scrip rather than cash. A survey found four thousand homeless in Cleveland, many of them taking refuge in several Hoovervilles jerry-built on the fringes of dumps and railroad yards.

But statistics, as Frederick Lewis Allen, a historian of the 1930s famously observed, are bloodless things. Some flesh as well as blood was provided for Cleveland's Depression victims in a sampling of case histories prepared for a congressional hearing on unemployment relief by Edward D. Lynde, general secretary of the Cleveland Associated Charities. One case was that of the Petocky family—John and Sophia and their six children, ranging in age from six months to fifteen years. Petocky (real names, of course, were changed in Lynde's report) had earned good money as a contractor before the Depression but had had no work for close to three years. The family occupied a modest five-room cottage surrounded by a large garden. Though Petocky had made many repairs and improvements on the home, he had lately fallen behind on his mortgage payments. Besides providing food, fuel, and clothing, Associated Charities had also been making interest payments to stave off foreclosure on the house. "To them it represents all that they had hoped to gain in coming to America," commented Lynde.

During the Depression, a man's home was not necessarily his castle. The Davis family, another example from Lynde, "once had a nice home, a piano, radio, and nice furniture" before Davis lost his $30-a-week job. Now they occupied four small rooms in a poor section of the city, dependent on the $5 a week an elder daughter earned doing housework. "All members of the family feel this change in standards keenly," observed Lynde. Another family of four, the Walterses, was compelled to move in with relatives. Andrew Kish, a duco finisher for the Hupp Motor Car Corporation, was able to purchase a home for his family of six. After three years of unemployment had exhausted all their resources, however, the bank foreclosed on them.

Among the saddest victims of the Depression were the children. Olga Kish faced not only eviction from home with her family but the termination of her education at West High School. Shabby clothing hadn't kept her from participation in school activities; lack of money for books, lunches, and bus fare nonetheless confronted her with the prospect of dropping out. Julius Matthew, son of a laid-off city worker, faced the same outcome to his business course at West Tech High School, where he no longer felt comfortable borrowing books and supplies from his classmates. The six children of the Duncan family, who had been sleeping on the floor since the family's bedding was repossessed, faced a more basic deprivation. One of the daughters of the Davis family had become self-conscious following the extraction of several teeth, with no funds available to replace them.

Even under such dire circumstances, families were initially reluctant to appeal for assistance. "The family borrowed from practically all their relatives before applying to Associated Charities," said Lynde of the Davises. Similarly, Enrico D'Amico had supported his family on savings during a year and a half of unemployment, "proud of the fact that they did not have to apply for charity." Even so, there was little enough Associated Charities could do once that bitter step was taken. Joseph and Ida Walters, for example, who together had brought home up to $35 a week when employed, received a weekly food order of $2.70 for them and their two preschoolers. For the Duncans and their six children, Associated Charities supplemented a weekly food order of $5 with a sack of flour.

What most of their clients wanted, which was work, Associated Charities couldn't supply at all. Relief in 1933 was still a local concern, and local resources weren't adequate to the scope of the crisis. Three years later, though the Depression lingered on, the New Deal had ameliorated its worst effects with direct federal aid. One of its programs, the Public Works Administration, approached the problem of Cleveland's homeless with three public housing projects: Cedar Central Apartments, Outhwaite Homes, and Lakeview Terrace. Not only did it replace 943 slum dwellings with new habitations for 1,849 low-income families, but it provided jobs for the workers who built them.

For most people—lay and learned, then and later—the archetypal New Deal relief agency was the WPA. Its approach to unemployment was to give jobs rather than outright relief, even if those jobs were nothing more than raking leaves or digging ditches. Some of the administration's projects were creative, such as murals painted by unemployed artists or state guidebooks compiled by jobless writers. Most of the jobs, however, were just plain, productive labor. As many as 125,000 Greater Clevelanders would pass through the WPA ranks in its eight years. The administration became the butt of many jokes, but it was no joke for those finally working after years of idleness—though most managed to

By 1935 the New Deal was providing federal work relief for the millions of unemployed during the Great Depression. More than a hundred thousand Greater Clevelanders worked in the ranks of the Works Progress Administration (WPA); in one of their earliest projects, they broke ground for the Lake Shore Boulevard that would soon bring many motorists to the Great Lakes Exposition. *Cleveland Press* Collection.

keep their sense of humor. Asked by onlookers what the initials on their project signs stood for, they were likely to respond "We Poke Along."

Early in 1936, the *Cleveland Press* ran a case study of a typical WPA worker. His name—no pseudonyms in this case—was Joseph Nowosielski, and he lived in the city's Polish neighborhood known as Warszawa. Nowosielski's story opened with the day of his "bitterest memory," that of October 8, 1932, when, after losing his job, he was compelled to apply for charity. He had come to Cleveland from Poland a quarter-century earlier to find employment in the Newburgh plant of the American Steel & Wire Company. He also found a wife, Jessie, and together they raised a family of four boys and two girls. Nowosielski made as much as $50 a week during good times, remaining on the job, save for four weeks due to a work-related injury, until the company shut down its Newburgh works for lack of orders. Several weeks later, he made that final desperate trip—not to the High Level Bridge but to the Associated Charities office at East 55th and Broadway. With him went his oldest son, Joey, whose English skills were better. Adding to his humiliation, the social worker taking their application told them to get rid of Brownie, the family dog, because they couldn't afford to feed him.

Their first food order of $9 was supposed to last for two weeks, but after weeks of belt-tightening, they blew it in three days. For the next three years, the family lived from hand to mouth, their biweekly food order supplemented with flour and cornmeal distributed by the Red Cross. Stanley, the youngest child, acquired probably a lifelong hatred of corn mush. They had difficulty with the rent, even after the South Side Savings & Loan reduced it from $22 to $12 a month. Both daughters, Angeline and Lottie, quit school and supplemented the family income by doing housework. Another son, Walter, was taken into the Civilian Conservation Corps, one of the earliest of Roosevelt's New Deal agencies. For six months, he lived in a camp in Sequoia National Park, doing forestry work with other unemployed young city men. He was given meals, shelter, and $30 a month, of which $25 was sent to the Nowosielskis back in Cleveland.

But Nowosielski remained idle except for odd jobs. Although American Steel reopened its Newburgh plant, he failed to pass the physical examination the company required of all workers, both new and recalled. They said he had a rupture; he claimed that if he did, he had gotten it on the job; they countered that it had to have occurred while he was laid off—case closed. Jessie went to the plant to plead on behalf of her husband, but all she got was the offer of a job for their son Joey. That still left the head of the family with nothing to do at fifty-two.

The WPA finally put Nowosielski to work, in the winter of 1935-36. He had to go all the way out to Solon to work on the roads with pickax and shovel, but he didn't mind. "I get fretful when I loaf, and fight with everybody. I like it now, even when I spend eight hours on the road and it is below zero," he said. "Lots of the men grumble. They'd rather loaf. I like to work." He was working thirty-two hours a week and bringing home $55 a month. It may not have been enough to catch up on the family's overdue dental needs, but he was able to take out life insurance again and drop a quarter in the basket at Saint Stanislaus Church on Sundays. And young Stanley didn't have to hide Brownie from the social workers anymore.

As the three-part series on the Nowosielskis unfolded in the *Press*, ground was being broken on the lakefront for the Great Lakes Exposition. Soon hundreds of Joseph's fellow WPA workers would be assigned to projects there. Nowosielski just might have been one of them.

On With the Show

2

June 27, 1936—By noon, a crowd of five thousand had gathered expectantly in front of the main entrance to the Great Lakes Exposition on St. Clair Avenue, filling the 170-foot-deep unoccupied plaza between the gates and the street. Though showers were forecast for later, they waited at present under a hot sun and blue skies. World War I veteran Paul J. Speno had been there for twenty-two hours with steamer chair and worn army blankets in hopes of being first through the gates. It was a well-dressed crowd, even overdressed by later standards, with women in their cotton summer dresses and men in hats, white shirts, and ties. There was nary a T-shirt or baseball cap to be seen. Glancing over their shoulders, they might have appreciated the appearance of that portion of the Mall behind them, cleared finally of temporary structures and parking lots, and attractively landscaped as originally envisioned in the Group Plan.

Most heads faced straight ahead, however, eyes fixed on the imposing entrance to the exposition. Looming seventy feet above them were seven monolithic pylons, spaced at equal intervals across the 460-foot width of the Mall. They were rectangular in shape, seven feet wide by ten feet deep, with flat white surfaces rising unbroken nearly to their tops. Capping each one were three horizontal fins or platforms, with open spaces between to provide contrast by day and special lighting effects at night. At its base, each housed a ticket booth, sheltered by a flat roof extending across and uniting the entire row of pylons.

It had been designed by Anthony Ciresi, an instructor at the Cleveland School of Architecture, the winning entry in a competition judged by the exposition's architectural advisory committee. What the wedge-like triangles of the Federal Building had been to Chicago's Century of

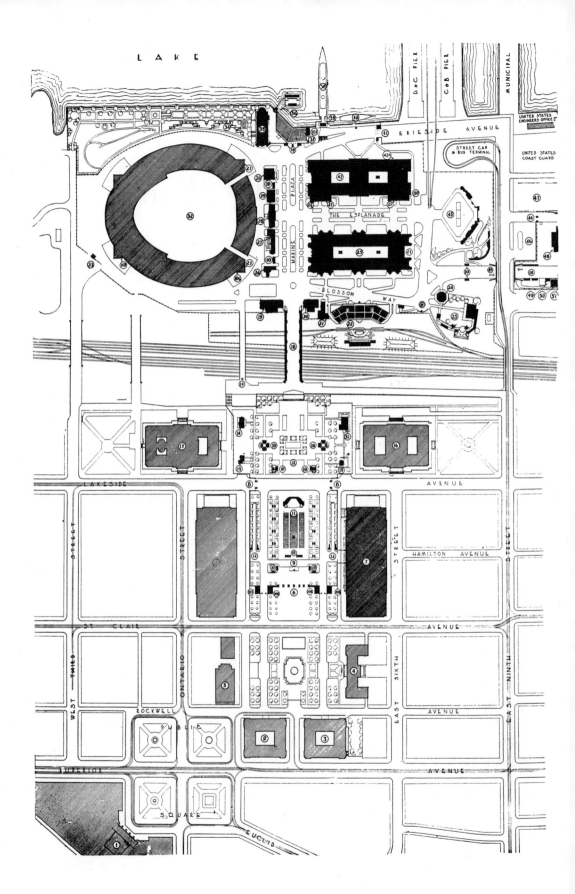

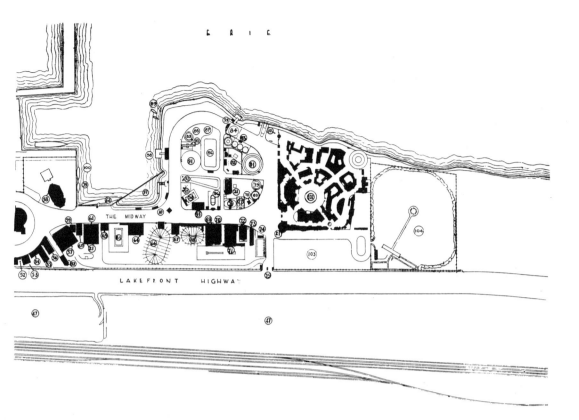

1	TERMINAL TOWER	44 EAST 9TH STREET ENTRANCE.
2	FEDERAL BUILDING.	45 EAST 9TH STREET UNDERPASS.
3	PUBLIC LIBRARY	46 TAXICAB STAND
4	BOARD OF EDUCATION	47 EXPOSITION PARKING LOT.
5	CLEVELAND COLLEGE	48 HERMAN PIRCHNER'S ALPINE
6	MAIN ENTRANCE PLAZA.	RESTAURANT & GARDENS.
7	PUBLIC AUDITORIUM-RADIOLAND	49 MAPLE SUGAR CAMP.
	- HALL OF THE GREAT LAKES	50 YE PHOTO SHOPPE.

GREAT LAKES EXPOSITION
CLEVELAND OHIO

SCALE

Extending for 125 to 135 acres in downtown Cleveland, the Great Lakes Exposition offered hundreds of exhibits and attractions in both preexisting facilities and newly constructed buildings. Its grounds in 1936 included most of the Mall, continued northward to Lake Erie, and then spread eastward across landfill hitherto used primarily as a dumping ground.

Several thousand Clevelanders were waiting for the main gates of the Great Lakes Exposition to open at noon on June 27, 1936, filling the plaza between St. Clair Avenue and the seven imposing pylons that dominated the entrance. Even for a summer exposition, dress codes in the thirties were far more restrained than in later days. *Cleveland Press* Collection.

Progress, Ciresi's menorah-evoking entrance would prove for Cleveland. In ads, brochures, and (of course) souvenirs, it would become the most recognizable logo of the Great Lakes Exposition. Even before the opening, the Bailey Company had mounted half-scale reproductions of the pylons over the entrance marquees of its downtown department store at Ontario and Prospect.

A lot of hopes were raised on what awaited behind those pylons. I. F. Freiberger, vice president of the exposition and the Cleveland Trust Company, estimated the total investment in buildings, exhibits, and landscaping at $25 million. Already, construction payrolls had returned a total of about $9 million back into the community, he observed, with "larger sums" to come in wages to "the thousands who will be engaged in actually operating the industrial show and its expansive amusement attractions over a period of more than three months." Others, such as the *Plain Dealer*'s Mary Hirschfeld, emphasized the project's psychological potential. "Our city is just beginning to emerge from under an unfavorable cloud, aggravated by the Depression, business setbacks, labor difficulties and several crime waves," she wrote, "and the Great Lakes Exposition affords an opportunity to prove to ourselves and to the nation that though we have been staggered a little, we are putting that behind us so that with our natural advantages, civic leadership and steady, earnest citizens, we may look forward optimistically to the next hundred years."

Hirschfeld's newspaper, comparing the record of Phineas Fogg's fictional voyage around the world with the eighty working days in which "the magic city on the lake front" had risen, declared "Jules Verne has been surpassed." On the eve of the opening, the *Cleveland Press* urged Clevelanders to see it early and "spread the word quickly. The success of this Exposition can be beneficial to every person who makes a living in this metropolitan community." "For weeks Clevelanders and their visitors have been on the outside looking in," said the *Plain Dealer* the following morning. "Now comes the hour of revelation."

When noon finally arrived, President Roosevelt pressed a button at his desk in the White House, and the gates between the pylons swung open in Cleveland. A large bell pealed atop one of the pylons, answered by a din of fireworks, factory whistles, and what seemed like every automobile horn downtown. Six army planes roared by overhead, and the sirens of all the fire engines in town were given a five-minute workout in front of their stations. A thousand carrier pigeons were released from the Mall, bearing messages of welcome from the exposition to various home cities on the Great Lakes. Only a colorful ribbon across the entrance separated the crowd from the grounds, and a great-great-great-great granddaughter of city founder Moses Cleaveland was on hand to cut it. A petite Ursuline College junior named Marguerite Bacon, she took several snips with her scissors to accommodate the photographers. First one in after the VIPs was sixteen-year-old east-sider John Soloky, who managed to beat out the ex-doughboy Paul Sperno. Some fifteen thousand Clevelanders surged in behind him in the next half hour.

■

Inside at last, those pioneering expo-goers might have stopped for a moment to take it all in, the lyrics of a topical song of the day running through their heads:

In a rick-shaw here, or a bus over there,
    Let's ride around through Fairy Land,
We will see many things, from "Romance of Steel,"
    To the great big Concert Band.*

---

*"Cleveland, We're Proud of You!" words and music by Margaret Ringgold.

Indeed, just past the entrance, the Cleveland Grays militia company was running Old Glory up the flagpole to the brassy accompaniment of the Great Lakes Exposition Band. Local bandmaster Angelo Vitale led the fifty-piece ensemble, resplendent in white naval uniforms. The Grays, organized in 1837, a year after Cleveland's incorporation, stood out in any crowd with their West Point cadet-style uniforms and towering black busbies. Other uniforms included the scarlet coats, black trousers, and white Sam Browne belts of the exposition guards under the command of Colonel John Hughes (USMC, retired). Scattered throughout the grounds were attractive young ladies known as Yeomanettes, outfitted in smart slacks and yachting caps, there to answer questions or simply pose prettily for shutterbugs.

Straight ahead was the main station for the Greyhound intramural bus service, with a fleet of ten blue-and-white buses waiting to transport visitors to any attraction on the grounds for ten cents a head. Designed especially for the exposition by streamlining virtuoso Count Alexis de Sakhnoffsky, their sleek profiles provided a dramatic contrast to the boxy buses familiar on outside streets. There was room for twenty-six in the free-swinging passenger section, which was attached tractor-style to a separate cab built by Cleveland's White Motor Company. Expansive open-air windows in the carriage provided maximum views for riders. At a separate station to the west of the main entrance, similar buses offered half-hour guided sightseeing tours of the entire grounds for thirty-five cents.

Although Greyhound had a monopoly on motorized transport within the gates, other options were available for the foot-weary. For a dollar an hour, one could hire a boardwalk-style wheelchair or an Asian-inspired jinrikisha, pushed or pulled by a hale young college student on summer vacation. The jinrikishas provided an especially exotic touch to the grounds once conservative Clevelanders overcame their ingrained aversion to appearing conspicuous. There was always the possibility that one might just happen to be hauled by young Bill Burton, son of Cleveland's mayor, who was earning funds for his senior year at Bowdoin College while staying in shape for its football squad. However visitors chose to get around, a spiral-bound *Official Souvenir Guidebook* was available for a quarter to direct them through the exposition.

Located also near the main entrance was a booth housing the "Golden Book of Cleveland." It was the gimmick of Clevelander Alexander von Seitz, who described it as the largest book in the world. Backed by measurements of five by seven feet, six thousand pages, and a weight of two and a half tons, its record likely was beyond dispute. All visitors were invited to register on one of its white linen rag pages, which offered enough space for the four million expected to attend that summer. Von Seitz had already gone to Washington, D.C., in April for his first autograph, "Good Luck to the Great Lakes Exposition" inscribed by Franklin D. Roosevelt. Expo-goers could add their signatures under the president's at no charge, although for a dime they might buy a four-page replica covered in gold foil to certify their registration. According to the booklets, "At the termination of the Centennial Celebration, the GOLDEN BOOK will be dedicated to the citizens of the City of Cleveland and will be placed in the Historical Museum to perpetuate the memory of this great event." By the close of opening day, a total of 61,276 visitors had the chance to record their attendance for posterity.

In homage to the Cleveland-based paint company, a major exposition backer, the entire section of the Mall between the entrance and Lakeside Avenue had been temporarily renamed Sherwin-Williams Plaza. It was dominated by a towering clam-shaped symphony bowl at the Lakeside end, with seating in front for four thousand. The massive proscenium arch framing the bowl rose to an apex of fifty feet and spanned a width of seventy-two feet, with space in the wings for dressing rooms, broadcasting facilities, and technical crews. It was the creation of architect Frank Meade and stage designer Richard Rychtarik, who further wanted the arch to be flanked by a pair of heroic statues personifying Beauty and Protection. Executing the twelve-foot female figures had been the job of five-footer Elizabeth Seaver, a graduate of the Cleveland School of Art. Working twelve hours a day with two tons of clay, she managed to sculpt the twin images in less than four weeks. Cast in plaster with a protective coating of lacquer, they were on their pedestals for opening day.

A small audience assembled in that impressive setting at 2:30 P.M. for the official opening ceremony of the Great Lakes Exposition. Serving as master of ceremonies was Dudley Blossom, who introduced Miss Bacon and reminded those on hand that it was 140 years that week since her forebear, General Moses Cleaveland, had founded the city which still, minus one vowel, bore his name. Mayor Harold Burton extended the city's welcome to the world and shared with listeners the congratulatory telegram sent by Mayor Kelly of Chicago. Senator Robert J. Bulkley took advantage of the occasion to remind constituents of his role in securing federal support for the exposition. Representing the federal government at the opening was Secretary of Commerce Daniel C. Roper, who delivered the nearest thing to a proper speech. "I compliment the people of the Great Lakes region on this striking significant exposition symbolizing the material and cultural progress of this beautiful and productive section of America," said Roper, who urged visitors to take advantage of "the marvelous opportunity to learn about [their] country, to gain a knowledge of our great natural resources and to obtain a better recognition of our nation."

Secretary of Commerce Daniel C. Roper was the featured speaker at the midafternoon opening ceremonies on Sherwin-Williams Plaza. Seated immediately behind him is Dudley Blossom, general chairman of the Great Lakes Exposition, with Mayor Harold Burton on his right. The young woman in the large hat is Marguerite Bacon, a direct descendant of Moses Cleaveland, who had cut the ribbon to open the show. *Cleveland Press* Collection.

Later that evening, Rudolph Ringwall, associate conductor of the Cleveland Orchestra, would enter the Sherwin-Williams music shell to lead an 80-member orchestra in the overture to *Mignon* by Thomas. Also on the opening symphonic program of the exposition were two movements from Dvořák's "New World" Symphony, a Strauss waltz, Elgar's "Pomp and Circumstance," and Tchaikovsky's "Nutcracker" Suite (the "1812" Overture would come the next night). Recruited largely from the Cleveland Orchestra, the Great Lakes Symphony Orchestra would perform nightly except Saturdays, but twice on Sundays. Signed up to spell Ringwall on the podium that summer were Hans Kindler, conductor of Washington's National Symphony; Erno Rapee, former leader of New York's Roxy Theater Symphony; Frank Black, music director of the National Broadcasting Company; Karl Krueger, conductor of the Kansas City Philharmonic; and José Iturbi, renowned pianist and conductor-designate of the Rochester Philharmonic. Afternoon concerts would be provided by Vitale's bandsmen.

Ringwall's inaugural concert was one of many exposition events broadcast both locally and nationally over radio, the mass medium of the day. The opening ceremonies in the shell had been aired, as had the excitement around the gates at noon. Roving microphones carried by local announcers Russell Wise, Gilbert Gibbons, Maurice Condon, and Wayne Mack had picked up the voices of Lincoln Dickey on how the expo had come into being and Marguerite Bacon on the thrill she had felt in opening the show. One of the radio highlights of the day occurred when Gibbons zeroed in on the youngest expo-goer in sight. It was a three-year-old identified as "Billy," who had traveled to Cleveland with his parents all the way from Fort Wayne, Indiana. "Billy," coaxed the announcer, "won't you say hello to the radio audience?" Thousands in radioland waited breathlessly in front of their living room consoles for the kid to say the darnedest thing. Billy, focused more on his ice cream cone than celebrity, just said "No."

■

Radio played a major role in the script prepared for the Great Lakes Exposition. Enclosing the entire eastern edge of Sherwin-Williams Plaza was the broad limestone facade of Public Auditorium, which the exposition had appropriated for Radioland. A canopied entrance in the building's western wall invited visitors into what the guidebook called "the world's largest broadcasting studio." Admission was free, as it was for the concerts outside, too. Running Radioland activities was Ralph B. Humphrey, a former advertising manager for local station WTAM. By chance or otherwise, he was also the husband of Peg Humphrey, the expo's sales director.

With a potential live audience of thirteen thousand, Humphrey no doubt really had the world's largest radio studio at his disposal. Ten thousand of those seats were contained in the building's nucleus, Public Hall, opened in 1922. An additional three thousand were available in the adjoining Music Hall, which was completed in 1928. The two halls were built back-to-back, sharing a single stage divided by a movable stage wall. Mention of a revolving stage in contemporary coverage, along with the thirteen-thousand seating capacity claimed by exposition publicity, would indicate that the most popular programs were witnessed by audiences from both halls.

Unlike television programming of today, network radio shows were produced by their commercial sponsors, not broadcasting companies. To attract shows to Radioland, the exposition offered not only to provide Public Hall rent free but to assume line charges for the broadcasts. In addition, standby musicians would be available through an agreement with the Cleveland Musicians' Union. A new public address system was installed, using state-of-the-art developments in radio pickup and transmission to carry every word uttered on the stage to the rear of the far balcony. In return for all this, the exposition received a big, glamorous attraction for its patrons as well as priceless national publicity for the length of the run.

Some of the earliest shows signed up for Radioland included *Fibber McGee and Molly, Cities Service Concerts, Kellogg's Singing Lady,* Standard Oil's *Stars Over Great Lakes,* and Ben Rubin's *National Amateur Night.* Also on Radioland's wish list were Paul Whiteman and his orchestra, Guy Lombardo and his Royal Canadians, Kate Smith and the A & P Gypsies, Walter Winchell, Rudy Vallee, and former Clevelander Bob Hope. Plans called for radio stars to appear in dry runs for matinee audiences, followed by live broadcasts in the evenings. Local programs on Cleveland's four AM stations (WTAM, WGAR, WHK, and WJAY; FM was still in the future) would also originate from Radioland.

One of the earliest stars to show up in person was singer and actress Irene Rich, who did a program two weeks after the expo's opening. A few days later, comedian Ed Wynn attracted an audience of seventy-five hundred on a Tuesday evening for his trademark lisping and giggling shtick. Though largely lost on the radio audience, part of Wynn's routine called for several costume changes into absurd getups for the benefit of the studio audience. (This was before the days of laugh tracks, when the comics really had to be funny.) Following the broadcast, Wynn and some of the other stars continued to perform for the live audience. Needing a couple of pianos positioned for an impromptu duet, the "Perfect Fool" turned to the wings and called for "Mr. Chrysler"—Walter Chrysler, his radio sponsor—and Mr. Chrysler promptly appeared to help set the stage for his star. (Actually, "Mr. Chrysler" was identified later as stage manager John Fitzgerald, but who in the far reaches of Public Hall could tell the difference?) Afterward, Wynn talked mostly about his son Keenan, who was then honing his acting chops doing summer stock in Maine.

■

After the show, Radioland audiences might head to the rear of Public Hall, where a staircase would take them down to the lower exhibition area, now known as the Hall of the Great Lakes. This was the room Lincoln Dickey had soundproofed for Paderewski's benefit. There were no poultry exhibits now, but with broadcasting going on above, insulation would still serve good purpose. According to the exposition guidebook, "Historical, educational and cultural exhibits by federal, state and local governments tell the story of the Great Lakes states and cities in the Hall of the Great Lakes." It was also the designated headquarters for visiting delegations from the four hundred groups allotted special days during the expo.

A prime attraction amid the thick posts in the sprawling, windowless space was the relief map of Cleveland fashioned by the artists and artisans of the WPA's Federal Art Project. According to the guidebook, it depicted the city as seen from an altitude of two thousand feet and was built at a cost of $12,000. A reporter later stated the perspective as being from fifteen thousand feet—maybe it depended on how far the viewer stood from the display. It must have been impressive from any perspective: its thirty-one-foot width represented an expanse of eighteen miles and contained a total of four hundred thousand miniature buildings. A "panoramic view" of the city in 1836, mounted on the wall behind, provided a dramatic contrast with the Cleveland of 1936 modeled below.

Cleveland past and present was the dominant focus of exhibits in this area. Much of the past could be seen in the display of the Western Reserve Historical Society, which contained objects and documents associated with Moses Cleaveland. One letter by the founder described how the Fourth of July had been celebrated in the year of Cleveland's birth: "Drank a few patriotic toasts and supped and retired in remarkable order and decency." There was also the sole surviving copy of the city's first newspaper, the *Cleaveland Gazette & Commercial Register* of July 31, 1818, with its fanciful front-page account of the sighting of a thirty-two-foot "Lake Serpent." Various artifacts of pioneer life, such as spinning wheels, lockets, and portraits of early Clevelanders, could be seen in the exhibit of the Early Settlers Association of the Western Reserve. Guides in period dress demonstrated such old skills as hackling, carding, spinning, and weaving. The feminine side of Cleveland history was highlighted in a booth of the Women's Centennial Commission of 1896, a group founded to observe the city's hundredth birthday and still extant forty years later. They had on display a replica of the aluminum time capsule containing various documents and artifacts, sealed in 1896 and slated to be opened in 1996. Also on view was a mural depicting women in various stages of Cleveland history, painted by Lurabel Long of Lakewood, a Cleveland School of Art student.

An entire "room" in the hall was set aside to honor Cleveland's most famous artist. This was Archibald Willard, a self-taught painter known largely for one work. He originally called it *Yankee Doodle,* but it became one of America's most familiar icons under the title *Spirit of '76*. It being the hundredth anniversary of the artist's birth, a Willard Centennial Commission had organized the display to memorialize the occasion. On view undoubtedly were samples of Willard's popular nineteenth-century genre scenes, such as *Pluck* or *Pluck II,* reproduced as chromolithographs by the thousands. Naturally the *Spirit of '76* was the highlight of the exhibit, although the record is unclear as to which version was on view. Willard painted it more than a dozen different times, including the one he did for City Hall, right across Lakeside Avenue. Conflicting accounts identify the expo's copy as having come from City Hall, the Western Reserve Historical Society, or even Marblehead, Massachusetts, home of the original version that had been the hit of Philadelphia's Centennial Exposition of 1876.

Contemporary Cleveland was also well represented in the hall, with booths sponsored by such service organizations as Dudley Blossom's Community Fund, the Convention and Visitors Bureau, the Chamber of Commerce, the Better Business Association, and the Ad Club's Come-to-Cleveland Committee. The Girl Scouts were there, as were the Cleveland Council of Parent-Teachers and the Cleveland Conference of Educational Cooperation. There was a display on local slum clearance housing projects by the federal government. Demonstrations on resuscitation and other lifesaving techniques were given by the Cleveland Fire Department, while the police department offered an exhibition on the process of fingerprinting. Of more morbid interest was the plaster death mask of a recent murder victim police were trying to identify.

Neighboring governments, ranging from adjoining suburbs to places on the far side of Lake Erie, also set up displays in the Hall of the Great Lakes. Bay Village, Bedford, Chagrin Falls, Cleveland Heights, Garfield Heights, Hudson, Parma, and Shaker Heights were among the former. Fairport Harbor, Lorain County, and Erie County were also represented, as were chambers of commerce from Akron, Lorain, Columbus, Newark, Marietta, and Cincinnati, all in Ohio. From out of state were displays by the state of Illinois and the Monroe (Michigan) Business Men's Association. Here, too, was the exposition's sole contribution from a foreign government, Canada, consisting principally of an exhibit from the recent Toronto Industrial Exposition. Canada also hoped to raise its profile with later visits by Canadian army and air force units and a troop of Northwest Mounted Police.

A series of drawings on the Romance of the Great Lakes began appearing that summer in the *Plain Dealer.* Rendered in chiaroscuro tones of black and white by the paper's editorial cartoonist, James H. Donahey, they depicted everyday scenes of work and recreation from the crowded

Yesterday a dump—TODAY—well, go take a look for yourself!

A *Plain Dealer* cartoon by James Donahey expressed the amazement of Clevelanders over the transformation of their lakefront on the opening weekend of the Great Lakes Exposition. On the site of a former city dump, tourists now surveyed the landscaped grounds in boardwalk chairs. Donahey also executed a series of drawings for the *Plain Dealer* on the "Romance of the Great Lakes," which was subsequently placed on exhibit at the expo. *Cleveland Plain Dealer*, June 30, 1936.

Cuyahoga to the distant locks of the Sault Ste. Marie. In September the entire collection of twenty-five originals was added to the attractions in the Hall of the Great Lakes.

■

There were 130,000 square feet of space in the underground exhibition area of Public Hall—but that was only the half of it. In 1929 a new subterranean exhibition area was added under the northern section of the Mall. Known as the Lakeside Exhibition Hall, it offered an additional 130,000 feet, the total of the two spaces being equal to the combined capacity of the two largest buildings just constructed on the lower grounds. Visitors could enter the Lakeside hall directly from Sherwin-Williams Plaza inside the main entrance via two gently graded ramps, but an underground passage beneath Lakeside Avenue also provided egress from the Hall of the Great Lakes. Those taking the latter route might linger for a minute between two concourse exhibits sponsored by the Cleveland Auto Club and the Museum of Natural History.

The entire Lakeside Exhibition Hall was devoted to nearly ninety exhibitors from business and industry, from light to heavy. In the former category were displays of "the food and canning industries on parade," led by a local grocery wholesaler, the William Edwards Company. With its label on everything from peas to catsup, Edwards was the Cleveland counterpart to Pittsburgh's H. J. Heinz Company—which was on-site with an exhibit of its own. Most of the local food exhibitors were from the dairy and confection sector, from Dairyman Milk, Fairmount Creamery, and Telling-Belle Vernon to Josephine Mae Candies and Quality Ice Cream.

Amid all this wholesomeness were somewhat incongruous displays by the M. & N. Cigar Company, Cleveland Home Brewing Company (makers of Black Forest beer), and the Distilled Spirits Institute. For some strange reason, the latter seemed more intriguing to newspaper reporters than ice cream producers. "The entire process of manufacturing whiskey takes place," recounted one in loving detail, "from the arrival of grain in freight cars to the emergence of little barrels to a shipping room by a conveyor belt." Sponsored by an association of national distillers and operating under the supervision of the Cleveland office of the Federal Bureau of Internal Revenue, the miniature plant could actually produce five gallons daily of the real McCoy. "The product is not sold or given away, but is, sadly enough, poured down the drain," observed the reporter soberly.

Cleveland's printing industry made an impressive showing in the Lakeside Exhibition Hall. There were five lithography companies and two publishing concerns, including the Penton Publishing Company, one of the nation's leading producers of business magazines. The mechanical branch of the industry was represented by the Addressograph-Multigraph Company and Harris-Seybold-Potter, a manufacturer of heavy printing presses. Other local concerns included the Chase Brass & Copper Company, Dougherty Lumber, Medusa Products, and the Grasselli Chemical Company. National exhibitors ranged from Coca-Cola and Scott Paper to National Cash Register (NCR) and International Business Machines (IBM).

"Chicago glorified science; California, climate," Lincoln Dickey had said. "Dallas will promote petroleum and agriculture, but Cleveland will present the romance of iron and steel manufacture." The industry was well represented by such exhibitors as the American Rolling Mill Company, National Malleable & Steel Castings Company, Superior Die Casting, National Steel, U.S. Steel, and the Lake Superior Ore Institute. Participants from northern Ohio included Cleveland-Cliffs Iron Company, which had brought the first iron ore through the Soo in 1855. Other local concerns involved were Pickand Mather's Interlake Iron Company, Lorain's American Shipbuilding, Youngstown Sheet & Tube, and Republic Steel.

At the heart of the Lakeside Exhibition Hall was "The Romance of Iron and Steel," the official Great Lakes theme exhibit. "It was made the theme of the Exposition because of Cleveland's position as the geographical center of the steel-producing district, the 'Ruhr of America'," wrote John M. Johnston in the *Cleveland Press,* passing on the fact that the Great Lakes district produced more sheet steel daily than the rest of the world combined. This was reinforced by the *Plain Dealer's* Dale Cox, who observed that the Great Lakes accounted for two-thirds of the nation's entire steel ingot capacity.

Sponsored by many of the participating steel companies, the exhibit was developed by a committee under the direction of Dr. Abram Alan Bates, professor of metallurgy at Case School of Applied Science. It sprawled over half an acre in the underground hall. Among the items contributed by various companies were models of mills, wire-drawing machines, an ore unloading dock, an electric steel furnace, and laboratory equipment. "The oldest veteran in the steel industry cannot recall any occasion when the steel industry has made a more elaborate attempt to exhibit its operations and its wares to the general public," reported Cox.

"It takes the visitors behind the scenes of iron and steel making," attested the guidebook. At the very beginning it plunged the expo-goer into the ocher-hued depths of an iron ore mine. Various chambers showed mining operations and early examples of iron making such as a medieval forge and a beehive furnace. Visitors eventually came to a bridge, under which lay a relief map of the Great Lakes region, with real water

Part of "The Romance of Iron and Steel" exhibit at the Great Lakes Exposition was this full-scale model of a beehive furnace, which was used to smelt iron ore prior to the Industrial Revolution. Located in the Lakeside Exhibition Hall, the expo's theme exhibit highlighted the importance of the Great Lakes region to the nation's steel production. Cleveland Public Library.

filling the lakes and running from Superior and over Niagara Falls into Ontario. Murals above showed scenes of the loading and unloading of the ore and the long boats that carried it from the mines of the Mesabi in Minnesota to the mills of Cleveland and Youngstown.

"Towering in the center of the exhibit is the cast house of a modern blast furnace," related Ralph Kelly in the *Plain Dealer,* "and wanderers along the way of steel may stand as dwarfed humans and feel as steel hands feel the might of the structure that rears above them." Through the interplay of color and lights, the cross section of a Bessemer converter gave the illusion of being in actual operation. In the course of their peregrination visitors came upon another full-scale replica, in this case one of a 125-ton pouring ladle. They might walk with perfect safety right into the fifteen-foot scoop, filled now not with white-hot liquid metal but "photographs picturing the entire open hearth method of refining iron into steel." Nearby a foundry floor was laid out to demonstrate the production of ingots from molten steel. There was also a thirty-four-foot model of a hot strip mill showing how steel slabs were rolled out in sheets one-thirty-second of an inch thick and then stamped into miniature auto body parts.

After their journey through the claustrophobic confines of mines and mills, it must have been a refreshing experience for visitors to take the stairways from the Lakeside Exhibition Hall and emerge on the sunlit Mall above. That would have put them on the northernmost section, flanked on the east by City Hall, on the west by Cuyahoga County Courthouse, and on the south by Sherwin-Williams Plaza, beyond Lakeside Avenue. It was called the Court of the Great Lakes for exposition purposes. Beyond attractive landscaping, on opening day it offered visitors four comparatively modest exhibits in the far corners of the space.

Cleveland past might be seen on the City Hall side in the form of two log cabins. The one closest to Lakeside Avenue was the Garfield Memorial Cabin, a replica of the 1831 birthplace of James A. Garfield, Cuyahoga County's contribution to the U.S. presidency. Said to contain logs taken from the original, the reproduction was designed to conform to contemporary accounts provided by the martyred president's descendants, one of whom was the expo's supervising architect, Abram Garfield. It contained furnishings contributed by members of the Early Settlers Association and was surrounded by a well and smokehouse, all enclosed within a zigzag rail fence. Behind it was another pioneer structure, representing the tavern of Lorenzo Carter, Cuyahoga County's first permanent settler. Designated the County Civic Exhibit Building, it housed historical, civic, and cultural displays. Whether any tavern fare was available remains unrecorded.

Two buildings in the shadow of the county courthouse might be said to have represented Cleveland present and future. They were model homes erected by Cleveland's building industry, which had also sponsored the cabins across the court to provide a dramatic demonstration of how home construction and comfort had been improved over the previous century. Though intended to showcase the latest in home plans and furnishings, the two models were anything but modern in design. A brick house put up by the Cleveland Builders Supply Company was described as of "Regency period design, reigning architecture of the 19th century." Furnishing the home's five and a half rooms (no separate dining room, just a "dining alcove" adjoining the living room) was the main exposition contribution of Bailey's department store. A specially reinforced beam beneath the foundation allowed for the permanent post-expo relocation of the structure.

Contrary to expectations, perhaps, the wooden house sponsored by the Cleveland Lumber Institute was decidedly the more upscale of the two. While the brick Bailey's home could be had completely furnished for

$12,000, it would take a cool $30,000 to duplicate the frame Georgian-Colonial manor known as the Halle House. The name partially explained the difference, but besides furnishings provided by Cleveland's premier department store, the all-wood home contained eight rooms and two baths plus breakfast room and "powder room for guests." There was black walnut paneling in the library, while the living room boasted woodwork and one entire wall of waxed Florida cypress. "Depression?" Halle's seemed to be saying, "What Depression?"

Something was missing from the Court of the Great Lakes on opening day, however—it lacked a centerpiece. That space had been set aside for an Ohio Building, but on June 27 there was no building, just grass. A $75,000 appropriation bill had been introduced in the Ohio General Assembly several weeks earlier, but was subsequently held hostage by the House Finance Committee. Some downstate representatives objected to spending the money for "a fair" while needs for poor relief and flood relief remained unmet. Republicans also objected to leaving the appointment of a planning commission to a Democratic governor. "Surely the Republican group at Columbus which is responsible for this muddle cannot fail to realize before long that its attitude is rather juvenile," editorialized the *Plain Dealer.*

Someone either grew up or cut a deal, because Governor Martin L. Davey got his appropriation, though belatedly. Even though A. N. Gonsior put a rush tag on the job, the building wasn't ready for visitors until four weeks after the exposition's opening—too late, in fact, to even get into the official guidebook. Whether by design or not, it was finished just in time to be dedicated on the governor's fifty-second birthday, July 25, which Lincoln Dickey designated as Governor's Day. Davey came up from Columbus in summery white shoes and trousers, blue blazer, and straw hat to dedicate the state exhibit and cut pieces of birthday cake provided by the Laub Baking Company for visitors.

Finally settled in its place of honor, the Ohio Building was an unassuming white stucco structure with an elevated entranceway under the greeting "Ohio Welcomes You." Inside, the windowless walls were covered with murals depicting such state assets as the Ohio River, Wright Field, McKinley's tomb, Ohio Stadium, and of course, a beaming Martin L. Davey. In the center was an open court containing a landscaped patio, spouting fountain, and plenty of chairs and matronly hostesses. Looking on the bright side, the *Plain Dealer*'s Roelif Loveland concluded, "it looks like one of the best places in the whole exposition area in which to rest."

The most impressive thing about the Court of the Great Lakes, however, wasn't what was on it; rather, it was the view *from* it. Turning away from the upper grounds, the visitor beheld a breathtaking panorama to the north: colorful pennants snapping in the breeze, gleaming white

Rising above a floral reproduction of the expo's logo are the upper grounds of the Great Lakes Exposition. To the right are the wooden and brick model homes on the Court of the Great Lakes. Seen beyond Lakeside Avenue are the back of the Sherwin-Williams music shell and the seven pylons marking the main entrance. Cleveland Public Library.

pylons reflecting the midday sun, and the expo grounds stretching eastward literally as far as the eye could see. In the words of one editorial, it was truly a "magic city on the lake front." And straight ahead—across a beckoning bridge and just beyond the landscaped grounds, within reach at long last—lay the glistening waters of Lake Erie.

Hardly a third of the Great Lakes Exposition lay behind them; expogoers still had a long way to go.

LET THERE BE LIGHT!

If not the biggest, promoters of the Great Lakes Exposition had no qualms about promising that it would be "the best lighted exposition the world has ever seen!" They based their certainty on "the fact that Cleveland is the center of the lighting industry, both research and practice of the entire country, and might even claim, very modestly, that same title in the world."

That claim rested primarily on the presence in East Cleveland of Nela Park, the pioneering industrial research campus of the General Electric Company's lamp division. Even as the expo's buildings were beginning to rise, engineers at Nela Park were revealing the development of a "frosty-white tubular bulb about a foot long and as thick as a [*sic*] ordinary walking cane," capable of producing "a brilliant white light . . . that would make the ordinary 85-watt bulb look yellow."

So fluorescent lamps came into the world on the eve of the Great Lakes Exposition, raising the bar even higher for lighting expectations in Cleveland's lakefront extravaganza. "Lighting engineers who are planning night illumination of the Exposition grounds are determined that the finished results of their work will come up fully to the standards which the country could reasonably expect from Cleveland," gushed the expo's publicists.

Given such advance buildup, turning on the exposition's lights for the first evening became as momentous an event as opening the gates had earlier that day. "That Man" in the White House, President Franklin Roosevelt, had performed the midday honors by pressing a button in Washington; for the nighttime ceremony, engineers enlisted the services, symbolically speaking, of the Man in the Moon.

It sounded somewhat like a Rube Goldberg arrangement, in which the telescope of the Warner & Swasey Observatory in East Cleveland was trained on a position in the sky where the moon was expected to be at precisely 8:22 P.M. When the earth's rotation brought moon and telescope into alignment, reflected light sped from the moon to a photoelectric cell at the lower end of the telescope. The resultant impulse was thence relayed several miles to the exposition grounds, firing off a bomb and starting the generators humming.

And voila! From the sky over Lake Erie sprang a man-made aurora borealis, spreading a rainbow-hued fan of light over the Marine Theater and across the lower exhibition grounds. "The aurora borealis makes an enchanted roof of moving, changing colors for the theater," wrote David Dietz, Scripps-Howard science editor, in the *Cleveland Press*. "Sitting beneath this canopy of light is a novel and thrilling experience. When the beams are spread wide apart, you can sometimes catch a glimpse of the stars behind them."

Varied lighting effects quickly flashed from one area to another throughout the grounds. In the plaza fronting the Marine Theater, batteries of floodlights, concealed in the faux crow's nests of sixteen poles representing masts, illuminated the pennants fluttering above and bathed the thoroughfare below in artificial daylight. Mercury Mazda

As the home of General Electric's Nela Park lighting laboratories, Cleveland was expected to put on a spectacular lighting show for the Great Lakes Exposition. GE and Westinghouse engineers created dramatic nighttime effects on the surfaces of such expo
structures as the Porcelain Enamel Building. "In fact," summarized one historian, "the use
of light was one of the major contributions of the Exposition." Cleveland Public Library.

lamps displayed the foliage of the Horticultural Gardens, while mush-
room lamps outlined the walkways between the plantings.

Pylons around the Hall of Progress and the Automotive Building were
revealed in the glow of indirect spotlights. Some glistened with colored
light reflected from chromium-plated corrugated metal facing. Four
banks of floodlights outlined the slender white shafts of the seven pylons
marking the main entrance on St. Clair Avenue, then were reflected by
the alternating red and blue horizontal planes at their summits. One
minute after the illumination of the exhibition area, another explosion
signaled the lighting of the glitzier amusement zone.

Engineers from both General Electric and Westinghouse had contributed to the overall effect. General illumination was provided by two hundred eight-foot standards, each containing a five-hundred-watt lamp in an
opal glass shade. No wires obstructed the view above, all wiring having been
installed underground. Fully lit, the Great Lakes Exposition consumed
enough power for a city of fifty thousand—roughly the size of Lakewood.

Beyond the special effects and the utilitarian illumination of the grounds, lighting was also intended to highlight the exposition's buildings to best advantage. Streamlining was declared one of the exposition's dominant architectural goals. Thought was also given to the general color scheme of red, white, and blue, particularly the last. Otto Teegan, an associate of *Ziegfeld Follies* designer Joseph Urban, came up with a hue he called "Great Lakes Blue." Avowedly inspired by Lake Erie, Teegan described it as "a combination of cobalt, ultra-marine and lapis lazuli." Not nearly as much care was expended on the red, which to Roelif Loveland seemed a "curious shade which was made just to go with the blue."

On the whole, the exposition's architecture received rather indifferent reviews. "The utter simplicity of these buildings, their frank expression of interior structure, and their generally 'realistic' or factory-like appearance were eminently suitable for providing economic exhibition space and were also expressive of the industrial theme of the Exposition," architectural historian Eric Johannesen summed up many years later.*

The dominant architectural leitmotif of pylons achieved inconsistent effects. Seen in proper proportion and perspective, as in the seven dramatic pylons of the main entrance, they were indeed impressive. As used indiscriminately in the lower exhibition area they proved distracting, forming, in the words of *Architectural Forum*, a "misshapen false front hiding the very interesting structure of the Automotive Building."

In the final analysis, light carried the day. "As a demonstration of the modern faith in scientific systems and functional design, the lighting and the architecture of the Great Lakes Exposition gave ample evidence of Cleveland's position in this movement," wrote Johannesen. "In fact, the use of light as an architectural element was one of the major contributions of the Exposition."

New York Times correspondent Lucius Beebe captured the overall effect from a fantastic night vantage point: "As with any fair on a similar scale of magnificence, it is best seen at night, and preferably from the air," he wrote.

> For then Cleveland's Great Lakes Exposition stretches in a broad demi-lune of multi-colored phosphorescence, under the shifting light of a hundred converging and retreating searchlights and the flicker of flowering bombshells, a bright pattern of avenues and terraces, promenades, midways and pavilions from the St. Clair Gates and the Court of the Presidents to the farthest stretches of the Streets of the World. . . .

---

*Eric Johannesen, *Cleveland Architecture, 1876–1976* (Cleveland: Western Reserve Historical Society, 1979), 190–93.

From 3,000 feet its esplanades and plazas gleam blue and white, while the Admiralty Club's caravel and the docked steamers of lake lines stand out like marginal splashes of illuminated animation against the unlighted background of Lake Erie. It is an exciting and glamorous setting from overhead, and at closer approach its multiple details of design and execution are no less imaginative.

The consensus seemed to be that the Great Lakes Exposition had fully justified Cleveland's reputation as the "World Capital of Light."

3

Bridge to the Lake

From the Court of the Great Lakes on the exposition's upper level, the way to the lower level led over the newly constructed bridge known as the Court of the Presidents. Straight ahead from the head of that bridge, one could see one of the most pictured vistas of the grounds. On either side in the foreground was a row of massive golden eagles that wouldn't have been out of place in Mussolini's Rome. The foot of the bridge opened into a broad promenade lined with pennant-draped poles in the form of ship's masts and yardarms. To the left loomed the huge mass of Municipal Stadium; to the right stretched the two principal freestanding exhibition buildings. In the far distance, the panorama culminated in the Marine Theater on the lakefront, crowned after sunset by the brilliant artificial lighting effect dubbed the Aurora Borealis. It was the nighttime view that turned up most commonly, in all its garish glory, on picture postcards.

To get there, one must first cross the bridge—pardon, the Court of the Presidents—which actually extended out from the Lakeside Exhibition Hall. Though jinrikishas and minibuses had their own lanes in the middle of the span, it must have been more fun to traverse its 350-foot length on foot. "A hundred booths line the sides of this broad bridge," read the official guide, "bringing to it the historic atmosphere of the medieval European bridges." Typical perhaps of the offerings along the way was the "hum-all" concession of the three Goldstein brothers. Described as "a species of buzzing instrument," it had provided the trio with a living for seven years. "It's a caution, the way some of the old people dance and cut up with these instruments," said Morris Goldstein. "They have a good time. I have a good time. We all have a good time." Probably akin to the novelties known as kazoos, the item undoubtedly contributed its

The Court of the Presidents bridge took visitors from the upper to the lower grounds of the Great Lakes Exposition. Its name memorialized the sixteen U.S. presidents from the Great Lakes states, each of whom was depicted on a pedestal surmounted by a sixteen-foot eagle. Built expressly for the expo, the bridge fulfilled citizens' long-held dreams of spanning the railroad tracks that separated downtown Cleveland from the lakefront. *Cleveland Press* Collection.

share to the desired festive note on the grounds. One can almost visualize a contemporary pied piper of Cleveland cavorting with his hum-all down Marine Plaza, followed by not rats, we hope, but a conga line of fair-going kiddies.

About those eagles: there were sixteen of them, eight to a side, lined up like monumental pharaohs along the banks of the Nile. Designed by Cleveland sculptor Frank Jirouch, each towered more than thirty feet above the bridge's surface—sixteen feet of gilded eagle with upraised wings on a sixteen-foot pedestal. As well as a decorative purpose, they also served an educational one. Each was intended to commemorate a U.S. president who was either native to or elected from one of the Great Lakes states (hence, "Court of the Presidents"). As the self-styled "Mother of Presidents," Ohio led the list with William Henry Harrison, Ulysses S. Grant, James A. Garfield, Rutherford B. Hayes, William McKinley, William Howard Taft, and Warren G. Harding. Pennsylvania had contributed James Buchanan; Indiana, Benjamin Harrison; Illinois, the towering Abraham Lincoln. New York's impressive delegation included Martin Van Buren, Millard Fillmore, Chester A. Arthur, Grover Cleveland, Theodore Roosevelt, and the incumbent, Franklin Roosevelt. The base of each memorial bore a portrait of its president with a plaque descriptive of his accomplishments (admittedly a challenge, in some cases).

Had anyone paused to look back from the foot of the bridge, he could have taken in an expansive floral display on the bluff below the Cuyahoga County Courthouse. This was the official logo of the Great Lakes Exposition—a somewhat busy design consisting of a map of the five Great Lakes enclosed within a border circumscribed by a mariner's divider with its pivot anchored pointedly on Cleveland. Blue petunias filled out the lakes, while dusty miller outlined the divider. Lacking the eye-riveting simplicity of the trylon and perisphere of the 1939 New York World's Fair, for example, the Great Lakes logo was generally replaced on souvenirs or brochure covers by such architectural standouts as the main entrance pylons.

■

Before exploring the lower level, expo-goers by this time might have stood in need of some creature comforts. Planners had anticipated their wants by placing a cafeteria and a drugstore on strategic corners at the gateway to Marine Plaza. To the right was a complete Standard Drug store, housed in a rectangular art deco building with a rounded corner at the main entrance. Here might be found a complete supply of emergency medicines, toiletries, cigars, candies, and of course, souvenirs. Like all other outlets in the fifty-one-store chain, it boasted a soda fountain as well—in this case a suitably expansive one running 120 feet along three of its four walls. Just beyond the drugstore stood a comfort station, which met other needs.

Opposite the drugstore, to the left was the exposition cafeteria, housed in a similar building with a tall vertical fin dividing the double entrance in its rounded corner. "Order a delicious, reasonably priced dinner at the big, clean, cool Exposition Cafeteria and then let our hostess suggest what is inexpensive and interesting to see at the great Fair," read an ad in the *Plain Dealer*. Entrees ran fifteen and eighteen cents, sandwiches ten or fifteen. A side of slaw or cup of joe cost a nickel; a slice of pie, eight cents. The cafeteria was open from 11:00 A.M. to 11:00 P.M., with table service available from 8 P.M. to midnight. For those in a real hurry, fast food 1930s style could be found in the ten hamburger and hot dog stands operated throughout the grounds by the Clark Restaurant chain.

At the end of the Court of the Presidents was one of the major crossroads of the exposition. Extending to the lake at upper left was Marine Plaza, while to the right, Blossom Way led to the amusement zone. On the corners of the intersection, clockwise from twelve o'clock, were the Automotive Building, the Standard Drug store, the expo cafeteria, and the Christian Science Reading Room. *Cleveland Press* Collection.

Suitably refreshed, the visitor might have continued toward the lake, straight down the roadway dubbed "The Street of Ship Masts" by the *Cleveland News*. To the west, the massive, pale yellow brick bleacher section of Municipal Stadium served as backdrop for four minor exposition buildings. First came the Christian Science Building, followed by the Newspaper Headquarters, the Porcelain Enamel Building, and the Western Reserve University Building. Christian Science buildings were inescapable fixtures in expositions of the period, having made appearances at Chicago and San Diego, currently in evidence at Dallas and Cleveland, and destined for resurrection in New York in 1939. The Great Lakes version was cut from the same cloth as the rest, with information booth, conversation room, reading room, and murals illustrating the history of the religion's official organ, the *Monitor*. It probably gave the Ohio Building stiff competition as a favored space to recover from exposition fatigue.

Much livelier, no doubt, was the Newspaper Headquarters next door. It must have been a second home for Roelif Loveland, who was churning out hundreds of words of expo copy daily for the *Plain Dealer*. John Johnston of the *Press* and Gerold Frank for the *News* were also assigned to the Great Lakes beat. At times Glenn Pullen and Josephine Robertson of the *Plain Dealer* and Jack Warfel and Winsor French of the *Press* put in their hours pounding out color pieces on the bulky Remingtons or Underwoods. Other facilities and tools at the disposal of local or visiting journalists included telephones, two darkrooms, a garage for press cars, and daily news releases from the expo's publicity director, Johnny Miskell. Early coverage of the exposition appeared in the *New York Times, Detroit News, Chicago Daily News, St. Louis Globe-Democrat, Newsweek,* and *Time*.

The truly unique attraction in the row along the Stadium was the Porcelain Enamel Building. If its gleaming bright walls of red, orange, violet, and blue didn't entice the eyes of passersby, the futuristic disk mounted on a spindle above its roof should have given them pause. Like a portent of the postwar flying saucers, it paraded the letters PORCELAIN ENAMEL on its slowly revolving rim. The building, with its aesthetic appeal, served a functional purpose as well. "The Porcelain Enamel Building at the Great Lakes Exposition is an example of the latest type of porcelain-on-steel construction," stated the exhibit's brochure. "This building is not intended to be permanent, but its attractive exterior would last for hundreds of years if necessary."

There were fifty exhibitors inside, extolling the application of porcelain enamel on everything from ashtrays and appliances to exterior siding. Stove manufacturers headed the list, with refrigerators and washers also in abundant evidence. A swinging steel ball demonstrated the material's toughness by failing to make an impression on a test panel. Local enamelist Edward Winter, who had created eleven murals in the medium for the building's walls, gave demonstrations of enamel firing. One of the hall's chief sponsors was Cleveland's Ferro Enamel Corporation, which provided an on-site model enameling plant and on Enamel Day took a hundred technicians out to view the real thing at its plant on East 56th Street. Four years earlier, Ferro had built the nation's first porcelain enamel house in a Cleveland suburb; unfortunately, no one asked the company for one to place alongside the traditional brick and wooden model homes on the Court of the Great Lakes.

Cleveland's major institution of higher learning at that time was Western Reserve University, which attested its preeminence with its own building at the exposition. Designed by Carl Guenther of the university's School of Architecture, its straight, modern lines were accented in the school colors of red and white. As "the greatest promotional opportunity Western Reserve University ever had," in the words of a school official, it contained an office for interviewing prospective students and displays illustrating the research of faculty members. Geology professor Jesse Hyde had persisted, despite ill health, in trying to perfect a model of flood control in the Muskingum Valley for the exposition; it was completed by two colleagues following his sudden death. There was also an alumni lounge, where a revolving three-foot world globe doubled as a pincushion to illustrate the far-flung homes of graduates.

■

Although the Marine Theater was the destination point at the end of the Marine Plaza promenade, a major attraction beckoned the traffic westward. It presented a fifty-foot-tall facade dominated by a mural depicting a female deity—possibly Chloris, goddess of flora—framed by scenes of planting and harvesting. Under the mural and above the entrance, providing a classical touch to the modern lines of the architecture, was a single word: "HORTICULTURE," with roman-style "U"s.

This was the doorway to the Horticultural Building and Gardens, which required an admission charge of twenty-five cents. There were some complaints about this, the first separate entrance toll within the exposition grounds, especially in view of the fact that the gardens were planted largely with the aid of federal funds. Lincoln Dickey answered by pointing out that the exposition had supplemented the $178,000 WPA appropriation with $100,000 of its own. In addition, after the expo both building and gardens would be conveyed to the city as permanent lakefront improvements. Noting that Chicago had charged forty cents for entrance to its horticultural exhibit, Dickey promised that for only a quarter, Great Lakes would deliver "a many times better show."

Behind its towering front, the Horticultural Building tapered down a 25-foot incline to the lake in a series of three terraces. Each level culminated in a graceful bay, putting viewers from the lake in mind of "the prow of an ocean liner." A uniform 60 feet in width, it stretched 190 feet from entrance to end. There were outdoor terraces off the upper two levels, with window boxes and umbrella-shaded tables on the middle deck. One entered on the top floor and descended to the ground level, which ended in a tearoom overlooking the lake.

All was under the general sponsorship of the Garden Center of Greater Cleveland, with contributions from allied groups ranging from the

Mentor Headlands Garden Club to Our Garden Club of Rocky River. Serving as chairman was Mrs. Elizabeth Mather, who had taken shovel in hand to plant the first tree outside back in April. Many area garden clubs took advantage of the invitation to conduct their meetings in the building. On the top level were changing flower shows, beginning with peonies in June and ending with mums in October, with roses, cacti, daisies, orchids, and dahlias among others blooming in between. The two lower levels were given over to exhibitors, both commercial and nonprofit. There was an insect zoo sponsored by the Cleveland Museum of Natural History, presumably located a safe distance from the Venus flytrap.

While all those shows and teas were undoubtedly pleasant and had their followings, for the majority of expo-goers the Horticultural Building's main function was to serve as antechamber to the gardens without. Accessible from the lower level, they received rave reviews. "This garden is an example of what may be accomplished by WPA labor when it is put to work on good plans under expert supervision," said the *Cleveland Press*. "The 500 men who worked on this job took great pride in it, and they are entitled to." To H. E. Varga, Cleveland's director of parks and public property, the gardens represented "an adventure in an awakened civic conscience. . . . Everyone who worked for these really magic gardens and who works for them now . . . to keep them as beautiful as they are, have [*sic*] earned great satisfaction and glory. They are among our proud possessions, pearls of rare beauty."

Taking most of the bows for these kudos was A. Donald Gray, the man assigned the task of designing them and supervising their construction. An intense, tireless perfectionist of forty-five years, he was Cleveland's leading landscape architect, known to the general public primarily as gardening editor of the *Press*. "I salute Mr. Gray," said Varga. "The very life-blood of his soul has gone into these gardens. Such an accomplishment was truly worth the heroic effort." Not the least of Gray's lifeblood was shed in putting the screws on Senator Bulkley to secure approval of the WPA appropriation. Word of his final success hadn't come until the end of March, leaving Gray only sixty-eight working days to get his garden in. Every shoot and shrub was in place by opening day, with the single exception of an Ohio State Highway plot delayed, as Gray dryly put it, by "a lot of red tape."

Gray had a gargantuan canvas on which to spread his floral oils: a strip of reclaimed land 1,000 feet long—a fifth of a mile! Situated directly north of Municipal Stadium, it gradually widened from 125 feet to twice that once past the curve of the building's facade. In area it covered three and a half acres, with Lake Erie as a northern border.

The plot fell away from the Stadium in a twenty-two-foot bluff, which Gray made imaginative use of in his scheme. He ran a pergola for five hundred feet along the top, overlooking a series of rock gardens, waterfalls, and naturalistic plantings of laurel, rhododendron, andromeda, ferns, mosses, and vines. "The view from this pergola walk will look down over the rock garden to the panel of lawn and bright flower borders across the promenade to the Lake beyond," he wrote. "The visitor might well be in some Italian Lake Villa."

According to the *New York Times,* informed opinion considered the display "among the best and most complete ever staged at an exposition of this kind." Its correspondent described how "water cascades, dashing down the hillside, amaze the gardener who is unaware of the modern electrical device which keeps the water in a continuous circular flow." Occupying a prominent position midway in the garden was a fountain presented by one of the expo's vice presidents, A. C. Ernst, and Mrs. Ernst. It spurted thirty-five feet into the air and gave a twenty-five-minute performance to colored lights at night. The expansive western end of the gardens was anchored by a sculpture, *Awakening,* by Clevelander William McVey, loaned to the exposition by the Cleveland Museum of Art. Here was also a "color organ" on which NBC artist Lew White gave daily concerts. "Special colored lights, revolving discs and other gadgets aid in building up an illusionary effect," reported the *Plain Dealer.*

Numerous special gardens filled the middle and lower levels. Annuals, perennials, evergreens, and roses all had their place in the sun. "Gardens of the Nations" were prepared with the aid of Cleveland's many nationality groups to demonstrate their contributions to American horticulture. One of the most popular attractions was a series of ten gardens illustrative of changing stages in Cleveland's gardening history. From a 1796 frontier garden, they advanced through the Civil War and the vegetable plots of the World War, to a silver and blue futuristic garden of 1950. "In a sun dial garden of 1900 were smooth lawns with croquet sets, and it wasn't hard to imagine the proper ladies in sweeping skirts and the men with high stiff collars who should have been having a dandy time there," wrote Josephine Robertson.

But perhaps the most rewarding spot in the gardens was one of the simplest: a broad gravel walk, lined with shade trees and benches, extending along the entire length of the garden at the very edge of Lake Erie. It may well have been from one of those benches that an editor of the *Cleveland News* saw the lesson the gardens held for the city. "It may seem to you like a lot of money—until you have seen this spectacle yourself and contrasted it in your mind with the ugly front porch the lakefront used to be," he—or she—wrote. "When the exposition ends let's win the rest of the lake front for Cleveland."

■

Covering three and a half acres between Municipal Stadium and Lake Erie, the Horticultural Gardens were widely regarded as one of the major triumphs of the Great Lakes Exposition. They were planned by local landscape architect A. Donald Gray and planted by workers of the Works Progress Administration. Among the garden's special features was a fountain contributed by A. C. Ernst, one of the expo's vice presidents, and his wife. *Cleveland Press* Collection.

As gratifying as it may have been to be able to sit and, metaphorically speaking, drink in the lake, the rest of expo couldn't be denied. There was too much to see yet! Retracing their steps through the gardens and Horticultural Building put visitors back in front of the Marine Theater, which consisted of a large amphitheater facing the lake, with a stage on the far side of a wide channel. Water shows were presented twice daily, with precision routines in the lagoon by a troupe of champion high school swimmers. Their marine ballets were swum to the strains of Strauss's "Blue Danube" and a new ballad by Walter Logan, one of the Radioland music directors:

> Meet me on the shores of old Lake Erie,
> Meet me where the summer breezes play—

Join the happy throng in song and laughter
Come where life is bright and gay—*

Professional acts such as an adagio dance team and five aquatic clowns supported the scholastic swimmers. The biggest waves were created by 250-pound "Tiny" Gorman, making his entrance from a diving board. Prior to the afternoon show and following the evening one, models on a runway in front of the stands presented a May Company Style Revue. Admission to the combined bill was free, save for a reserved section at a dime a seat.

Continuing eastward along the lakefront, one passed a large sandpit and two ships: a steamer and a sailer. The sandpit was an arena for sand sculptor Claudie Bell of Atlantic City. One exposition publicity stunt that hadn't floated was a plan to have Radioland opened by the two-year-old Dionne quintuplets pushing a button from their Ontario nursery—an idea killed by prohibitive costs. Bell soon compensated for that loss by reproducing little Marie, Cecile, Yvonne, Annette, and Emilie in sand right on the southern shore of Lake Erie. The feat took him three days.

Anchored stern to shore, the steamer was a 350-foot former car ferry out of Conneaut christened the *Marquette-Bessemer II.* It had been refitted in the West 54th Street yards of American Shipbuilding into a floating nightclub, the SS *Moses Cleaveland.* Mrs. Martin Davey, Ohio's first lady, baptized it with water from the five Great Lakes (some of which certainly hadn't had much of a trip). There were two clubs aboard the vessel, one public and the other private. On the lower deck was the Show Boat, offering nationally known dance bands and a "nautical bar with attendants in sea faring attire." One could board the nightclub from shore via a gangplank or from a speedboat by a hanging ladder, at a toll of a quarter during the day, half a dollar at night.

It took considerably more to gain access to the ship's top two decks, which were restricted to members of the Admiralty Club. Limited to a socially select four hundred, membership was by invitation only and extended to such luminaries as Mayor Burton, Dudley Blossom, Eben Crawford, Lincoln Dickey, Walter Halle, Leonard Hanna, Philip Mather— the usual crowd, in other words. For a $25 fee, the select received entry in the form of a "passport" good for the season. Among the amenities was a Limoges china service from Higbee's, featuring red sailboats on

---

*"Meet Me on the Shores of Old Lake Erie," words and music by Walter Logan (Cleveland: Evan Georgeoff Music, 1936). This was designated on the sheet music as "Official Song of the Great Lakes Exposition."

a sea of black waves, designed by renowned local artist Viktor Schreck-engost. There was dancing to music by Russ Lyons, piano playing by Roger Stearns—but no gambling. Thinking that a floating nightclub might give a wide berth to state and local antigambling ordinances, a syndicate had sounded out Dickey on the possibility of stocking the *Moses Cleaveland* with roulette wheels. "We shall have a few games of skill, certainly, but we shall not have one game of chance on the grounds," proclaimed Dickey in refusal. One thing "Linc" may have found room for aboard the *Cleaveland,* according to at least one report, was his own administrative headquarters. That would have put his desk a hop, skip, and a jump from his table at the Admiralty Club.

Next to the *Moses Cleaveland* was a three-masted sailing ship, identified by large letters along the entire length of its hull as "BYRD'S SOUTH POLE SHIP." For a quarter's admission, expo-goers could board the vessel, the *City of New York,* which had carried Admiral Richard H. Byrd on his first Antarctic exploration expedition. Descending into the hold, they could view not only the crew's quarters but a model of Byrd's Little America base on Antarctica. The ship by this time was as familiar with the Great Lakes as with the Antarctic Ocean, having spent two summers anchored at Chicago's Century of Progress.

Just beyond the bowsprit of Byrd's vessel, the walk along the lake-front ended in the Erie-side entrance to the expo grounds, anchored by a thirty-foot-tall lighthouse capable of casting a beam of 14 million candlepower. Outside were the piers for the Detroit & Cleveland and the Cleveland & Buffalo lines. Excursionists from those two cities at opposite ends of Lake Erie could thereby sail right up to the back door of the Great Lakes Exposition.

■

South of the wharf harboring the *Cleaveland* vessel extended a low building, so long that the word "PROGRESS" was repeated twice along its side. This was the Hall of Progress, one of the two main exhibition buildings constructed on the lower grounds. Doubling back to Marine Plaza, visitors might enter at the head of the 180-by-540-foot structure whose building had kicked off construction the previous March. There were no windows to take up space that might be devoted to displays; lighting was totally artificial, natural ventilation being supplied by means of horizontal louvers in the sides of the hall. Two interior landscaped courtyards provided some relief from the building's utilitarian starkness.

A hundred exhibitors filled the 110,000 square feet of floor space. The state of West Virginia was one of them, joining Illinois, Ohio, and

Florida as the only states represented on the grounds. A good part of the building, 30,000 square feet in all, was given over to the official U.S. government exhibit. There was room enough for two military pursuit planes as well as contributions from the Departments of Agriculture, Justice, and Labor, the last including a display of bottled lungs showing the progress of silicosis, or black lung disease. New Deal programs on view included public housing projects by the Public Works Administration and flood control efforts of the Tennessee Valley Authority. A local connection was added to the exhibit with the presentation of the flag of Cleveland's Lakeside Medical Unit, the first American military outfit to reach Europe in the First World War. All was under the supervision of U.S. commissioner A. Harry Zychik, a local attorney appointed in recognition of Cleveland's large Polish population.

Although national prohibition had been repealed three years earlier, the Women's Christian Temperance Union continued to battle demon rum with an exhibit in the Hall of Progress (hoping, perhaps, to squelch any cravings aroused by the Distilled Spirits Institute display back in the Lakeside Exhibition Hall). Roelif Loveland described side-by-side specimens of water and alcohol containing bread, candy, and goldfish, in illustration of the maxim "alcohol kills everything that's living and preserves everything that's dead." Sure enough, the goldfish in water was "swimming about, seeking his identity. In the other, alas, was a goldfish which was dead and somewhat bleached." Providing entertainment as well as instruction, another section of the exhibit pictured a gentleman in the various stages of sobriety, from "Dry and Decent," down, alliteratively, through

Delighted and Devilish
Delinquent and Disgusting
Dizzy and Delirious
Dazed and Dejected

to the final depths of "Dead Drunk." Nonetheless, Loveland couldn't help noting that "Not everyone purchases the greenish limeade which is for sale at the exhibit at a nickel a throw."

Cleveland's printing industry had as strong a presence in the Hall of Progress as in the Lakeside Exhibition Hall on the bluff. Here were displays by, among others, the Braden-Sutphin Ink Company, Central Paper, William Feather printing, and typesetters Schlick-Barnes-Hayden. Also in force were the appliance makers. Several modern model kitchens were on display by the Electrical League of Cleveland, supplemented by separate exhibits from American Stove, United Vacuum Cleaner, and White

Sewing Machines. Westinghouse presented a twelve-minute pantomime in which an actress on a revolving stage demonstrated the evolution of household chores through five historical periods, from drudgery by hand to leisure with electricity. General Electric wowed onlookers with the world's tiniest and largest light bulbs: a third of a watt surgical lamp and a fifty-thousand-watt behemoth. Although the latter was also exhibited in Chicago, San Diego, and Dallas, Cleveland's was apparently the only expo with enough juice to actually light it up—four times every hour.

Also on hand were the area's three major public utilities. Like so many others in the hall, Cleveland Electric Illuminating was pushing electric kitchens. Home heating was a major theme of the East Ohio Gas Company. One of the most crowded exhibits was that of the Ohio Bell Telephone Company, which featured two popular attractions. One was a device that allowed visitors to hear how their own voice sounded on the phone. Even more entertaining was a drawing every fifteen minutes for a free long-distance call—in an age when long-distance calls were usually matters of births or deaths.

There was only one catch to the free-call jackpot: Ma Bell provided the phone and the connection, but no booth. Winners had to put up with dozens of eavesdroppers around the Bell concession, who got to listen in on both ends of the conversation. To their titillation, one wife getting a surprise call from hubby at the expo greeted him with a testy "Where the hell have you been?" Most calls were more banal, such as a mother in Toledo repeatedly advising sonny to wear his rubbers if it looked like rain, or a nephew being informed "Aunt Hannah's teeth fit fine and she can eat again." But every so often the audience was rewarded, as when a young winner used his prize to call his sweetheart with a long-distance proposal of marriage. Of course she said "Yes, dear," presumably to a chorus of "Aww"s from the gallery.

■

Having gone methodically through the Hall of Progress, from Marine Plaza on the west to the eastern exit, visitors would have emerged to the sound of music and a vision of dancing waters. These were the renowned Singing Fountains of Firestone, a row of six domes of water rising from a pool stretching 120 feet in width and choreographed to a musical accompaniment. Colored lighting added to the overall mood at night, as the waters changed from red at the lower end of the musical scale to green and blue in the treble clef. "It is said to be the only feature of its kind in the world," boasted the guidebook.

One of the most popular exhibits in the Hall of Progress was sponsored by the Ohio Bell Telephone Company. There, expo-goers might hear what their own voices sounded like over the phone or, if their names were chosen, even win a free long-distance call. There was only one catch to the freebie: bystanders all got to listen in. Cleveland Public Library.

This was merely a prelude to the huge exhibit of the Firestone Tire and Rubber Company, at 180,000 square feet the largest exhibitor on the grounds. As such it occupied its own building, a broad structure shaped like a shallow, inverted "V," cradling the fountains in its gently curving arms. Inside were displays depicting "the romance of tires," from the materials that went into them to examples of specialized lines such as the 510.5-pound monster manufactured for earth-moving equipment. Also on display was Louis Meyer's 1936 Indy 500–winning race car; the pungent smell of hot rubber emanated from an on-site vulcanizing press, on which demonstrators were turning out toy rubber automobiles.

Through a large archway in the rear of the building lay the third component of the Firestone exhibit: a complete model farm like the one Harvey Firestone still operated for nostalgia's sake on his ancestral homestead in Columbiana County, Ohio. There were real animals in the fields as well as the latest in farming machinery, the latter all equipped with Firestone

WHITE MOTOR EXHIBIT

Cleveland's White Motor Company was one of the major exhibitors in the Automotive Building. While Detroit's Big Three filled their spaces largely with passenger cars, the local manufacturer presented what was billed as the "largest motor truck and bus exhibit in the world." From the pioneer White Steamer in the foreground, borrowed for the occasion from the Smithsonian Institution, the display culminated in the "Dream Coach of 1950," the world's first air-conditioned bus. Cleveland Public Library.

ground-grip tires. All was under the care of farmer Frank Kline of Amherst, Ohio. "Country people are less interested than are city dwellers from Cleveland, Pittsburgh, Detroit," noted the *Cleveland Press.* Some of the effects were necessarily artificial; real farmers paused only long enough to wonder why they would hear roosters crowing at 10:00 P.M.

From the bucolic setting of the Firestone farm, expo-goers might double back and reenter the urban scene via the Automotive Building, the slightly larger sister of the Hall of Progress, longer by only a foot but wider by nearly fifty. Designed by Antonio Dinardo of the expo's architectural advisory committee, it was distinguished mainly by thirty-two pylons along the perimeter of the twin-gabled structure. Seventy feet high, not counting their thirty-foot flagpoles, four were posted at each of the eight entrances. The cluttered effect was more suggestive of a walled medieval town than streamlined modern industrial design.

Inside was streamlining enough (at least 1930s style), as the Big Three and other American automakers displayed their wares. Ford led the way with a crowd-collecting display known as the "Car in the Clouds." Designed by marionette-maker Tony Sarg and recycled from previous auto shows, it produced an optical illusion in which a pretty (naturally) girl appeared to be driving a Ford V-8 through the sky above a model town. Behind the surreal scene, produced by an arrangement of seven mirrors, were a real car and a live girl, the latter able to interact with viewers through the means of earphones and a microphone concealed in the car's horn.

More down to earth, Chrysler nonetheless managed to grab its share of the spotlight by installing an elaborate English garden in which to showcase its Plymouths, Dodges, DeSotos, and Chryslers. Filling an entire wing of the Automotive Building, it was designed by the landscape engineer of the Detroit Flower Show and maintained by its own staff of gardeners. The cars were displayed on a series of terraces that gracefully led visitors down to the edge of a sunken pool filled with lily pads, turtles, and goldfish. "The greenery and the fountain combine to create an effect of light without heat, which in a glaring afternoon is worth considering," noted one reporter. "From the standpoint of being artistic, the Chrysler exhibit is in a class by itself," commented another.

General Motors, perhaps preoccupied with planning its Futurama exhibit for the coming New York World's Fair, seemed content to let its rivals steal the show at Cleveland. The company did bring in a boatload from headquarters to visit the expo, including President William Knudson, the Pontiac Male Chorus, and the Chevrolet Glee Club. Its display included an engine from its Cleveland Winton Diesel plant, and by the end of summer it was able to show off the 12 millionth Chevy to roll off its assembly lines.

Cleveland's White Motor Company rivaled Detroit's Big Three with its Great Lakes display, billed as the "largest motor truck and bus exhibit in the world." Leading the parade was the first White Steamer, a 1900 model borrowed from the Smithsonian Institution for the show. It was followed by two dozen current models of White delivery and other specialized trucks, culminating in the "Dream Coach of 1950," the world's first air-conditioned bus. Other historic vehicles on view included World War trucks loaned by Ford's Dearborn museum. All were displayed in a setting designed by White's streamlining guru, Count Alexis de Sakhnoffsky.

Studebaker was there with a display of its historic wagons and a modern model. Among the former were carriages that had borne Presidents Lincoln, Grant, Harrison, and McKinley and the Marquis de Lafayette. The current Studebaker was uniquely shown at a forty-five-degree angle, allowing viewers to inspect its undercarriage without crawling underneath. Though still in business, there were no Hudsons, Nashes, or Packards on the premises. Automobile-related companies based in Cleveland were well represented, including Sohio, Willard Storage Battery, and Thompson Products.

■

Working through the Automotive Building from east to west, one would come out again on Marine Plaza. A sharp left turn would place visitors at the head of the last major thoroughfare of the lower exhibition section, which bore the honorific of Blossom Way. Transportation was the theme of the first attraction along the way, the *Parade of the Years* pageant. Like the Singing Fountains, this was another retread from the Century of Progress. It was the brainchild of Edward Hungerford, a writer and railroad buff who saw history through the prism of transportation progress. His initial variation on the theme was the *Fair of the Iron Horse* pageant, produced for the centennial of the Baltimore & Ohio Railroad in 1927. It led eventually to *Wings of a Century,* which ran up more than a thousand performances during two years at Chicago.

For the Great Lakes production, Hungerford prepared an expanded, updated, and localized version of his Chicago effort. "His show has been described as a combination of drama, grand opera, comedy, circus, and radio, all in one," Loveland told readers of the *Plain Dealer.* Beginning with pioneer Conestoga wagons and flatboats of the westward movement, the *Parade of the Years* went on to reenact the introduction of the steamboat, the *Baltimore Clipper;* the iron horse; the "gas buggy"; and finally, the Wright Brothers' airplane. All moved in stately progression three times daily across a 265-foot stage designed by Cleveland's Richard Rychtarik. One of the two narrators of the seventy-five-minute show was Noel Leslie of the Cleveland Play House.

Driving, drawing, or occupying these conveyances was a reputed cast of 200 actors (though only 124 were named in the program) and 50 horses. The actors were largely recruited from Clevelanders, and most enacted their roles in pantomime. The real stars were the carriages, vessels, trains, and cars either borrowed from collectors or reproduced in replica. Henry Ford had lent some stagecoaches, automobiles, and a vintage Brooklyn streetcar. James R. Garfield contributed a carriage his father had used while in the White House, while carriages used by Lincoln and McKinley came from Cleveland philanthropist Harold T. Clark.

Stealing this show, however, were the locomotives that steamed past Rychtarik's sets on a spur run from the New York Central tracks along the lakefront (for once a convenience rather than an obstacle). From the Central itself came a replica of the *DeWitt Clinton* and the original No. 999, the locomotive that had set a speed record of 112 mph in 1894. From the

A dramatic highlight of the *Parade of the Years* pageant was the completion of the first transcontinental railroad in 1869. Actors portrayed the human participants, but the locomotives were represented by members of the original cast. On the left was Locomotive No. 9 of the Union Pacific Railroad, which was met by the Central Pacific's *Thatcher Perkins. Cleveland Press* Collection.

B & O came a replica of the *Tom Thumb* and the original *William Mason* from Lincoln's funeral train. The Union Pacific provided Locomotive No. 9, one of the two engines that met at Promontory Point in 1869 to mark the completion of the transcontinental railroad.

Cleveland scenes included the arrival of President-elect Lincoln in 1861 and the return of his remains four years later. The reenactment was taking place close to the same spot where the actual events had occurred seven decades earlier. For a scene from the 1890s, feminist Anna ("Newspaper Annie") Perkins was seen selling the *Cleveland Press* on Public Square. Harry Horner, the pageant's costume designer, had fashioned her nonconforming knee-length trousers from an eyewitness account (more authentic, certainly, than the wristwatch spotted by a keen-eyed observer of the 1849 Gold Rush segment). Also in the scene were early Cleveland-made Winton and Baker Electric automobiles.

"Episodic, compact and complete, it has a 'March of Time' air about it," wrote Charles Schneider of the show in the *Press*. Seating up to four thousand, the open-air pageant was billed as the largest concession on

Beckoning the crowds at the end of Blossom Way was the colorful gateway to the exposition's amusement zone. Visitors entered through an underpass or subway, excavated under East 9th Street by WPA labor. It cost nothing to pass through, but nearly every concession on the other side had its own price or entrance fee. *Cleveland Press* Collection.

the grounds. It represented an investment of more than $100,000 over the value of the borrowed properties. With an admission charge scaled from forty cents to a buck ten, it was also the most expensive individual ticket on the grounds. It appeared well worth the price to the *Plain Dealer*'s Eleanor Clarage, who wrote, "The greatest difficulty I've had at performances of 'The Parade of the Years' has been to keep from crying, just from the thrill of it all and the historical significance of every scene."

Emerging from *Parade of the Years*, expo-goers might focus their misty eyes on a tall spire down Blossom Way bearing the vertical legend "HIG-BEE." It rose out of a distinctive octagonal concession sponsored by the Higbee department store, a kind of Buck Rogers version of a Burmese temple. Dubbed the Tower of Light, its seventy-five-foot height made it the exposition's tallest building. Each of its eight sides opened to a separate specialty shop selling clothing, gifts, and other merchandise. It was a miniature version of the mother store on Public Square, with the bonus attraction of Great Lakes Exposition motifs on much of its offerings.

Just behind the twenty-first-century image of the Higbee Tower, one might step back into the antebellum South of the nineteenth century. Set amid lush subtropical greenery was a white-columned manse with a two-story portico and balustrade extending across the entire front. It might have served as a setting for *Gone with the Wind,* the instant best-seller published the same month the Great Lakes expo opened. The letters along the roof line read "FLORIDA," however, not Georgia.

Aside from Ohio, Florida was the only state boasting its own stand-alone exhibit on the grounds; the Sunshine State in fact outspent the Buckeye State more than three to one, with a total investment of a quarter-million dollars. The lavish display was under the supervision of its own landscape engineer, who garnished the one-and-a-half-acre spread with its own fountain and pergola and three varieties of palm trees. "In a real orange grove, negroes sing and dance as in typical plantation life," stated the guidebook, in the lingering spirit of the plantation legend.

All was calculated, of course, to attract tourists and even future residents to the southern peninsula. A bronze statue of Ponce de León at the entrance was intended to symbolize "the lease of life Florida guarantees to those who go there." Along the pergola and in the big house were murals, dioramas, and displays celebrating the state's history, industries, scenery, and recreational opportunities. The exhibit's general manager extended invitations to tour the "educational display" to "every school child in Cleveland." A seven-day "Florida fiesta" was declared for the first week in September, culminating in a state visit by Governor Dave Sholtz. "If you have never been to Florida for your winter vacation, go to the exposition this week and take a synthetic Florida vacation," shilled a Cleveland reporter.

Returning to the cooler reality of Cleveland, perhaps licking at a cone of "Florida orange sherbet" from a stand near the exit, expo-goers would find themselves at the end of the lower exhibition area. Any kids in tow were probably pretty antsy by then, even after walking through the giant molten iron ore ladle or lighting the world's largest light bulb. Relief was in sight, however.

Ahead, the amusement area beckoned through the WPA's East 9th underpass, its tunnel embellished overhead by a frieze depicting a procession of chimps, elephants, and giraffes outlined in bold primary colors and masking the street above. This might have been a good time to send the kids ahead with Aunt Helen, find a bench to recuperate, and review some of the outstanding events of Cleveland's exposition summer of 1936.

GARDENING MAN

Hearing of a chance remark by one of the workers on the Great Lakes Exposition to the effect that he must be getting "rake offs" from nurseries doing business with the Horticultural Gardens, A. Donald Gray shifted into high dudgeon. Before the end of the day he had fired off an indignant letter to A. N. Gonsior, the expo's chief of construction.

"Clevelanders who know my reputation and integrity would not believe such reports, but just in case you do not happen to know my reputation in this community, may I state that my professional ethics cannot be attached," he wrote. "I choose to operate my business on the basis of getting the best prices for my clients. . . . You can see that this is not only ethical on my part but good business sense."

By 1936 Gray had reached the pinnacle of his profession as Cleveland's, and probably Ohio's, preeminent landscape architect. He had not only laid out the city's great private estates and public places but advised thousands of small homeowners on how to make their gardens bloom. "He behaved like a good doctor," observed civic leader Thomas L. Sidlo. "He would go to see a poor 'patient' as quickly as a wealthy one. If the owner of a shanty wanted Gray's help in fixing his surroundings Gray was ready to go out and see what could be done."

Born in Tyrone, Pennsylvania, Gray received his bachelor's degree from Bucknell University and went on to postgraduate work at the Harvard School of Landscape Architecture. He served his apprenticeship in the Brookline, Massachusetts, firm of the Olmsted brothers, founded by Frederick Law Olmsted, designer of New York's Central Park. During World War I, Gray was a lieutenant in the U.S. Army Corps of Engineers.

Gray would later recall a picture of Cleveland's Euclid Avenue in his grammar school geography book as having impressed him with its stately beauty. It may have been one of the things that brought him to Cleveland in 1920 to establish his own landscaping business. Among his private commissions were those for the residences of Crispin Oglebay in Gates Mills, James E. Ferris in Bratenahl, and the Sherwin estate in Waite Hill.

Equally involved in the city's civic appearance, Gray promoted the Cultural Gardens in Rockefeller Park and personally designed the Irish portion, which he laid out in the shape of a Celtic cross. Cahoon Memorial Park in Bay Village and Forest Hill Park in the eastern suburbs were also among his creations. During the 1930s, he beautified the grounds of the Cedar Central and Valley View public housing projects.

In conjunction with the *Cleveland Press,* Gray launched a "Make Cleveland Beautiful" campaign in 1932. "At one time Cleveland was one of the most beautiful cities in the United States," he stated. "Then came

Landscape architect A. Donald Gray was Cleveland's prime exponent of the City Beautiful movement. Besides designing the Horticultural Gardens for the Great Lakes Exposition, he conducted a private landscaping business and served as gardening editor of the *Cleveland Press*. He is pictured with a model he used to illustrate lectures at the Cleveland Garden Center, forerunner of the Cleveland Botanical Gardens. *Cleveland Press* Collection.

industrial development. . . . As the city grew industrially, a period of neglect developed. The city was no longer kept beautiful. This has been an economic as well as an aesthetic loss. At the present time, much property in Cleveland is useless simply because it has been neglected."

Gray outlined his campaign on two fronts. On the individual level, he would plant demonstration gardens in ten different city neighborhoods to show homeowners what might be done in their own yards. On the public side, he urged increasing and improving playgrounds and parks and planting more trees in what was once known as the Forest City. He became an especially forceful advocate of preserving Cleveland's lakefront for common and recreational use. Gaining a forum for his views at the same time, Gray became the gardening editor of the *Press*.

A. Donald Gray's columns for the *Press,* later carried also by the *Akron Times-Press* and the *Youngstown Vindicator,* consisted primarily of practical tips for the backyard gardener. He advised readers to purchase plants on the basis of quality rather than price and to feed birds in winter to ensure better pest control in the summer. When he wrote that the grass-planting season had passed, sales of grass seed slumped accordingly.

With his habitual tweed suits and military-style mustache, Gray was the image of the English country gentleman. In 1928 he married Florence Ball, daughter of jeweler Webb C. Ball. They had one daughter and in 1931 moved into a new development on Fairhill Road designed in the style of a Cotswold village and landscaped, of course, by Gray. According to a story attributed to another resident, Rowena Jelliffe, the place soon acquired a popular nickname by way of the Great Lakes Exposition: a visitor who couldn't remember the address described the development to his cabbie, who, probably with visions of the expo's Streets of the World in his head, exclaimed "Oh, you must mean the Belgian Village!" and promptly drove him out to Fairhill.* The name stuck, and Gray possibly was pleased with the association.

For his own contribution to the exposition, Gray received $500 for his plans and drawings, plus an additional $2 per hour spent in supervision. It was hardly a princely sum, and he undoubtedly put far more into the job than he received. A luncheon was given in his honor at the Horticultural Building in September, at which Lincoln Dickey presented him with a gold medal "for distinguished service to the Great Lakes Exposition."

Far from resting on his laurels, Gray if anything intensified his civic involvement following the expo. He dispensed advice freely to the Works

---

*The nickname story was related to the author by Cynthia Reese, who heard it from Mrs. Jelliffe. With her husband, Russell, Rowena Jelliffe was the cofounder of Karamu House.

Progress Administration on landscaping aspects of its numerous city and county projects. Involved with the Garden Center of Greater Cleveland since its inception in 1930, he helped with the enlargement of that organization's building in Wade Park in 1939. While declining their request that he assume active directorship of the group, he assured them of his continued time and advice without compensation.

One of Gray's pet causes was the preservation of Dunham Tavern, one of the last original structures remaining on Euclid Avenue. For years he used it as his business office, but he ultimately hoped to have it restored to its former condition as a museum. A model of the old inn was the centerpiece of the 1836 garden in the period section of the expo's Horticultural Gardens. As his museum plans neared fruition, Gray moved his office to Carnegie Avenue.

Widening his scope of concern, Gray also became involved in the activities of the Cleveland Citizens League. Named in 1937 to its executive committee, he headed a subcommittee concerned with developing a plan for city-county reorganization.

Still, the quest for the City Beautiful remained Gray's foremost and ceaseless passion. Returning from a tour of South American urban gardens early in 1939, he inveighed against the ugliness that greeted him back home. Granted, it was the northern hemisphere's dreariest part of the year, with its barren trees and sooty residue of melting snowbanks, but Gray saw this as all the more reason to renew his crusade.

Three months later, with flowers once again in full bloom on the eve of Memorial Day, Gray returned home to the "Belgian Village" after a full day spent working at the Garden Center and finishing his column for the following day's *Press*. Though it was 3:00 A.M., he made sure he had hung out an American flag for the holiday before turning in. He rose late the next day, ate breakfast, complained of indigestion, and was dead of a massive heart attack within an hour.

His death at forty-eight was unexpected enough, but what must have seemed even stranger was the thought of A. Donald Gray in repose. "He was outstanding in his profession and so well suited to the work to which he devoted his life that it will be difficult to replace him in the important place he occupied in Cleveland's civic and cultural life," said Mrs. Lucia Otis, a member of the Garden Center.

4

Sizzling Summer of '36

It was the city's summer of the century. Not only did it see Cleveland's biggest bash ever, but it brought four of the country's most important political conclaves to the Forest City. It had fireworks, celebrities, and the longest parade in America. It saw the launching of the city's two most legendary sports careers. If anything more were needed, it also had record-breaking heat and one of the nation's most notorious serial murder cases. That was Cleveland's summer of 1936, and at least to some degree, it was planned that way from the outset.

"During 1936, Cleveland is due to get a lot of attention from the nation at large," editorialized the *Cleveland Press* on New Year's Day. "In this city, the Republican Party will meet in convention to nominate its candidate for the presidency. Here the American Legion will hold its annual convention. Here the city will entertain a vast throng of visitors at its Great Lakes Exposition. . . . There are important conventions, in addition to those mentioned above, too numerous to mention here. There is a baseball club under new leadership; it might turn out to be a pennant winner under the inspiration of all these other civic activities."

Baseball fortunes aside, the *Press* saw "better reason for confidence and hope" at the beginning of 1936 than it had for any of the previous half-dozen years. There was discernible progress toward economic recovery in the country, with "substantial reduction in the number of people without work or wages."

Cleveland had not only shared in those gains, but, according to the editorial, "in many respects it has done far better than average for the country." It was a view seconded by *Business Week* magazine, which saw Cleveland's comeback from business reverses and bank failures as a result of the residual strength of the city's core industries. This revival was part of "a general rebirth of trade and industry throughout the Great Lakes area," which was responsible for more than half the nation's industrial output and business activity.

If anything more were needed to keep the economic engine humming, Cleveland was looking for visitor spending to grease the gears. By one count, city promoters had lined up 170 conventions and trade shows for the year, attracted by such facilities as the Public Hall and Municipal Stadium as well as the allure of the Great Lakes Exposition. Some quarter million or more delegates were expected to make local cash registers cha-ching to the tune of $12.5 million, not counting the additional visitors and money attracted solely by the exposition.

The invasion began promptly in January with the American League against War and Fascism, followed by the American Road Builders Association. February would bring the National Association of Groundskeepers of America; March, the Men's Apparel Club of Ohio; April, the Classical Association of the Middle West and South; May, the Loyal Ladies of the Royal Arcanum Supreme Council. Summer visitors would range from the Republicans to the Ohio Order of Rainbow; from the Men's Garden Clubs of America to the American Legion.

And so the beat went on. As summarized by historian William Ganson Rose, "Cleveland entertained as never before." Or since, it might be added.

■

Serving as a warm-up act for the exposition was the Republican National Convention, which met in Cleveland the second week in June. It was gaveled to order in Public Auditorium, the same hall in which Calvin Coolidge had received the Republican nomination in 1924. Almost brand new then, the facility unfortunately was showing signs of wear a dozen years later. Anxious to make a good impression, Republican mayor Harold Burton must have swallowed hard before doing the unthinkable: he appealed for help to the Democratic administration in Washington. The WPA sent six hundred workers to fix, paint, and clean the place for the party bent on putting them out of business if elected. There was no record in the convention proceedings of any resolution of thanks for their efforts.

While preparations for the Republicans went on in the auditorium upstairs, other workers were assembling exhibits for the exposition in the exhibition halls downstairs. Several pages of the thick, official *Book of the Republican Convention* were devoted to a preview of the Great Lakes Exposition in hopes of enticing delegates and observers to stick around or come

Cleveland decked out its Public Square with Great Lakes Exposition themes for the millions of visitors expected in the summer of 1936. Turning from Ontario Street onto Superior Avenue is a presidential cavalcade, with President Roosevelt's open car in the lead. Over the entrance to Higbee's department store is a mock-up of the Higbee Tower located on the expo grounds, while the seven pylons of the expo's main entrance appear atop the portals of the Terminal Tower. *Cleveland Press Collection.*

back for the show. One United Press correspondent on a preconvention reconnaissance "walked into the wrong door" and stumbled on the expo's "Romance of Iron and Steel" theme exhibit. "And there we were," he wrote in mock alarm, "in a gigantic iron mine, red-walled, strewn with iron ore. Even as we write this, we're tapping, tapping, tapping on the walls in hope a Republican rescue squad will arrive before it's too late."

Reporters might have appealed with more reason for rescue from the tedium of the events that followed back upstairs. One of the highlights was an address by former president Herbert Hoover on the second night. It received a thirty-five-minute ovation despite the fact that many in the hall couldn't hear it due to the speaker's microphone shyness. *Cleveland Press* pundit Jack Raper, who did hear it, said it was worth several million votes—for the Democrats. A Republican mayor from Massachusetts died of a heart attack in the Hotel Statler that night, but no one thought the Hoover oratory had anything to do with it.

Needing only two hundred more votes when the convention came to order, Kansas governor Alf Landon picked them up before the first ballot and was nominated by acclamation. Though there had been talk of an acceptance speech in Municipal Stadium, the Kansan became the last nominee to remain at home and await formal notification by a specially appointed committee. There were those who thought he actually had a chance.

No one gave Norman Thomas a chance, but the Socialists had already met in Cleveland and nominated him as their standard-bearer for the third time. Then, in the wake of the Republicans, a group capable of upsetting the whole political applecart assembled in Public Auditorium. Officially, it was the second annual convention of the Townsend Old Age Revolving Pensions movement, which brought eleven thousand followers of Doctor Francis E. Townsend of California. Townsend had proposed that the government issue $200 monthly checks to every person sixty years or older, with the single proviso that it all be spent within thirty days, thus providing the economic stimulus that, theoretically, would lift the country out of the Depression.

Behind the scenes, the gathering of old folks masked a cabal of the nation's foremost political intriguers, jockeying to gain the votes of the doctor's estimated 3 to 10 million supporters for the third-party presidential candidacy of North Dakota congressman William Lemke. There was the Reverend Gerald L. K. Smith, who claimed to be the inheritor of assassinated senator Huey Long's "Share the Wealth" movement. There too was the Machiavellian Father Charles E. Coughlin, the Catholic "Radio Priest," who claimed his own millions of followers as head of the National Union for Social Justice.

A trio of political right-wingers joined forces in Cleveland at the convention of the National Union for Social Justice in August. Playing to the crowd are the Reverend Gerald L. K. Smith, protégé of the late Huey Long; Father Charles Coughlin, the "Radio Priest"; and Dr. Francis Townsend, promoter of the Townsend Old Age Revolving Pensions Plan. They were backing third-party candidate William Lemke against Roosevelt in 1936. *Cleveland Press* Collection.

In an oratorical shout-out, Smith mounted the rostrum, Bible in hand, to deliver a fiery diatribe against both Wall Street and the New Deal. "Never in my life, in truth, have I heard a more effective speech," wrote H. L. Mencken, whose standards may have slipped after he fought off drowsiness through the Republican speechifying of the previous month. Smith was "the greatest rabble-rouser since Peter the Hermit . . . the gustiest and goriest, the loudest and lustiest, the deadliest and damndest ever heard on this or any other earth," pronounced the Sage of Baltimore, no matter that when it was over, "no one could remember what he had said."

Following an act like that, the radio-trained Coughlin was initially at a disadvantage in a contest of stump-speaking. Halfway through his effort, he stepped back and removed his black coat and his Roman collar, handing them to Gerald Smith behind him. Whether a calculated gesture or simply a concession to the heat, it got the attention of the crowd as he launched into his peroration against "Franklin Double-crossing

Roosevelt." Though Lemke ended up with the endorsements of Smith, Coughlin, and Dr. Townsend, he could draw no more than five thousand to his closing-day speech in Municipal Stadium. Interested more in pensions than politics, most of the Townsendites had left for home.

One month later, the same cast of characters returned to Public Auditorium for the first convention of Coughlin's National Union for Social Justice. Not surprisingly, the eight thousand delegates elected Coughlin NUSJ president and endorsed Lemke for U.S. president over the single objection of a delegate from Pittsburgh, who thereafter left the hall under the protection of a police escort. Carried away, perhaps, during an eighteen-minute demonstration in favor of the Lemke endorsement, Coughlin made a grandstand play for the benefit of watching newsmen. "I will give Lemke . . . 9,000,000 votes in November, or I'll quit broadcasting forever," the *Plain Dealer* reported him saying. "If I can't do that I'm washed up and there is no use of going on."

■

Not all the fireworks that summer were generated by visiting orators. There was a ten-minute fireworks display four nights a week, propelled above the exposition grounds from two barges anchored offshore. A special show was planned for the Fourth of July, one week after opening day. So spectacular that it required a "dress rehearsal" on the eve of the Fourth, it was billed in advance as "bigger than that put on at the Chicago Century of Progress." Adding to the drama was the unrehearsed rescue of eleven people near the scene when an expo speedboat sheered into a private launch.

A huge civic parade took place July 22 in observance of the 140th anniversary of the coming of General Moses Cleaveland to found the city named after him. A crowd of seventy-five thousand lined Euclid Avenue to watch three thousand participants march from East 22nd Street to the Exposition gates on St. Clair. Local bands and organizations were augmented by such expo representatives as the Yeomanettes, exposition guards, coaches from *Parade of the Years,* and some of the exotic inhabitants of the midway. Two weeks later, Cleveland was out-flown by the upstart city of Akron in a balloon race launched from Municipal Stadium. Forced down after 222 miles by a thunderstorm in Pennsylvania, Cleveland's *Great Lakes Exposition* saw Akron's *Goodyear X* float on for an additional seventy-five miles.

Nature itself seemed determined to be part of the show that summer, as record-shattering heat prostrated Cleveland and the Midwest. From July 8 to July 15 the mercury topped 100 degrees in Ohio, including a record 106-degree reading in Columbus on July 14 and a torrid 110 the day before that in Middletown. Cleveland wasn't quite that broiling, but the temperature hit a local peak of 98.7 degrees on July 11 and 94 four days later, when a record nineteen heat fatalities taxed the county morgue's resources and kept the coroner's staff working late into the night. Cleveland police set the week's toll at forty-eight deaths, while Ohio's losses approached three hundred.

While there were no reported deaths on the exposition grounds, there were numerous cases of heat prostration. Five teenaged girls were treated at the expo's emergency hospital on the first day of the heat wave, followed by slightly higher numbers of victims of all ages on succeeding days. One exhibit which experienced sudden popularity was the joint display of the Ohio Association of Ice Industries and the City Ice & Fuel Company in the Lakeside Exhibition Hall. What had been designated as "Ice Day" happened to coincide with the onset of the hot spell on July 8. Even more attractive than the sight of Ice Queen Virginia Cipra must have been the opportunity to get an inside look at the "world's largest refrigerator," a twenty-five-foot-high monster capable of cooling off two dozen expo-goers at a time.

Heat wasn't the only killer stalking Cleveland that summer. On June 5, a few days before the Republicans gathered in Public Auditorium, two young schoolboys were playing hooky in Kingsbury Run, a wooded ravine feeding into the Cuyahoga River a couple of miles south of downtown. Coming across a pair of trousers rolled into a bundle, they prodded it in hopes of finding something of value. To their horror, the decapitated head of a man rolled out instead. They hightailed it home and told one's mother, who sent them to the police. The heavily tattooed body that went with the head was discovered in the area the next day.

It wasn't entirely surprising to the police; in fact, it was beginning to seem monotonous—this was victim no. 4 in a series of brutal killings that left behind the common calling card of expertly dismembered corpses and were, fittingly, called the "torso murders." The first two had been discovered the previous fall in the same area, an overgrown urban enclave that harbored nests of hobo jungles or Hoovervilles. Victim no. 3 was a woman whose headless torso cropped up not too far away in January.

While the second and third torsos had been identified, the first victim remained nameless, as did the latest. Police had a plaster death mask made of victim no. 4 and displayed it in the Cleveland Police Department exhibit in the Hall of the Great Lakes, hoping that some passing expo-goer might provide a name. Tens of thousands looked at the closed eyelids and slightly parted lips, but none recognized the face.

Before the end of summer, two more victims turned up. Victim no. 5 was discovered on July 22, body first, then head, far afield in Brooklyn Village on the west side. For the sixth victim, pieces of whom were found on September 10, the killer had apparently returned to his customary haunts in Kingsbury Run. At the request of the mayor, Safety Director Eliot Ness assumed personal control of the investigation. Cleveland's police obviously had a far more serious problem on their hands than the rotary left turn.

■

Neither heat nor serial killer could keep visitors, both ordinary and extra-ordinary, away from Cleveland and its exposition. Foremost by far was what might be regarded as a state visit by the man who, with the push of a button several hundred miles removed, had opened the gates of the Great Lakes Exposition. It was part of a three-day trip by President Franklin D. Roosevelt, which began with a stop in Johnstown, Pennsylvania, to examine the scene of a flood the previous spring. He arrived at the Pennsylvania Railroad station at East 55th Street and Euclid Avenue at 10:00 A.M. on August 14, coincidentally diverting the city's attention from the opening of Father Coughlin's NUSJ convention in Public Auditorium.

First on the presidential agenda was a review of the progress of four thousand WPA workers in enlarging and repaving the runways at Cleveland Municipal Airport on Brookpark Road. This necessitated a fifteen-mile motorcade through "a canyon of cheers" downtown and on the west side, witnessed by an estimated one hundred thousand Clevelanders. Mayor Burton provided a considerably higher figure, perhaps carried away by his vantage point alongside the president, telling FDR that he guessed there were "about three million" people lining the streets. "I congratulate Cleveland on its growth," quipped Roosevelt, who was also amused by a salute from the horns of cars parked in Lovers' Lane at Edgewater Park.

Returning downtown, the motorcade then proceeded to inspect the city's other major ongoing WPA project, driving out on Lake Shore Boulevard to East 53rd and back. By 11:45 they were back at the main gate to the exposition on St. Clair Avenue. Holding on to his hat against a stiff lakefront breeze, the president was given a tour of the grounds. A portion of the fence shielding the Horticultural Gardens had been removed to allow FDR to admire yet another local result of WPA labor.

At noon, the president was taken aboard the SS *Moses Cleaveland* as guest of honor at a luncheon for four hundred invited guests. FDR opened his brief remarks by saying that he had no intention of delivering

President Franklin D. Roosevelt, who had opened the Great Lakes Exposition with the press of a button in Washington, came to Cleveland in person seven weeks later. Seated in the back of the 1934 Lincoln, with custom Brunn phaeton body, are Ohio's Governor Martin Davey, Cleveland's Mayor Harold Burton, and FDR. After inspecting some of the larger WPA projects around town, the president toured the exposition grounds and delivered a few "nonpolitical" remarks at a luncheon aboard the *Moses Cleaveland. Cleveland Press* Collection.

a political speech. Right on cue, a waiter behind the scenes dropped a full tray of china as if in shock, Roosevelt himself joining in the resultant laughter. "Everything he did was so theatrical—the way he picked up his cigarette, rolled his eyes," recollected Herman Pirchner after more than half a century. "He was a master showman."

There was a fittingly theatrical finale to FDR's visit, completely unrehearsed, when they brought his special train down a spur to pick him up right on the grounds. The grade back up the bluff proved too steep for the switch engine assigned to the job, however, leaving the presidential party stranded. To the rescue came John Ross Reed, director of the *Parade of the Years* pageant, who ordered *Old 999* from the show fired up. Like the Little Engine That Could, the historic old locomotive proved equal to the occasion, hauling the heavy special back to its regular engine waiting above.

(The next stop on the presidential itinerary was Chautauqua, and Cleveland thereby just missed being witness to one of Roosevelt's most memorable utterances. He chose the educational institute in upstate New

York for a major pronouncement on the darkening foreign situation, closing with a somber reminder: "I have seen war. . . . I hate war.")

Two more New Dealers came to the expo soon after the visit of their chief. Secretary of agriculture, Henry A. Wallace, appeared the following week, Farm Week at the exposition, to defend the administration's farm record. The final week of the exposition brought Frances Perkins, secretary of labor and first woman to hold a cabinet-level position. At a luncheon sponsored by the Federation of Women's Clubs of Cleveland in the Horticultural Building, Perkins talked about the recently passed Social Security Act, the New Deal's answer to the Townsend revolving pension plan. "Perhaps no act ever passed by Congress received more careful study," she said, pointing to the bipartisan support received by the social security measure. Between the two Democrats, Senator Arthur Vandenberg of Michigan put in an appearance for the Republicans.

Harvey S. Firestone was guest of honor on Firestone Day in September. Receiving the exposition's Distinguished Service Medal in a ceremony in front of the Firestone exhibit, the rubber baron responded by congratulating "the people of Cleveland on the development of such a wonderful Exposition, and . . . Ohio for having the inspiration to build a lake front fair such as this." Firestone's friend Henry Ford appeared to be in one of his cantankerous moods during his visit a couple of weeks later. While Mrs. Ford toured the Horticultural Gardens, her husband took in *Parade of the Years*, possibly to see how the vehicles he had loaned were being handled. Asked what he thought of the expo, "Oh, I think it's fine," he snapped.

Getting a reception second only, perhaps, to that for FDR, was crooner Rudy Vallee, who came in August for a gig at Radioland. He was greeted by thousands of fans on his arrival at Union Terminal, and his four shows over two afternoons and evenings attracted an estimated forty thousand to Public Auditorium. His appearance was credited with bettering the expo's next-best Monday attendance by eight thousand. Vallee responded by extending his shows an extra half hour and pleased Clevelanders by "shooting" them on Euclid Avenue with his new camera.

Some visitors became celebrities only after passing through the expo's turnstiles. One young lady from Youngstown was mildly shocked to be taken in hand by two red-coated exposition guards as soon as she stepped through the gates. As the five-hundred-thousandth visitor, she was photographed, interviewed, and showered with gifts including a season pass, a set of Firestone tires, and a free call home at the Ohio Bell booth. She also would have received the last of five hundred thousand "Charter Associate" scrolls distributed to the first half million to go through the gates.

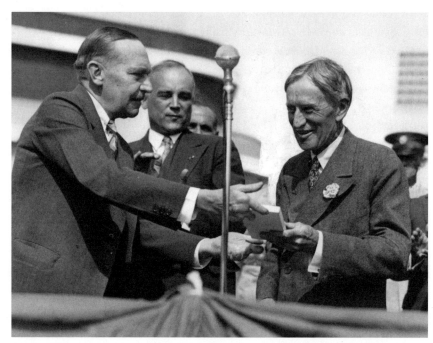

Among those expo-goers receiving the red-carpet treatment was Harvey S. Firestone, founder and chairman of the Akron tire giant. His company was the largest exhibitor on the grounds with a stand-alone building, a model farm, and the fabled Firestone Singing Fountains. Dudley Blossom responded to these contributions by presenting him with the exposition's Distinguished Service Medal. *Cleveland Press* Collection.

Even more fuss was made over the millionth expo-goer a couple of weeks later on the fair's thirty-third day, and publicist Johnny Miskell couldn't have asked for a more homespun hero. Ira Henning, a sixty-three-year-old farmer from Louisville, Ohio, said he would have come earlier but had to wait until he got his oats in. "I thought it was a holdup at first," he said of his reception. "I'd heard about a lot of robberies up here." He and his wife, though, got the haul, including a Firestone tire set, airline and baseball tickets, cigars, photographs, jewelry, perfume, and two dozen roses. He took a rain check on an Admiralty Club dinner, because "we got to get back home in time for milking. That's about six o'clock tonight." Other celebrities for a day followed. A railroad conductor from Massillon was the 2 millionth; number 3 million was an eight-year-old boy from Pittsburgh.

Evidently not all expo-goers, however, prizes or no, were willing to enter the gates in approved style. Ted Robinson ran the following limerick from a contributor in his "Philosopher of Folly" column in the *Plain Dealer:*

A young man of vaulting ambition
Tried to crash the Great Lakes Exposition,
    But a vigilant guard
    Hit him once, very hard—
Which is now called a Fatal Admission.

■

Except for boxing and high school and college football, sports were still largely a summer pastime in 1936. Given its proximity to Municipal Stadium and Lake Erie, the Great Lakes Exposition hoped to benefit from sporting enthusiasm, both participatory and spectator. Only two days after opening day, ten thousand members of German turnverein organizations descended on the stadium for the American Turnerbund's thirty-fifth national Turnfest. Included in the four-day meet were volleyball, tennis, track, and other sports besides the dominant gymnastic events. It all culminated with mass demonstrations and fireworks for Turnfest Day at the expo on July 3.

Two weeks later, action shifted to the lakefront for the Great Lakes Regatta. Stands lined the shore in the amusement zone from East 9th to East 26th Streets for two days of aquatic racing events preceded by an evening pageant of cabin cruisers decorated with flags and lights. The thirty-four events included contests for various classes of sailing and motorized craft. The most exciting happening was an unscheduled one, when an outboard motorboat careened out of control. Aptly named the *Flying Harps,* it ejected its operator and zoomed off on an uncharted course inside the breakwall, menacing its bobbing skipper and dozens of dodging boats. The rogue vessel was finally stopped involuntarily by the cruiser *Dorothy R.,* at the cost of a foot-wide hole in its side.

Another gymnastic and track meet, dubbed the Workers Olympiad, took place outside the grounds in July. Organized as a protest against holding the 1936 Olympics in Nazi Germany, it was sponsored and hosted by the local chapter of the Czech Workers Gymnastic Union. Gymnasts and athletes from all parts of the country and from Czechoslovakia came to compete in an east-side hall and the John Adams High School athletic field. Related cultural events also took place in the union's camp at Taborville in Geauga County.

Most Clevelanders, however, had good reason to remain focused on the Berlin Olympics. Two East Tech High School alumni, high jumper Dave Albritton and multiple threat Jesse Owens, were prominent members of the U.S. team. The latter had been in the national track spotlight for a year, ever since breaking or tying six world records in one day for Ohio State at the Big Ten meet in Ann Arbor, Michigan.

Owens more than lived up to expectations in Berlin. On the first day, as Albritton took a silver medal in the high jump, Owens set a new world record in the 100-meter sprint. He went on to establish new Olympic or world marks in the 200-meter sprint, the 400-meter relay, and the long jump on his way to picking up four gold medals. Even more memorable than those feats, though, was Owens's subsequent snub from German chancellor Adolf Hitler, self-proclaimed champion of the "master race," who left the games prematurely, apparently to avoid having to congratulate a Negro. The incident made Owens not only a champion athlete but a powerful symbol for the antifascist movement.

Cleveland waited eagerly for the triumphant return of its champion. In the meantime his wife, Ruth Owens, served as hostess at the African Village in the expo's Streets of the World. When Owens finally arrived home near the end of August, he was given a thirteen-mile motorcade through the east side, from East Cleveland to downtown. Following a half-hour tour of the exposition grounds, he was taken to Public Hall for a civic reception. Among the honors he received was the Distinguished Service Medal of the Great Lakes Exposition.

Baseball was still the national pastime, of course, even in an Olympics year. Exposition officials had secured the tournament of the National Baseball Federation for Municipal Stadium in September. In the final round, Cleveland's Fisher Foods team took two out of three from the Dayton Delcos to win the national sandlot championship.

Lincoln Dickey set his sights on bigger game, however, when the Cleveland Indians suddenly made a run for the American League pennant in July. Seeing it as a great draw for the Great Lakes Exposition, Dickey proposed moving a Sunday game with the league-leading New York Yankees on August 2 from League Park to Municipal Stadium. Seeing twice as many marketable seats as in the team's everyday haunts, Tribe president Alva Bradley readily agreed. Dickey, Bradley, and 65,342 fans got more than they bargained for, as the two teams battled for more than four hours, through sixteen innings, to a 4–4 draw. With night baseball still a thing of the future, umpire George Moriarty called the game at 7:15 P.M. on account of darkness. Publicists were able to salvage something out of the marathon, calling the crowd the largest in baseball history to witness a sixteen-inning game.

That crowd watched something even more memorable though, when the Indians gave them a pregame look at a pitching demonstration by

A hero's welcome awaited sprinter Jesse Owens when he returned home to Cleveland with the four gold medals he had won in the 1936 Berlin Olympics. He and his wife, Ruth, were greeted by an enthusiastic crowd at the New York Central station in East Cleveland. Following a motorcade through the east side, Owens was given a VIP tour of the Great Lakes Exposition and a civic reception in Public Hall. *Cleveland Press* Collection.

an Iowa farmboy who wasn't even out of high school yet. Bob Feller was his name, and he belied his teenage gawkiness by firing five straight pitches through a paper target set up at home plate, outshining such seasoned veterans as George Uhle, Denny Galehouse, and Mel Harder. As of then, he had appeared in only two major league games—three innings in an exhibition game against the St. Louis Cardinals and a relief inning against the Washington Senators in a game that counted.

Back in League Park on August 23, the Indians let Feller start a game against the St. Louis Browns. He repaid their trust with a 4–1 victory, striking out fifteen batters in the process. "He was tested in every possible way, and in every way he came through like a veteran," wrote Gordon Cobbledick in the *Plain Dealer*. "He proved that his control is good enough to make him a sound gamble in a tight spot, and he proved that he can still fog that fast one trough [*sic*] after nine tough innings, which is something no one knew for sure until yesterday."

By that time the Indians were out of the pennant race, but Feller wasn't through yet. Facing the Philadelphia Athletics September 14 at

League Park, he struck out one hitter for each of his seventeen years, tying a record set by Dizzy Dean in 1933. Feller then went back to Iowa to earn his high school diploma, while Indians fans at least had something to look forward to for the next season.

■

José Iturbi's musical pitch undoubtedly was as perfect as Bob Feller's baseball delivery. That wasn't the problem as the temperamental Spaniard mounted the podium at Sherwin-Williams Plaza in August to conduct the second half of a Great Lakes Symphony concert. Rudolph Ringwall, the regular conductor for the series, announced that the guest maestro would lead the orchestra in *Impressions of Buenos Aires* by José Andre. When no music came forth, Ringwall shot Iturbi a questioning glance and got the single word "Piano" in reply. Does he mean "pianissimo"—quiet?—Ringwall wondered. No, it seemed Iturbi wanted a pianist. Ringwall thought they had agreed to do the piece without the piano part; Iturbi obviously disagreed.

There was no time for debate; the concert was being broadcast over the Mutual network, and announcer Maurice Condon desperately ad-libbed while Ringwall frantically searched for a pianist. Finally he drafted Boris Goldovsky, the Cleveland Orchestra's choral director, who came onstage after nine minutes' delay to give a totally unfamiliar score his best shot. Iturbi then made up for lost time by finishing five minutes too early and further endeared himself to Ringwall by refusing to play an encore, leaving Ringwall and Condon, like baseball announcers during a rain delay, to fill the air time with color commentary.

It soon became clear that Iturbi had other issues besides encores and pianos. While Ringwall had been scouring the plaza for a pianist, the conductor had confided to the orchestra that he had just wired to New York asking for a release from his contract. "Understand—the trouble is not you," he said. "You played beautifully. But I can't stand these hot dogs—pop—whistles and street cars." Ringwall later responded that none of the previous guests had objected to concert conditions. As for hot dogs, he growled, "Iturbi himself ate a hot dog Monday night while he was listening to Walter Logan conduct the orchestra."

Actually, Iturbi admitted that he had consumed three of them but insisted that he had finished them before going into the plaza. "Hot dogs! The audience eating hot dogs while we play the Second Symphony of Jan Sibelius," exclaimed the haughty maestro to a reporter who quoted him phonetically. "People scraping their feet over the floor. Like thees: Scrape! scrape! Madre Dios, it ees disgraceful. Diabolo! It ees undignified!" To show

Assistant conductor of the Cleveland Orchestra at Severance Hall, Rudolph Ringwall provided the downbeat for many of the same musicians as musical director of the Great Lakes Symphony. Though relieved periodically through the summer by guest conductors, he was on hand to step in after one of them objected to the consumption of hot dogs and other distractions during the outdoor concerts. *Cleveland Press* Collection.

he was "just a plain regular fellow," he confided that he also happened to like—no, adore—hamburgers. "But you do not give me hamburger when I am invited to a formal dinner. No respect for the artist."

If necessary, Iturbi said he was prepared to fulfill his obligation; orchestra officials decided it was not necessary, and Ringwall provided the downbeat for the rest of the week. A *Plain Dealer* reporter (probably Loveland) dropped in to review more the audience than the concert. "They are expo visitors, and they are mainly from downstate, because they go home when the concerts end at 9:45–10 P.M., fishing in pockets for auto keys and staggering under souvenirs," he wrote. "They stop by the orchestra's 'outdoor hall' when they have seen most of the expo they are going to see, and, tired, they decide to try the benches for a rest and see what this music is like." They entered "as quiet and unobtrusive as possible," but more important, many remained to find themselves "being emotionally stirred." If any felt insulted by Iturbi, they could look for revenge on the midway, where, Winsor French recalled, for the rest of the summer, hot dogs were known as "Iturbis."

Another bit of news came out of the expo grounds the following month, when it was announced that a new gas had been discovered in the Western Reserve University Building. Christened thionyl chlorofluoride, it was the culmination of two years of experiments by Harold S. Booth of the university's chemistry department. Moving his glass tubing, pumps, liquid air containers, and electrical relays from campus to exposition, he continued his search under the curious gaze of an estimated four hundred thousand visitors until his "Eureka!" moment.

It didn't get a fraction of the coverage the Iturbi blowup did. Booth, who now had sixteen such discoveries to his credit, couldn't provide a specific use for his latest, because "you discover a gas and then find a use for it afterward." Though highly toxic, he didn't think it had a future in warfare. Had he wanted more publicity, he should have gone into a tirade about people munching hot dogs while witnessing a serious scientific experiment.

■

As the days of September imperceptibly but inexorably shortened, natives and visitors alike seemed determined not to loosen their grip on summer. Newspapers had been warning Clevelanders in particular that their chances to take in the big show on their own doorstep were fast running out. In blatant appeals to local pride, reporters and editorialists were estimating that up to 80 percent of expo-goers were from out of town.

Both natives and strangers seemed to get the message on Labor Day weekend, when a total of 274,092 fun-seekers passed through the gates in three days. Sunday saw a record crowd of 125,192, which so jammed downtown streets that police looked on with tolerant smiles at out-of-state cars ignoring "the famous Cleveland turn at intersections." Records fell inside the grounds, as *Parade of the Years* played to a total audience of ten thousand in four shows, and Cliff Wilson's Snake Show on the midway had its best day in twenty years of show business.

Two weeks later, WPA Day drew a record Saturday crowd of eighty thousand. Those from the east side likely came via the new Lake Shore

Near the end of the city's sizzling summer of '36, cartoonist Willard Combes pictured Moses Cleaveland reviewing some of the highlights with evident satisfaction. With its two huge parades, the American Legion convention would provide a fitting climax. *Cleveland Press*, August 13, 1936.

Boulevard they and their fellow workers had recently completed. On the grounds, they could have inspected the scale model of Cleveland crafted by WPA artists in the Hall of the Great Lakes, then headed to the lakefront to enjoy the Horticultural Gardens installed by other relief workers. Then they could walk to the midway through yet another WPA project, the East 9th Street underpass.

Mingling with the WPA crowd that Saturday was the advance guard of the American Legion, pouring into the city for their annual convention the coming week. Rudy Vallee arrived on Sunday to do another broadcast from Public Hall and then made an unscheduled appearance at a stag and smoker for Legion journalists. He planned to extend his visit a couple of more days to join in the camaraderie of his fellow Legionnaires.

Two huge parades provided the highlights of the week's events. Monday witnessed the antics of the Forty Men and Eight Horses parade, marked by colorful costumes, outlandish floats, and unrestrained high-jinks along the route. Watched by an estimated crowd of three hundred thousand, the cavalcade passed down Euclid Avenue from East 21st Street, headed north at Public Square, and finished with a turn around the field in Municipal Stadium. That was only a curtain raiser for the main Legion parade the following day, when seventy thousand marchers followed the same path past half a million onlookers. From advance to rear guard, it lasted eleven and a half hours.

Legionnaires made their presence known throughout the exposition grounds. Legion musicians competed for the title of best band in Sherwin-Williams Plaza. In the Court of the Great Lakes, veterans of the 26th "Yankee" Division dedicated a memorial to their late commander, General Clarence Edwards, near the site of his boyhood home. The Singing Fountains of the Firestone exhibit serenaded the visitors with such wartime tunes as "Over There," "My Buddy," and "Rose of No Man's Land." In Streets of the World, the Swiss Village evoked the wartime experience with a display of sandbags and barbed wire.

Of course, in light of the Legion's reputation for rowdiness, the Swiss Village may have been thinking in terms more of self-defense than tribute. If so their precautions proved unnecessary, as little damage was reported, beyond one broken show window on Euclid Avenue. "The fact is that they did not tear up the Great Lakes Exposition—not even the midway; they did not tear up the restaurants," observed the *Plain Dealer* in almost palpable relief. Considering the nearly $3 million estimated to have been spent in the city by Legionnaires, that single shattered window must have seemed like a bargain.

Exposition officials were undoubtedly buoyed by the September surge in attendance. They couldn't do anything about the shortening days, but they could extend the show by a few more days. A week after Labor Day, expo president Eben Crawford announced that the Great Lakes Exposition, originally booked for a hundred-day run, would be held over for a week—eight extra days of lakefront enjoyment. Autumn would arrive a little late in Cleveland that year.

ART GETS ITS DUE

Early in 1936, William Milliken looked up from plans for the Great Lakes Exposition and asked, in effect, "Where's the art?" As director of the Cleveland Museum of Art, Milliken had not only the right to ask but the clout to do something about it. Since 1936 would also mark the museum's twentieth anniversary, the obvious thing to do would be to mount a special exhibition.

Prompted by Milliken, museum trustees met with exposition officials in February to plan a major loan exhibition in conjunction with the Great Lakes Exposition. They pledged a $25,000 guarantee against loss, although a twenty-five-cent admission fee was expected to cover costs. Because of the value of the objects included, it would necessarily be housed in the museum's classical-style home in University Circle. The entire main floor would be placed at the disposal of the exhibition, with most of the permanent collection relegated to the ground floor.

Now Milliken had just four months to get his act together. He was only the second director in the museum's two decades, having succeeded Frederick Allen Whiting in 1930. Described by *Time* magazine as "suave, dapper, erudite," the forty-six-year-old bachelor began calling in his chits from neighboring museums and local collectors.

From Detroit came *Saint Jerome in His Study* by Christus; Chicago sent Toulouse-Lautrec's *At the Moulin Rouge* and five others. Sixteen paintings, including Turner's dramatic *Burning of the Houses of Parliament,* came from the estate of the late Cleveland philanthropist John Long Severance. Leonard Hanna lent his early Picasso, *Figures (Pink).*

Milliken's net quickly expanded from coast to coast and even beyond. From New York, Mrs. John W. Simpson sent Chardin's *Soap Bubbles* and the Adolph Lewisohn Collection parted temporarily with Van Gogh's *L'Arlesienne.* Washington, D.C.'s Phillips Collection contributed its prize attraction, *Luncheon of the Boating Party* by Renoir; Walter C. Arensberg of Hollywood offered the sensation of New York's 1913 Armory Show, Marcel Duchamp's *Nude Descending a Staircase.*

One of Milliken's biggest coups was the promise of four items from the Rockefellers in New York, who made an exception to their rule against lending art works. Especially symbolic was the inclusion of Sargent's portrait of oil baron and family patriarch John D. Rockefeller Sr. It was interpreted by some as a sign of renewed affection by the nonagenarian for the city where he had begun his fortune. His son sent a pair of altarpiece panels by the Siennese Duccio, which Milliken considered "the prize catch of the show."

On one of Milliken's early fishing expeditions he had been on Washington's Embassy Row in hopes of catching some European loans. It paid off in contributions from collections in London, Paris, Bologna, Florence, Milan, Rome, and Venice. Overall, the museum director reported a 98 percent success rate in getting what he wanted.

A total of 385 works of art were deployed in the show, of which fewer

William Milliken, director of the Cleveland Museum of Art, assembled 385 works of art for the Official Art Exhibit of the Great Lakes Exposition. Although nearly half the show came from the museum's own collection, Milliken used his extensive connections to secure works on loan all the way from Los Angeles to Paris. *Cleveland Press* Collection.

than half, 160, came from the museum's own collection. Accorded the place of honor in the catalogue was the museum's medieval Guelph Treasure, Milliken's first and ultimately most significant purchase as director. Also on view was the museum's most recent acquisition, Cezanne's *Pigeon Tower at Montbriand*.

Touted as a $12 million review of six centuries of Western art, the Twentieth Anniversary Exhibition of the Cleveland Museum of Art was unveiled on June 26, the eve of the Great Lakes Exposition opening. Comparisons with Chicago's Century of Progress art exhibition were inevitable, and there seemed a consensus of critical opinion that, while smaller in quantity, the Cleveland show excelled in quality.

"The Cleveland Museum of Art has tried to build its permanent collection on quality alone, and it has never stressed the quantitative," Milliken explained in the *New York Times*. "The Twentieth Anniversary Exhibition expresses this same philosophy—a philosophy which has animated not only the museum but Cleveland collectors as well."

"Director Milliken's unique achievement was to get all his masters into one museum without letting them fight," said *Time* magazine. "So natural was the progression of pictures and schools, so considerately was each of the 385 paintings displayed in its place, that visitors were last week amazed to feel no museum fatigue after making the rounds."

There were two empty spaces on those rounds for the first week of the show. Then, on July 3, police met a Railway Express Agency shipment in Union Terminal and escorted two paintings from the Louvre down Euclid Avenue to University Circle. One was *The Holy Family* by Titian; the other, Raphael's *Portrait of Two Men*. They had been sent by the Paris museum as a special tribute to the late Myron T. Herrick, former Clevelander who had twice served as ambassador to France. They had been delayed, in typical French fashion, by changes of government and strikes in Paris.

A potential handicap for the "Official Art Exhibit of the Great Lakes Exposition" was its physical separation by some three miles from the grounds downtown. "It is worth a trip to Europe," stated the exposition guidebook, "and all that is necessary is to take the Euclid Avenue street car from the Public Square to East Boulevard or Adelbert Road, or a Hough Avenue trolley bus to the end of the line. The Museum is just a few minutes' walk from either stop."

Both Clevelanders and visitors made the trip in gratifying numbers. From one thousand on opening day, considered a favorable sign, crowds swelled to more than five thousand daily in the closing weekend. Some waited in line for hours for the galleries to clear. On Sundays Milliken was giving four talks a day to capacity audiences in the museum's five-hundred-seat auditorium, reclining backstage in exhaustion between lectures.

One distinguished visitor even came back from the dead, in a manner of speaking, to view the exhibition. This was the French modernist Marcel Duchamp, listed erroneously in the catalogue over the dates 1887–1933. Said to have been "immensely entertained" when informed of his reported demise, the artist stopped in Cleveland on his way back to France from the West Coast, both to see the CMA show and to demonstrate, à la Mark Twain, that rumors of his death had been "greatly exaggerated."

Duchamp may also have been amused to learn that his *Nude Descending a Staircase* was the best-selling reproduction of the show. It couldn't have been the result of prurient interest, since his cubist rendering had been famously described as "an explosion in a shingle factory." Most of the purchases, according to the lady at the sales desk, were "from the standpoint of levity."

In a more serious frame of mind, visitors voted for Whistler's *White Girl* as their favorite in the show, followed by Hals's *The Merry Lute Player.* In third place, reputedly propelled by the votes of young schoolboys, was the museum's own *Stag at Sharkey's* by Bellows. Like the exposition itself, the art show was extended an extra week in October, in part to give more local schoolchildren a chance to see it. Milliken later claimed a total attendance in excess of 180,000.

Not all the borrowed artworks had to be given up by the museum. During the exhibition, it was announced that the sixteen works from the Severance estate had been left to the Cleveland museum. They included not only the Turner but paintings by Gainsborough, Hobbema, Lawrence, Rembrandt, and Reynolds.

The experience undoubtedly was all highly gratifying to William Milliken, but it didn't come without personal cost. Traveling to Europe that winter for rest and recuperation, he suffered a nervous breakdown in Sicily. Happily, he bounced back to head the Cleveland Museum of Art for another two decades.

5

Down the Midway

Finally! At last, expo-goers had reached the amusement zone. Those exhibits and displays in the grounds west of East 9th Street were impressive and instructive; they showed off the region to advantage, and most visitors would have admitted to having learned something—some of them, a lot. Having paid their educational dues, they were ready for some serious fun.

"Forty acres of thrills, laughs and fun to attract the millions of Exposition visitors, await the opening of the big show on the lakefront," planners had promised. Fully a third of the grounds had been given over to the amusement zone. "The range of choice is very wide. Whatever one may call his or her favorite 'fun,' it will be found in the Great Lakes Exposition."

"Also, there was a midway, as honky-tonk as Coney Island," Winsor French would fondly recall fifteen years later, "and it served as a great safety valve for people who had lived too long with talk of depression and unemployment." He had good authority for that opinion—no less than that of President Franklin Roosevelt. Regretting that he hadn't time to see all the scientific exhibits during his 1936 visit, FDR also put in a plug for the midway attractions with the observation that "a good many people in this country are entitled to a good time after what they have been through."

People evidently were in no need of presidential prompting, many of them opting for play before work. "Rowdy and rollicking was the Midway with live pythons and motorized dinosaurs," observed *Time* magazine of opening week. "But almost deserted was the underground Lakeside Exhibition Hall, where visitors were invited to prowl through plaster of Paris mines, gaze at blast furnaces and Bessemer converters, store away such bits of knowledge as: 'It takes five tons of material to make one ton of steel.'"

Exposition officials were more than willing to give the people what they wanted. While exhibitors in the rest of the grounds pulled down the shutters nightly at 10:00, it was announced, "The midway will be kept open as long as the volume of business warrants it." Jean Skelly, working for the expo's public relations firm, Miskell & Sutton, was assigned an office right on the grounds that summer. "When we closed the office, we didn't go home," she remembered.

Save for food and a handful of special attractions, most of the sights in the upper and lower exhibition areas were free; in the amusement zone, nearly everything had a price. Even the comfort stations, besides free "sanitary toilet facilities," offered "smaller pay accommodations for those who desire them." Tickets for most of the rides and concessions cost from a dime to a quarter. Adding up all the admission charges in the *Cleveland Press*, Jack Warfel came up with a grand total of $15.15. Seeing everything at the Century of Progress, he pointed out by way of comparison, would have set one back to the tune of $69.50 (though admittedly, there had been more to see in Chicago). As for food and drink, expo officials pledged that prices would be "no higher than one is accustomed to paying for food of the same quality in the same environment anywhere." One freebie viewable from all sections of the grounds was a nightly display of $1,500 worth of fireworks.

So, in the words of the *Plain Dealer*, "Step into the Midway, folks, and let yourself go. Enter with a stout heart, a strong stomach, and a pocket full of change; you'll use them all. . . . Here is building after building filled with things that will thrill you or make you laugh. There are good things to eat and cool things to drink. In fact, there is everything that makes for a hilarious time."

■

Whether they entered through the underpass or came in directly from an outside entrance on East 9th, visitors to the amusement zone were greeted first by the Continental flair of Herman Pirchner's Alpine Village. It occupied an island of an acre or so right between the two entryways, which would merge into the midway past Pirchner's nightspot and beer garden. "Because I, in a sense, inspired the Great Lakes Exposition, Lincoln [Dickey] was generous," recalled Pirchner. "'Pick your location,' he said." Without a doubt, the Village occupied prime expo real estate.

Regardless of whether or not Pirchner had been the expo's prime instigator, Dickey had ample reason to grant him special consideration. Not only had the Austrian native anteed up a thousand dollars for Dudley Blossom's starter fund, but he became the first nightclub operator to actually sign up for a concession. His contract called for an investment of more than $50,000 to provide a restaurant, beer garden, and sidewalk café on approximately twenty-two thousand square feet. From the outside, his operation wasn't much different from the expo's overall generic modernistic design, save for the large "LEISY'S" sign advertising Cleveland's oldest and largest brewery.

Inside, however, expo-goers would find themselves amid the log walls, timbered rafters, and rough wooden tables of an Alpine tavern. "It was a good beer-drinking atmosphere," said Pirchner. "It was by far the largest dining room in the expo." There was room for five hundred in the dining room officially and two hundred more in the terraced beer garden. Including the bar, Pirchner claimed he could squeeze in a thousand. A total of some thirty-two hundred was accommodated in shifts on opening night, and the Village turned away more for lack of room.

Besides a hearty Central European menu and endless streams of Leisy's Dortmunder, Pirchner's establishment overflowed with gemütlichkeit. It was supplied by some 150 employees, with those on the floor outfitted in full Alpine regalia. Apparently one condition of employment was an ability to yodel. Otto Thurn led an oompah band of a dozen lederhosen-clad musicians in a colorful Tyrolean bandstand; a Viennese quartet in blue-and-white student uniforms sang as they marched around the large dance floor; Mildred Smith sang tunes from *The Merry Widow* "in a high, clear soprano that never needs the aid of a microphone." If that weren't enough, Pirchner had Jeanne ("Little Egypt") Farah waiting in the wings with an exotic dance act.

But the main attraction was often the proprietor himself, never to be outdone in costume or yodeling. "Bubbling over with energy, Impresario Pirchner is somewhat of a genius in making people feel at home or putting them in a singing mood," observed a reporter. "Within two minutes after his first revue started he had his guests singing 'Ein Prosit' and 'Tipperary' at the top of their voices." His specialty was carrying a tray piled high with filled beer steins across the room without spilling a drop.

Having established a record of thirty-six steins at his Playhouse Square location, Pirchner was determined to set a new high at the Great Lakes Exposition. Perhaps to a drumroll by Otto Thurn, the feather-hatted host started across the dance floor with fifty foaming beer steins stacked on his tray. Cautiously, he crab-stepped to the middle of the room, then suddenly went down in a Niagara of broken glass and Leisy's best. Nursing sundry bruises and abrasions, he pointed to a wad of carelessly discarded gum as the cause of his downfall.

Though running simultaneously with his Playhouse Square operation and another on the far east side, Pirchner's exposition venture quickly

"Ein Prosit!" Lifting their steins in a toast to guest Frances Srjanzak at the Alpine Village are Otto Thurn, Herman Pirchner, and Paul Klatt. Located on the threshold of the Great Lakes Exposition's amusement zone, the Village was an expo version of Pirchner's popular nightclub on Euclid Avenue. Thurn was the leader of the oompah band, while host Pirchner might be seen schlepping dozens of foaming beer steins at a time across the dance floor. *Cleveland Press* Collection.

became one of the city's favorite gathering places that summer. Mayor Harold Burton spotted William McDermott, the *Plain Dealer*'s globe-trotting columnist and drama critic, fresh from another European sojourn. "I suppose McDermott is here to get a little foreign atmosphere," loudly bantered His Honor. In the early morning hours, the old-timers from the midway would often turn up there for story-swapping sessions. They were presided over by the Alpine's seventy-seven-year-old doorman, August Siefert, who claimed to have taken in every important exposition over the previous forty years.

∎

Some of the overflow crowd waiting outside the Alpine Village may have found themselves accosted by a young man in red cloak and tights. His name was "Shorty" Fuller, barker for the Old Globe Theatre, and his job was to get patrons into the reconstructed Elizabethan theater on the north side of the East 9th entrance for a serving of Shakespeare. No one would have considered that an easy sell on the midway. His main selling point to a pair of young boys was a graphic description of the murder of Julius Caesar to be seen inside for only fifteen cents. "Don't be a sucker," said one of them to the other; "For ten cents we can go across the street and see Hauptmann electrocuted." Fuller wasn't without support in his task, however. Members of the company staged free Morris dance exhibitions and Punch and Judy shows on the green outside the theater to entice passing expo-goers.

Dr. Thomas Wood Stevens, a theater scholar, poetry editor, and Shakespeare enthusiast, was the impresario behind the Old Globe. Stevens, as head of the Carnegie Institute of Technology Drama School in Pittsburgh a dozen years earlier, had advised the Cleveland Play House to hire a Carnegie student named Frederic McConnell as its first professional director. Under McConnell the Play House had matured into one of America's leading regional theaters. Now Stevens proposed to bring Shakespeare to the Cleveland masses in a format similar to that in which he had first been seen by the masses of "Merrie England." He had tried it out with considerable success at the Century of Progress in 1934. He would be repeating his experiment in San Diego, Dallas, and Cleveland, the three exposition cities of 1936.

Stevens was savvy enough to know that few expo-goers would be willing to invest an entire afternoon or evening in a classic play—in verse, yet! His gimmick was to offer them "tabloid" versions of the Bard, each pared down to under an hour in length. "Nothing important will be left out," Charles W. Lawrence assured readers of the *Plain Dealer,* "just a lot of the stuff you couldn't see any sense in when you were in high school, anyhow." Ward Marsh would review a thirty-six-minute *A Comedy of Errors* and a forty-two-minute *As You Like It* in the same paper. Even a Bard devotee such as William McDermott could see the benefit of brevity under the circumstances. "With all his great genius, Shakespeare is long-winded for a modern audience," he noted in his column. "He can stand the cutting which he invariably gets in one degree or another."

While not averse to altering the text, Stevens aspired to a faithful realization of Shakespeare's theater. His Old Globe was a half-timbered replica based on specifications for London's Fortune Theatre, a contemporary of Shakespeare's own Globe. It was somewhat smaller, seating about six hundred, and it placed the audience on benches in the pit, where the masses of Elizabeth's day had to stand. Due to fire regulations there would be no seating in the galleries, where the gentry of old were wont to sit. All in all, McDermott observed without complaint that the Great Lakes version was "more comfortable and a good deal more sanitary than the original ever was."

In another stab at presumed authenticity, the players performed everything in Elizabethan dress, merely draping togas over their breeches and doublets to suggest the Rome of *Julius Caesar*. Ten-year-old Bob Andree of Rocky River, taken to the Globe by his grandfather, experienced an unintended touch of verisimilitude. He doesn't recall exactly what play he witnessed; much clearer in his memory was having his pocket picked by a modern version of the Elizabethan cutpurse.

Some thirty young troupers were recruited for the Great Lakes Globe, several coming from Stevens's former bases in Pittsburgh and Chicago. There were five Clevelanders: Kenneth Bates, John Johnston, Rita Koval, Wayne McKeekan, and Jay Pozz. McKeekan was originally a Michigander who had come to town to work for Sherwin-Williams and study drama with Barclay Leathem of Western Reserve University. Though consigned to several thankless roles such as First Merchant or Fourth Citizen, he would be heard from again, as would two out-of-towners in the cast. Like McKeekan, Chicagoan Sam Wanamaker had to pay his dues by impersonating a colorless variety of servants and attendants. A John Kennedy, who hailed from Massachusetts via Carnegie Tech, managed to snare meatier parts and later claimed to have earned forty dollars a week against the prevailing eighteen.

Whether for $18 or $40, they obviously earned their wages. There were seven performances a day, eight on weekends, from a repertoire of six plays: *A Comedy of Errors, The Taming of the Shrew, A Midsummer Night's Dream, As You Like It, Julius Caesar,* and *King Henry VIII*. Most plays were given at least once daily; most players appeared in five of the six but were allowed to miss one performance a day.

Besides the grueling schedule, there were other trials to contend with. Kennedy recalled a nightly stench emanating from a sewage outlet blocked by a submarine berthed near the Globe. When a storm loosed the sub's stern line one evening, the actors finished the job by pushing the vessel out into the lake for at least temporary relief. They weren't doing *Macbeth*, so *Julius Caesar* seemed to be their jinxed play. "Scarcely a performance ends without a skinned knee, bruised eye or cracked elbow having been received during the mob scene," reported Jack Warfel in the *Press*. Then there was the night when Mark Antony's funeral oration over the body of the dead Caesar was interrupted by the cry of a barker from the midway: "Your dime back if he's not alive!"

Even more discouraging must have been the sparse houses early in the season. While the Alpine Village was turning them away across the road, one Play House observer was counting the Globe's audiences on his fingers. "One night we were livid because . . . we had an audience of two," said Kennedy.

The Old Globe Theatre

Thomas Wood Stevens, *Director*

Presenting in Brief the Plays of Shakespeare (and certain of his Friends) in a Replica of Shakespeare's Playhouse.

Before the Plays, on the Village Green, the Morris and Country Dances of Merrie England.

*Can this cockpit hold
The vasty fields of France? or may we cram
Within this wooden O the very casques
That did affright the air at Agincourt?*
—SHAKESPEARE

WEEK OF AUGUST 24th, 1936

●

GLOBE THEATRE PRODUCTIONS, LTD.

Present

THE BLACKFRIARS COMPANY

In the Plays of

WILLIAM SHAKESPEARE

JULIUS CAESAR

Julius Caesar	*Karl Weber*	Second Citizen	*Samuel Wanamaker*
Marcus Brutus	*Hubbard Kirkpatrick*	Third Citizen	*A. Vance Hallack*
Marcus Antonius	*Joseph Curtin*	Fourth Citizen	*Wayne McMeekan*
Caius Cassius	*John Kennedy*	Lucius	*Rita Koval*
Casca	*Wyman Holmes*	Calpurnia	*Charity Grace*
Trebonius	*Jerome Stein*	Portia, wife of Brutus	*Dorothy Tynan*
Decius Brutus	*Jay Edward Pozz*	Senator	*Lee Haydn*
Metellus Cimber	*William Robertson*	Citizens	*Wyman Holmes,*
Cinna	*Kenneth Helmbock*		*Jerome Stein, Jay Edward Pozz,*
Artemidorus	*Rex Roberts*		*William Robertson, Kenneth*
A Soothsayer	*Kenneth Bates*		*Helmbock, Charles Moyer, Rex*
Popilius Lena	*A. Vance Hallack*		*Roberts, Kenneth Bates, A. Vance*
First Citizen	*Kenneth Helmbock*		*Hallack, Josef Knabel.*

SCENE: Rome. The play staged by Thomas Wood Stevens.

Tabloid versions of half a dozen Shakespearean plays were on the bill at the expo's Old Globe Theatre. They were staged in a reconstruction of one of the Bard's original playhouses and pared to less than an hour apiece in length. Out of this cast for *Julius Caesar*, John Kennedy, Wayne McKeekan, and Sam Wanamaker would be heard from again. Author's Collection.

Things eventually picked up, aided no doubt by good reviews. "The plays are presented in a swift, no-intermission, vigorous style. 'Streamlined' and shortened without undue damage to Shakespeare's deathless lines," summarized Charles Schneider in the *Press*. "And there's a pleasant absence of the artful, mincing mannerisms," added Arthur Spaeth of the *News*. "It's truly a case of the play's the thing—and the play's entertaining." Within a month the players were drawing in excess of a thousand a day, and Kennedy remembered full houses by summer's end.

Kennedy had no cause for complaint about his own reviews. "John Kennedy plays Petruchio with broad and bold strokes, with good humor and with vigor," wrote Warfel of *The Taming of the Shrew*. "He is admirable in catching the king's fierce temperament if not the finer nuances," said Glenn Pullen of Kennedy's Henry VIII in the *Plain Dealer*. "There's a real Shakespearean tang to his arrogant strut and deep voice which delivers the history-making speeches so fluently." Also admired was Kennedy's delivery of the "All the world's a stage" monologue as Jacques in *As You Like It*.

In September Stevens freshened up the repertoire by importing a production of *Romeo and Juliet* from his San Diego Globe. Longer at eighty minutes than the other plays, it would be given once nightly at a premium admission of seventy-five cents. Though many of the leads came from the West Coast production, Elizabeth Robinson of the local troupe landed the role of Juliet, and Kennedy was rewarded with the plum part of Mercutio. Thanks undoubtedly to Stevens's publicity man, Roy Harvey, a good-luck wire along with a rose bush from the "Romeo and Juliet garden" in California came to the Globe from Norma Shearer, star of the current movie version of Shakespeare's tragedy.

■

That submarine that inadvertently fouled so many Globe performances was actually the next act on the north side of the midway. It was moored in a basin which, cutting deeply into the amusement zone, normally served as the home of the local U.S. Coast Guard station. For the duration of the expo, the artificial harbor also provided a venue for several water-related attractions.

First came the 240-foot, 1,000-ton S-49, a former U.S. Navy submarine launched in 1922 and decommissioned nine years later. It was a sister ship of the S-51, which had sunk off Long Island in 1925 with a loss of thirty-four crew members. The S-49 herself had once lost four submariners, when the batteries underneath their sleeping quarters exploded. An entrepreneur named F. J. Crestensen had purchased the S-49 from the navy and exhibited her at the Century of Progress.

"As honky-tonk as Coney Island" is how one reporter fondly recalled the midway of the Great Lakes Exposition. Another counseled expo-goers to "enter with a stout heart, a strong stomach, and a pocket full of change." On the left, they might have taken a boat ride on the lake or inspected a real submarine; on the other side were such attractions as Cliff Wilson's Snake Show behind its tall bamboo facade and the "real southern cooking" of Mammy's Cabin farther down the strip. Cleveland Public Library.

No longer equipped even to maneuver in reverse, let alone dive, the S-49 was towed to the Great Lakes Exposition by tug from her home base in Erie, Pennsylvania. For thirty cents, a nickel more than the price of most Old Globe performances, visitors might board her and inspect such curiosities as its four-by-ten-foot galley and the emergency escape hatch. Sharing the water with the S-49 was a nearby "paddle-about" concession. These ungainly craft may not have been so glamorous, but at least they were capable of navigating the waves under their renters' own powers.

Once past the Coast Guard basin, the strip expanded northward into several acres of amusements. On a conspicuous corner was an attraction called the Front Page, aimed at the public fascination in the 1930s with gangsters and G-men. It opened with what seemed like a surefire draw in John Dillinger Sr., father of America's first "Public Enemy No. 1." Garbed in one of his late son's suits and armed with the wooden gun used by junior in his prison break, the elder Dillinger prepared to impress upon young visitors the futility of a life of crime. "There was nothing I could say to him then," said the seventy-one-year-old former shopkeeper about his son's sudden reappearance at home after his escape. "He had already gone too far. All John had when he died was seven-odd dollars, a watch and a few personal things."

Alack, crime proved no more profitable for the father than for the son. After a run of only three days Mrs. J. R. Castle, proprietress of the concession, felt constrained to give the old man his notice. It had been nearly two years since young Dillinger had been gunned down by federal agents, and several Public Enemies No. 1, including "Pretty Boy" Floyd and "Baby Face" Nelson, had come and gone in the interim. "I hate to let him go, but . . . I don't know what I can do. People around here just don't seem to be interested," explained Mrs. Castle. "He's such a nice old gentleman, and he tells how he ran a store while John ran around loose and got into bad company."

Other anti-crime crusaders were on tap to fill out the Front Page. They may not have been the real thing, as was Mr. Dillinger, but they tried to make up in acting ability for what they lacked in pedigree. One John Caterino, for example, demonstrated the gruesome death throes of a criminal undergoing electrocution. "A black cap is put over his head, and he writhes in three different movements as a man . . . pulls three different switches," related Roelif Loveland in the *Plain Dealer.* "A black velvet curtain is then drawn across the stage in front of the chair, and we leave poor Mr. Caterino apparently paying for his sins."

To Loveland's professed surprise and relief, Caterino turned up again a few minutes later, but only to undergo this time the tortures of hanging. "Yes, I am hanged as many as 24 times a day," he told the reporter after surviving yet another execution. "It is quite safe. I have about twelve inches of extra rope. That has always been enough." He had never witnessed an execution himself but learned the fine points of muscular contractions from Mrs. Castle, who in turn received her instruction secondhand from talks with penitentiary wardens.

If one left the Front Page in search of lighter fare, the exposition had anticipated the need right next door, with Monkey Land. For a dime, one might watch real monkeys riding miniature automobiles and capering on other mechanical devices. (Of course, one could see monkeys disporting in a natural habitat for no extra charge on Monkey Island, which opened that same summer at Cleveland's Brookside Zoo.)

One magnet after another led expo-goers young and old uncritically through the amusement zone. Leading an imaginary nephew by the hand, Gerold Frank of the *News* announced, "On our left is a small island of entertainment: the Hey Dey ride, a golf driving course, the Watermelon gardens, the Ridee-o, the Lion Motordrome, the Tumble-Bug ride, the kiddy rides, the merry-go-round, the Iroquois Indian village, the pony track, the airplane ride, the flying trapeze, a riding school, a Ferris wheel, the Flying Scooter, the Loop the Plane, the—I'm out of breath, Rollo."

Perhaps the Loop the Plane was "that midway scissors business" on which Winsor French spied local patricians Charlie Otis and Len Hanna mixing with the masses. Hanna was hit in the eye by his own cigarette case "during that breathless, upside-down moment." Such moments were all in the day's work for the Four Lorenzos, whose trapeze act was the major free attraction, with shows twice daily, in the middle of the rides section. It took a dime, however, to see the Iroquois from New York's Tonawanda reservation demonstrate "the tribal dances, songs, athletics and other life of the 'vanishing race.'"

Working their way through the rides would have led thrill-seekers up to the lake and back around to the Coast Guard basin, where a fleet of water launches, including speedboats and seaplanes, awaited to transport those so inclined around the lake before they returned for further midway adventures.

■

Having circumnavigated the northern half of the amusement zone, expo-goers would have found themselves back at the Front Page, facing the yet unsampled southern strip of the midway. An unbroken line of concessions nearly half a mile in length, this was probably closer to the popular conception of midway fare—certainly to Winsor French's evocation of Coney Island honky-tonk. The term itself came out of Chicago's 1893 Columbian Exposition, when planners filled a mile-long stretch between two parks—the "Midway Plaisance"—with exotic foreign villages, the world's first Ferris wheel, and risqué acts of which "Little Egypt" became a prototype.

The Great Lakes version began innocently enough, with a maple sugar camp just inside the East 9th underpass. It was the concession of W. S. Richards of Geauga County, who had outdoor workers in nineteenth-century dress demonstrating the traditional process of tapping a pair of maples and boiling down the syrup in large iron kettles over an open fire. Inside a log sugar cabin, other attendants demonstrated the modern process, using a mechanical evaporator, and offered the product for sale. Thinking more of what awaited expo-goers further down the midway, *Cleveland Press* columnist Jack Raper cracked, "And we suppose there'll be many a sap tapped, too."

Raper may have been thinking of experiences such as one related by John Straka, who visited the exposition as a young man of nineteen or twenty. "There was a sideshow," he recalls after seven decades. "For ten cents, you could see a diver go into the water with a real octopus. I remember walking past a couple of times and trying to decide whether to spend a dime or not. At that age I didn't have much money, and even a dime for an octopus was somewhat extravagant." Curiosity finally overcame Depression-bred scrimping. "So we paid our dime, and the octopus was real, but what they neglected to advertise was that the octopus was dead." Straka may have recouped some of his investment afterward, in the entertainment he found in standing outside "to watch the faces of the people coming out."

Fred Schuld tells a similar story from his memory as an even younger visitor. "My mother and sister went to see a two-headed baby," he says, "but it was in formaldehyde!" Fred himself felt that he did better by going into a sideshow "where they had cars—FBI cars, crime cars, I don't know." (It may have been the International Crime Prevention Exhibit from 1937, billed as "Reproductions of major crimes portrayed by living actors showing that crime doesn't pay.") "One was supposed to be Dillinger's car—anyway, I believed it," continues Fred. "I'd never seen bulletproof glass. It was really thick."

Similar attractions in the southern strip included the Pantheon de la Guerre, filled with "World War trophies and relics gathered from the Battlefields of Europe." It was buttressed on one side by an embryological exhibit called the Bouquet of Life and on the other by The World a Million Years Ago. Animated models of some fifty prehistoric creatures filled the latter, from a twenty-three-foot stegosaurus to a forty-thousand-pound mammoth. Guides outfitted in khaki and sun hats were on hand to provide educational commentary.

From a million years in the past, expo-goers might stroll to the next exhibit for a preview of things to come. It was television, a modest concession that reached out to midway traffic by letting them see themselves passing on an outside screen. "The first time people just would not believe it," remembered Herman Pirchner. "They would walk by, see their picture, do a double take, and come back." Less impressed was the ten-year-old Bob Andree, perhaps still regretting the loss of his seven dollars. "I didn't really pay attention to it, I'll have to admit," he says. The Cleveland stringer for *Variety* was equally dismissive. "A show that would appear doomed is Television—long waits and hokum," he wrote in a classic off-the-mark prediction.

Food was available throughout the midway. There were the usual pretzel and taffy stands, naturally. Offering more substantial fare, as well as a touch of novelty, was a sit-down eatery called Mammy's Cabin. "In a typical Southern log cabin," said the guidebook, "colored women and chefs

One of the most popular concessions on the midway, seen at extreme right, was John Hix's Strange As It Seems, which offered "animated objects . . . and many other oddities" ranging from a one-man band to a three-legged woman. After cocktails at the Hollywood Studio Cafe, promenaders might step next door to view doubles of Hollywood stars demonstrating how movies were made. Cleveland Public Library.

prepare spring chicken, waffle potatoes and biscuits for visitors who enjoy real southern cooking." The novelty came in the presentation. "There will be no silver in the place," warned the *Plain Dealer.* "The chicken must be eaten with the fingers, and when the patron has finished he is served a bowl of warm water with a piece of lemon, soap and a towel."

While more than willing to provide African Americans with service jobs, Mammy's Cabin was accused of being less eager to serve them—with or without silver. According to Cleveland's black weekly, the *Call and Post,* a group of local blacks was bringing suit against Mammy's and two other expo venues for denial of service on the basis of color. The charges were denied and the suits apparently dropped; presumably the claimants were quietly accommodated.

Cleveland's smart set had no complaints about the service anywhere on the grounds. They got together one evening for a progressive dinner that began with tomato juice at a stand on the Court of the Presidents, continued with the full Southern course at Mammy's Cabin, corn-on-the-cob at a midway stand, and finally orange sherbet back at the Florida exhibit. "Everybody had a grand time, and got a lot of healthful exercise out of it," reported Eleanor Clarage.

Adjoining Mammy's Cabin, and run by the same concessionaire, was another bistro with a gimmick. Sportsmen's Paradise featured an eighty-by-thirty-foot pool stocked with perch, pike, and bass. Patrons were provided with baited rods and reels with which to catch their own dinner, which was then taken from the hook by a nautically attired attendant, then prepared and served inside. It sounded like a nifty idea, and it might have succeeded but for one of the peculiarities of Lake Erie's ecosystem.

That summer brought the annual infestation of the pesky winged insects known locally as midges, muckleheads, or, more colorfully, if erroneously, Canadian soldiers. Clarage overheard one feminine expo-goer telling her friend, "By the way, never in my life have I seen so many Canadian soldiers," in response to which, the other asked, "Were they good looking?" Evidently they looked good enough to the fish in Sportsmen's Paradise, who gorged on so many that they refused to bite for the paying customers. (No dumb bass in that pool.) Then the drain to the pond somehow slipped open, releasing half the stock into the lake. By August, Sportsmen's Paradise had reinvented itself as the Black Forest skating rink and dance hall.

■

People of all degrees could be found on the midway. Spotted by Winsor French was the noted journalist and boulevardier Lucius Beebe, stopping passersby in their tracks by "wearing enough plaids to clothe all of Scotland." Overheard at the Ohio Bell exhibit was a young girl using her free call to breathlessly tell Sis, "A guy guessed my weight wrong and I won a free parasol, and we went on that loop-the-loop thing, and I had my fortune told and the woman said I'm going to marry a dark, handsome fellow with lots of money." Sis's pleas that she needed help at home caring for their sick mom fell on deaf ears: "This is the first good time I've had in days and I won't have it spoiled," said the expo girl. The midway's lure was not to be denied.

Amplifying that lure was the job of a special breed of midway denizens known as barkers, though they preferred to be called "talkers." Shorty Fuller of the Old Globe wasn't truly representative of the fraternity, having been cast in that role as just another acting assignment. Much more typical were old-timers such as Robert Markus of the Creation exhibit, who was described by Glenn Pullen as "A neat juggler of adjectives and startling facts [who] learned his trade on the tanbark trail and still has a circus air in dress." They had their own jargon, in which audiences were "tips" and "casing a tip" was, as another reporter explained, "to estimate during the course of the ballyhoo just what per cent of the crowd that is listening will go inside and how many drift away to the next stand."

Johnny Meyers, who considered midgets an easy sell, was in his element talking up Graham's Midget Circus on the midway. He had retired two years previously, he said, but only until the seductive tooling of a circus calliope on the radio had him back on the road the very next day. The midget circus may have been an easy gig for Meyers, but it proved less so for some of the performers. On the expo's second day a twenty-one-inch dancer, billed as the "smallest girl in the world," fell off a forty-eight-inch stage and was taken to Charity Hospital with a possible fractured skull. Several weeks later, a storm threatened to bring down the big top overhead, until the show's only full-sized performer, an elephant named Pit, eased the tension by loosening some tent poles with its trunk. Graham's Circus was beginning to look as jinxed as *Julius Caesar* at the Globe.

Patrons of the neighboring 13 Spook Street expected the unexpected, as they wended their way through a haunted castle replete with creaking doors, banging shutters, and a "ghost dinner" in its repertoire of special effects. Known in the business as a "walk through," the Great Lakes version was modeled after a similar attraction at Coney Island. Coincidentally or not, it was heralded as the thirteenth concession signed up for the Cleveland exposition.

Scarier even than Spook Street for many would have been Cliff Wilson's Snake Show. Wilson hawked his own show, standing in front of its bamboo facade and talking up his slithery menagerie of caged reptiles. Centerpiece of the collection was a pit full of giant serpents fourteen feet or more in length. The show's twenty-eight-foot headliner was Elmer, the Borneo Reticulated Python. (One can imagine the loving emphasis with which Wilson articulated each syllable, "re-tic-u-lat-ed.")

For some reason Elmer had been off his feed of late, and Loveland witnessed a fearful exhibition of forced feeding. Mixing up a batch of seven dozen eggs and four pounds of hamburger, with proportionate dashes of sugar and olive oil, Wilson then had an assistant pry open the python's mouth. Inserting a length of rubber hose with a funnel on the end, he proceeded to ram his concoction down Elmer's maw with the aid of a bamboo pole. To the admiration of the watching crowd, the assistant coolly shook off his bleeding hand with a smile.

One of the most popular attractions on the strip, thanks to previous exposure in newspaper cartoons, was John Hix's Strange As It Seems.

Spielers were a vociferous presence in the amusement zone, as they pitched its shows to entice customers, or "tips," to part with their change and bid them, "step inside, folks." Roland Taylor, one of the fraternity, talked up the accomplishments of dancers in the Syrian Temple. Popularly known as "barkers," they preferred to be called "talkers." *Cleveland Press* Collection.

Described unabashedly as "A collection of animated objects, freaks, human or otherwise and many other oddities," its offerings included a flea circus, a one-man band, a three-legged woman, an armless girl who could sew and write, a sword swallower, Flexible Freddie the India-rubber man, and the Westinghouse robot. Santelle the strongman made the kids' jaws drop, as he ripped phone books to shreds and drove nails through boards with his bare hands! For the benefit of the tenderhearted, the show's manager offered a consoling thought: "All of these people would be dependent upon society if it weren't for their present occupations. As it is, they are self-supporting."

Strange as it seems (thank you, Mr. Hix), barkers . . . er, talkers, regarded "girl shows" as a relatively hard sell. "The public has been fooled by peep shows and girl shows so often that a talker has to be really good to sell them," explained Meyers. That's not to say they didn't try. The midway's outstanding specimen was Creation, described in the *Plain Dealer* as "a girl spectacle, illusion show. There are twenty scenes which change faster than the pennant hopes of the Cleveland Indians." One scene delivered a fleeting glimpse of an Eve in the company of a cloth serpent, to the piano accompaniment of "In the Shade of the Old Apple Tree."

Girls were also a part of some of the more general attractions. The Sport Show and Outdoor Exhibit on the midway found room for a "California sun or nudist colony." Others sought to bolster lagging attendance by adding some spice. A pair of "prehistoric hula hula dancers" named Oola and Boola were added to The World a Million Years Ago, while Princess Najda brought her Aztec drum dance to the Hollywood cocktail bar and show. After only two weeks, the Front Page ended its run and gave way to an attraction called "Rhumba." Loveland predicted it would be "a girl show of some sort, because the word 'naughty' has been prominently displayed on the side of the building."

Crime did make a comeback on the midway before long, in the form of a reenactment of the recent electrocution of Bruno Hauptmann for the slaying of the Lindbergh baby. Though done with animated wax figures and purportedly with an anti–capital punishment slant, the show promised enough gore to lure young boys away from the more edifying entertainment at the Old Globe.

Once past Creation, the southern strip faded away into the relatively innocuous concessions of Gulliver Land, an archery course, and then a roadway between a walled area to the north and an army encampment to the south. A detachment of the 11th Infantry from Fort Benjamin Harrison was stationed there to demonstrate camp life and contribute to the pageantry of exposition events. At the end of the road was the Goodyear blimp field, where for $3 a head, one of the silver leviathans waited to give prospects a ride over the expo grounds, the lakefront, and downtown Cleveland.

One of the first sights from the blimp must have seemed the most fantastic. Just over that walled area adjoining the field, one could see an assemblage of towers and rooftops suggestive of all lands and civilizations, separated by colorful winding streets, with even a mountain thrown in. The visitor still wasn't done with the Great Lakes Exposition—he had yet to walk the Streets of the World.

....

CARNY CHARACTERS

A few weeks before the opening of the Great Lakes Exposition, downtown pedestrians on St. Clair Avenue heard cries for help coming from the open door of a storefront. First to investigate happened to be a boy, who asked a distraught person in the doorway what the trouble was. When informed that the occupant and his partner were in the coils of a huge snake, the boy took off screaming.

Other onlookers, thinking it was some kind of stunt, merely laughed at the man's desperate plea—"For God's sake get the police." Someone finally took him seriously, but when a pair of cops arrived on the scene with drawn guns, the victims objected on the grounds that the man-killing python would go right on squeezing them to death even after its own demise. Three of their friends arrived at that point and managed to extricate the two men from the serpent's deadly grip.

Once out of peril, Cliff Wilson explained that he and his assistant had been trying to bathe the reptile in preparation for an exposition side-show, when the monster wrapped some of its twenty-eight-foot length around the helper's arm and leg and clamped its jaws down on Wilson's hand. Local newspapermen recognized Wilson from the "Sandusky sea-serpent scare" of some years earlier. It seemed Wilson had been part of a circus at Public Hall, when reports of monster serpent sightings began coming in from fishermen around the Lake Erie islands. Wilson went out in a rowboat to investigate and returned with one of his prize speci-mens, which he claimed had slithered away from the circus. "Of course I didn't report the escape," he had explained. "A snake like that at large was likely to have gobbled up a few horses or something, and I thought it would be just as well if it wasn't known that he was mine."

So reporters received the story of Wilson's cliffhanger on St. Clair with a modicum of skepticism, though duly noting the snake handler's heavily bandaged hand. It was Cleveland's first, but far from last, encounter with the carnival characters brought to town by the Great Lakes Exposition.

They were most in evidence on the midway, where Cliff Wilson would set up his snake show. Tattooing was a rare enough sight in the 1930s that onlookers were attracted to the arms of Curt McClelland, who put on Punch and Judy shows outside the Globe Theatre. McClelland ex-plained his ink as "a relic of his circus days." Other expo-goers may have done a double take at a Clark Gable sighting, only to discover that the handsome features of the movie idol actually belonged to midway weight-guesser Sam Snitman.

There were half a dozen weight-guessers on the midway. For fifteen cents, they promised to guess the expo-goer's avoirdupois within three pounds or else surrender a prize—generally a cane or a parasol. Men were subjected to a pat-down before the guesstimation, but women had to be sized up by sight alone. Guesser Danny Krassner related how he had once underestimated the "deceiving figure" of Eleanor Roosevelt by ten pounds. Snitman informed the crowds from his own experience that voluptuous Mae West tipped the scales at 140 pounds.

John Hix's Strange As It Seems exhibit was a veritable warehouse of uncommon humanity, ranging from tiny Bernice Weeks, billed as the "legless wonder" or "half woman," to Aurelio Tomaini, reputedly the "tallest boy in the world" at eight feet, four inches. As surely as opposites attract, the two fell in love at the Great Lakes expo. Since Miss Weeks, a minor, would have needed the consent of both parents to marry in Cleveland, the pair took leave from the expo to tie the knot in Ripley, New York.

Hix couldn't have been too happy about their elopement destination, since Ripley was also the name of his great rival. As it happened, Bob Ripley's Believe It or Not Odditorium succeeded Hix's show the following year at the Great Lakes Exposition, with its own cast of curious characters. Among them was elastic man Clarence E. Willard, a native of nearby Painesville, who claimed to be a descendant of artist Archibald Willard. Archibald had been a self-taught painter; Clarence had taught himself to add five or six inches to his height simply by stretching his pliant bones. He could also stretch an arm or a leg four inches longer than the other, which he claimed came in handy for walking along street curbs.

Not all the carnival types were confined to the midway. Keeping the aisles of the Florida exhibit swept was a janitor known as "Whistlin' Willie" Williams, who regularly entertained visitors with his imitations of birds, hens, roosters, rattlesnakes, and automobile horns. He styled himself as Willie L. Williams, adopting the initial in order to stand out from all the other Willie Williamses in his neck of Florida. His fifteen minutes of fame came when he did his rendition of a railroad train for the Major Bowes amateur radio hour.

Cleveland itself contributed to the expo's cast of eccentrics. Directing a crew of guidebook sellers was a small man in a pith helmet, who could show them how to do it himself. Ed Murray had begun his career in theater sales as a "candy butcher" in the old Cleveland Theatre and worked shows here and across the country ever since. He had cornered the theater market in Pittsburgh and made a fortune; he had bought a carnival and lost everything. He sold half a million guides for Great Lakes and was setting his sights even higher for the 1939 New York World's Fair. In the fifties he would still be hawking programs for Musicarnival in Warrensville Heights.

During the heat wave of 1936, John and Regeva Mulak earned their pay the hard way by dressing as Eskimos on the Byrd South Pole ship at the expo. There weren't really any Eskimos in the Antarctic, of course, but at least Mulak could claim to be a full-blooded Eskimo from Alaska, and

One was more than eight feet tall, and the other was billed as only a "half woman," but Aurelio Tomaini and Bernice Weeks didn't allow such disparities to stand in the way of love. They took a leave from the Great Lakes midway to tie the knot in Ripley, New York. *Cleveland Press* Collection.

his wife was half-Eskimo. They called themselves "impersonating advertisers," and the sidewalks of Euclid Avenue often served as their stage.

Mulak had sat in an electric chair in front of the Allen Theatre, made up as Boris Karloff and drooling on cue, with a wad of gum in his mouth, to publicize a movie entitled *The Walking Dead*. Playing a divorced couple, he and Regeva had staged a quarrel ending in blows to ballyhoo another show. To publicize *The Good Earth*, Mulak became a Chinese coolie pulling a rickshaw along Euclid. In 1937 he was again working for the expo, dressed this time as a penguin for the benefit of the Winterland ice spectacle. It was even worse than the Eskimo gig, since he had to waddle in the heat with both arms pinioned inside his suit.

Appropriately enough, the last word on carnival characters must be given to the fortune-tellers. They were often associated in the popular mind with Gypsies, who in turn were often linked with fairs or carnivals. One writer in the *Plain Dealer*, for instance, asserted that the Great Lakes Exposition had "lured a record number of these strange people into Cleveland." He tracked some down to a storefront decorated with gaudy trinkets on East 9th Street, not far from the expo's midway. "You would learn in a few visits with gypsies that they would constantly be telling your fortune if you permitted it," he observed.

Following up his leads, the writer drove out to visit a Gypsy encampment in rural Twinsburg, some twenty miles outside the city. There they had rented a field from local farmers, parked their cars, "some of them new and expensive," and pitched their tents for the summer. "Girls began to grab for our hands. The fortune telling had started," he related. "Turning to one of the girls, I asked where they did their fortune telling. 'Sure—in Akron, in Cleveland,' she said."

Some of them conceivably may have joined the exposition's sizable contingent of fortune-tellers. One reporter counted thirteen of them, most plying their trade in Streets of the World. Their methods included handwriting, astrology, phrenology, palmistry, tea leaves, and crystal-gazing. Madame Lea Bijou, a palm reader in the Egyptian Temple of Knowledge, could have had Romany blood in her veins; so may have another palmist known as Madame Rose.

Actually, the ethnic origins of most fortune-tellers seemed as diverse as their techniques. Mrs. W. H. Davis, a tea-leaf reader in the Shamrock Tearoom, didn't sound very exotic; neither did Miss Bertha Klein of the Romany Tearoom, who read futures in playing cards. As for crystal-gazer Vishnu Ranade, the gentleman may have been a real Hindu—or maybe just a good fakir.

One seer emerged from the competition to become a favorite of the expo's café society. She went by the name of Madame Zouiza and practiced the esoteric art of Egyptian sand-divining in a stand opposite the

Swedish Village. Zouiza (pronounced Zoo-aye-zah) supposedly came from Morocco, a heritage reinforced by the Arab headdress that provided an enigmatic touch to her otherwise unprepossessing appearance. She had been selected as the future bride of a plantation owner at the age of eleven, went her story, then educated and later married in Paris, where she gravitated in the orbit of such luminaries as Sarah Bernhardt and the Duke of Windsor.

Zouiza first discovered psychic powers by reading her husband's unopened mail. They would provide her with a livelihood after his death and the loss of the family's fortune. She read the plays of Noël Coward, listened to Chopin impromptus, and peppered her conversation with such conundrums as "Each time we live is but a day in school."

Her biggest promoter was Winsor French. "I found my way to her tent the afternoon the expo opened and to this moment she remains a mystery to me," he would recall two decades later. "She was a rather terrifying woman, Zouiza." He conducted Harpo Marx, undistinguished without his stage wig, to her presence one afternoon, and she administered a scolding that sent him into a sulk for the rest of the day. "You make nonsense all the time," she admonished, charging him with disappointing his mother and wasting his life. To a prominent Cleveland matron who had lost her star sapphire, Zouiza predicted that she would find it in filth. One wonders whether the woman was more relieved or insulted, when it turned up that night in her hairbrush.

Evidently Zouiza remained a Cleveland fixture long after the Great Lakes Exposition dimmed its lights. French passed on a rumor that after the first season she would be practicing her calling at the Mayfair Casino, the art deco nightclub that briefly operated in the Ohio Theatre on Playhouse Square. Following the expo's second and final summer, she set up shop in a flat at the foot of East 9th Street. One of her clients was a prominent Akron industrialist who overcame alcoholism with her aid. Cleveland department-store heiress Kay Halle once received an airmail missive from Zouiza warning her to keep a close watch on one of her friends, only to learn only hours later that the woman had just committed suicide.

Yet Zouiza left behind letters after her own death denying any paranormal powers, according to French. Furthermore, she had come from Maine, not Morocco. She had entered show business via burlesque in Boston and developed her cabalistic persona while working the carnival circuit en route to the Great Lakes Exposition. Thus Winsor French closed the book on Madame Zouiza; but, as was said of the death of George Gershwin, one didn't have to believe it.

Global Village

6

"The entrance will probably be built along the lines of a European castle, and from the moment visitors step inside they will leave America behind," promised Richard Rychtarik. Back in January he had been named to design one of the major attractions of the Great Lakes Exposition: the Streets of the World. As envisioned in the official guidebook, "The gayety of the Exposition reaches its peak along these colorful streets. Seeking diversion and pleasure, one may choose the typical nightlife of almost any nationality. There are alluring Parisian girls. From a nearby village comes the strange piping of music of the Far East. Rumba rhythms and spirited Spanish dancers enliven another cafe. The happy comradery of singing and lifting steins of beer beckon from a German beer garden. The strains of languorous European waltzes float into the night from the Viennese cafes. Each foreign land presents its own special attraction."

As with so many other features on the grounds, Chicago once again had provided the model. Its "Midway Plaisance" of 1893 had contained villages from Egypt, Algeria, Dahomey, Ireland, and Austria. There were half a dozen in the 1933 Century of Progress, including the Streets of Paris and the Belgian Village. "The village is inhabited by craftsmen in the costumes of hundreds of years ago," said the Chicago guidebook of the latter. "Ancient folk dances are a feature of the main square. Typical Belgian milk carts drawn by dogs and driven by merry milkmaids add to the picturesqueness of the village." The frolicsome Belgians proved so popular that Chicago opened half a dozen additional villages the following year, among them Hawaiian, Irish, Italian, and Tunisian.

Such expansiveness was beyond the scope and means of the Great Lakes Exposition. Making a virtue of necessity, planners came up with the idea of accommodating even more ethnic communities within a single area. It would be an "international village" in which dozens of different nationalities would share the same streets in true cosmopolitan fashion, anticipating the "salad bowl," as opposed to "melting pot," model of later immigration historians.

It would also be a microcosm of the population of Greater Cleveland. Following various censuses of the early twentieth century, Cleveland was said to be the world's third-largest Slovene city, second-largest Hungarian city, and largest Slovak city, presumably not even excepting Bratislava. Although down from 30.1 percent in 1920, Cleveland's foreign-born white population still constituted one of every four residents (25.5 percent) in 1930. Czechs led the list, followed in order by Poles, Italians, Germans, Hungarians, Yugoslavs, and Russians. Black Clevelanders reversed the overall trend by doubling their numbers during the twenties, rising from 4.3 to 8 percent of the general population.

Despite the drastic decline of immigration in the wake of the quota acts of the 1920s, ethnic influence was still strong in Cleveland at the time of the expo. Perhaps the most prominent evidence could be seen in the chain of Cultural Gardens planted in Rockefeller Park, beginning in 1926 with the Hebrew Garden; by 1936 there were a dozen. Another example during the early 1930s was a Theater of the Nations series sponsored by the *Cleveland Plain Dealer* for three seasons in the Little Theater of Public Hall.

When John H. Gourley was appointed as director of Streets of the World, he wisely enlisted the input and participation of the various nationality groups. He had taught English for the foreign-born in Milwaukee before coming to Cleveland to serve as a director of the Cleveland Recreational Council and then as the city's recreation commissioner. His work kept him in contact with the various ethnic groups, for whom he developed a genuine sympathy. "These people are real citizens, but they rightfully retain something of their old country culture," he stated.

Some five thousand meetings among the different nationalities went into realizing the Streets of the World. Gourley estimated that the final result would represent the heritage of more than 70 percent of the Greater Cleveland population. No group seemed too small to want a piece of the action. There were only twenty-five Belgians in Cleveland, but with the aid of their countrymen in other cities, they were planning a café, food shop, and novelty concession. Even the city's seven Hindus signed up for a restaurant and tea shop. Many saw participation as an opportunity to raise funds for national halls, cultural gardens, or charitable causes. By the expo's opening date, three dozen different nationalities could be found in Gourley's global village.

Here is Streets of the World, as it would have appeared from one of those blimps circling in 1937. Squeezed within its walls were ten acres of faux Old World churches, palaces, towers, and rathskellers. It was bordered by the rides of the amusement zone (bottom), the U.S. Army encampment (right), and the Goodyear blimp field (top). Stretching into the distance was Lake Shore Boulevard, recently completed by the WPA. Author's Collection.

It was up to Richard Rychtarik to provide these disparate groups with a workable setting or showcase. He was a Czech immigrant of broad artistic abilities, from watercolors to furniture design, but his chief interest lay in designing stage scenery. His work in that medium had been on prominent view at the Cleveland Play House and most recently in the operatic productions staged by the Cleveland Orchestra in Severance Hall. Now he had been handed a vast outdoor stage, ten acres in extent, and told to fill it with dozens of different sets. In a sense he would be doing what the WPA artists were doing in the Hall of the Great Lakes with their miniature model of Cleveland—but on a human-sized scale. It was either a stage designer's biggest nightmare or a dream come true.

Rychtarik freely scattered replicas of world-famous structures throughout his streets, giving visitors the satisfaction of seeing storybook views come to life. On the whole, however, he emphasized the burgher architecture of shops and restaurants, the everyday haunts of the average man. While he worked with many different materials, the most prominent in view were the common ones of plaster and rough logs. When available, old lumber was preferred for its appearance of authenticity. Many of the individual buildings were constructed in outside shops, dismantled, and then reconstructed on their assigned streets. Providing focal points for the eye were the slender towers of Ireland and the rectangular campaniles of Italy. He not only supplied the Swiss with chalets but gave them a background of the Matterhorn large enough to accommodate real shrubbery and an Alpine torrent.

Logically, the more populous ethnic groups occupied the largest clusters. Internal "villages" of from half a dozen to twenty buildings were allotted to the Poles, the Germans, the Czechs, Irish, Italians, Hungarians, and the British. As much as possible, countries were to occupy both sides of their respective streets. Each street was provided with a distinctive view, whether castle, fountain, or lagoon. Countries that bordered on the sea, such as Denmark, Holland, and Italy, were preferably given locations on the lakefront.

Viewed from the air, the expo's global village roughly resembled a bull's-eye within a square, intersected by an "X." Around a central circular plaza was a larger, concentric circle, the "X" providing avenues between inner and outer circles. From above one could spot here and there the wooden struts supporting false facades as in the western towns of a movie set, but on street level the structures appeared as convincing as in the movies. All radiated from or wound around that central court, the International Circle. A hundred and fifty feet in diameter, it con-

Richard Rychtarik drew upon his Prague roots in designing this medieval-looking entrance to the Streets of the World complex of the Great Lakes Exposition. Located at the end of the midway, its portals gave access to restaurants, shops, and entertainment representative of some three dozen nationalities. It was a microcosm of Cleveland's ethnic population, which played a major role in its planning and operation. Author's Collection.

tained a large open stage with seating for five hundred spectators, for the presentation of ethnic programs and cultural exhibitions.

If Rychtarik had any nightmarish moments, they weren't evident in the finished product, which earned universal praise. He had seamlessly maneuvered 150 buildings into his ten acres, representing "Typical architecture of more than 30 foreign lands," in the words of the guidebook. "On one street a niche in the wall holds the plaster statue of a gnarled and bearded Italian saint," observed the *Plain Dealer*. "Near by, the tiled and tiered roofs of a pagoda ascend to the skyline to stand outlined against the white bulk of an imitation Swiss Alp." Perhaps the ultimate praise came from a Chicago priest, the Reverend Ernest J. Zizka: "Chicago's attempt to bring Europe to its door by scattered single units was lost in the great conglomeration of the surrounding attractions. Cleveland, in the compact area of the Streets, has admirably solved the difficult problem."

It was a gated community, with its main gate prominently visible at the end of the midway. A pair of wide gothic arches separated by a tall, slender tower and spire provided entry. Bert Todd, former manager of the Priscilla Theatre on East 9th Street, was in charge of seeing that everyone paid the entry fee of a quarter for adults, fifteen cents for children.

Inside the gates, the myriad inhabitants of Streets of the World worked in various ways to convince visitors that they truly were on foreign soil. Dressed in native costumes, they demonstrated Old World crafts and offered the goods of many lands for sale in nationality shops. Exotic music and dances were formally staged in the International Circle and performed informally in the "quaint winding streets." Ethnic foods as well as entertainment could be found in dozens of cafés, rathskellers, taverns, and tea shops. Father Zizka, relaxing in the Slovak Village tavern, found the intimate atmosphere conducive to reawakening memories of his travels in Europe.

A short broad boulevard led from the entrance to the International Circle. There, at regular intervals, one might hear the piercing tones of a trumpet calling from the direction of the lake, ending suddenly on a broken note. It came from one of the twin towers of a reproduction of Saint Mary's Cathedral of Krakow, Poland. In the thirteenth century a sentry atop the original Saint Mary's had begun a similar signal to warn the city against invading Tartars—until silenced by an arrow. Resounding the unfinished alarm hourly, day and night, had become a tradition in Krakow to commemorate the original bugler's sacrifice. Eve Klonowski of Cleveland's Polish community, dressed in the uniform of a medieval Polish guard, carried on the tradition in the Polish Village of the Great Lakes Exposition.

With the advice of a local Polish historian, Rychtarik had re-created much of Krakow's public square, dominated by the huge mass of the Sukiennice, or Cloth Hall, originally built in the sixteenth century to house the city's trade guilds. Like its Krakow prototype, the Great Lakes version contained a bazaar offering a variety of Polish products, with the proceeds earmarked for maintenance of the Polish plot in the Cultural Gardens. Inside the cathedral was a large exhibit of Polish religious objects, mostly imported. Alongside the church was a mountain tavern stocked with a Polish menu, delicacies, and Gypsy fortune-teller. In a palatial building abutting the International Circle could be found a Polish coffeehouse, antique shop, and perfumery.

Historical verisimilitude was also a feature of the Hungarian Village, tucked into the northeastern corner of the Streets. Here the centerpiece was another bastion against invading Turks, the fourteenth-century castle Vajda-Hunyad. Surrounding it were shops displaying shawls, table covers, jewelry, and other Hungarian goods. Facing the leaded-glass oriels of the castle was its social antithesis, a reproduction of a Hungarian peasant cottage. Close by, the Hungaria restaurant enticed the senses with Magyar dishes and a "genuine gypsy orchestra."

While boasting no castles or cathedrals, the Italian Village claimed the distinction of being the largest enclave in Streets of the World. Not surprisingly, most of its more than a dozen buildings were devoted to the selling and serving of Italian dishes. Its pièce de résistance was the Trattoria Santa Lucia, a Lake Erie version of the cafés found on the island of Santa Lucia in the Bay of Naples, right down to the outdoor patio. Among its culinary competition were a winery, a spumoni shop, a waffle shop, and several other cafés. Walking off a heavy pasta repast, patrons might pause in the streets and dig into their pockets for pennies to toss to Julia, the dancing monkey of strolling organ grinder Domenic Fantine.

Bavaria's Rathaus architecture dominated the stuccoed, half-timbered buildings of the German Village. "To those of us who have not traveled, especially in Germany, the German Village on Lake Erie is just what we always thought a German village would be like," wrote John Mihal in the *Cleveland News*. A tall, square, three-story tower on the eastern rim of International Circle served as an entrance to the Alt Heidelberg, a large German café. A store operated by the German Trade Alliance offered such wares as amber jewelry and cigarette holders, canned pumpernickel bread, marzipan candies, camel's-hair slippers, and a party game known as *Mensch ärgere Dich nicht,* which was loosely translated as "Men don't get excited."

Readers of Charles Dickens would have been drawn to a modest cottage with a second-story overhang on which was printed "Dickens' Old Curiosity Shop." A copy of an original in London, it was the chief attraction of the British Village. Here members of the British Commonwealth Club could be seen in the garb of Little Nell and other characters from the novel that immortalized the shop. Prints of Dickens scenes were also on hand, and an English tearoom nearby offered light refreshments. Scotch and Welsh cottages also graced the village, the latter occasionally the setting for stirring choral singing. A small Irish Village contained a shop run for the benefit of a new motherhouse for the Sisters of the Incarnate Word in Parma Heights.

Each of the thirty-eight nationalities represented added its characteristic colors to the international kaleidoscope. The cool blue of Royal Copenhagen china could be viewed and purchased in the Danish cottage; Assigi spears and Congo leopard skins were among the sights in the African Village; Russian costumes and embroideries were on display in the Russian café; murals of typical Slovakian scenes added atmosphere to the Slovak Village tavern.

Even tiny Belgium established a unique presence with a Brussels Lace and Linen shop and the small workshop of John Vrombaut, who demonstrated the art of carving wooden shoes. Some of those shoes would get a warm workout that summer in the International Circle.

■

Though Streets of the World was located at the very end of the grounds, expo-goers would have been well advised to hold off on food and entertainment until they passed through its portals. Practically every one of its villages had nourishment to offer, some in multiple stands, from a casual bite to full-course dinners. In view of the ethnic emphasis, Clevelanders and visitors alike had a rare opportunity to sample exotic flavors not available in their own neighborhoods.

There were gastronomic opportunities in more than half of the hundred concessions in the global village. "Among the many colorful eating places where the hungry visitor may appease his appetite," summed up a reporter for the *American Restaurant Magazine,* "are an African tea room, a Syrian delicatessen, a Syrian coffee shop, Italian tea room, Spanish restaurant, Slovak sandwich shop, a Lithuanian cafe, and a Swedish coffee shop—to mention only a few."

"Sir, try these special Syrian delicacy," a spieler in the Syrian Village entreated a *News* reporter. "It is called 'Kibbee,' and nowhere else in the city—only in Damascus and Beirut—can you buy it." For further details he referred the newsman to his mother, who explained that kibbees were made from leg of lamb, "cut up, fixed with dried whole wheat and many oriental spices and sauces." So Cleveland may have had its first taste of kibbee, whose time would come some fifty years later.

Similar Middle Eastern treats could be found across the way in the Armenian Village, which adopted the name Mousa Dagh in recognition of the current popularity of Franz Werfel's novel of Armenian history, *The Forty Days of Musa Dagh.* There the main dish was kofte, described as a seasoned ball of lamb wrapped in an exterior of cracked wheat. Dessert consisted of paklava, a mixture of chopped walnuts and butter wrapped in layers of paper-thin dough, obviously a relative of Greek baklava. All might be washed down with a glass of fermented milk, known as masoun, or a cup of syrupy Armenian coffee.

There were other challenges for the adventurous palate, from Indian curry to Russian borscht, or beet soup. Somewhat less exotic, perhaps, were the chicken paprikash and stuffed cabbage available at Hungaria, or the scaloppini Romano, ravioli à la Milanese, and chicken à la cacciatore on the carte at Trattoria Santa Lucia. Even a relatively pedestrian

While ethnic villages of various nations had long been a mainstay of world's fairs, uniting them within a single compound was a unique feature of the Great Lakes Exposition. Walking down one of its streets, one might encounter the pagodas of the Orient, cafés of the Middle East, and shops and crafts of Europe. "To those of us who have not traveled," wrote a local reporter, "the German Village on Lake Erie is just what we always thought a German village would be like." Cleveland Public Library.

One of the Continental experiences readily available in Streets of the World was al fresco dining. Frank Monaco's restaurant on the lakefront was one of several bistros offering outdoor seating in the global village. "The town has accustomed itself to eating out of doors," approvingly observed *Press* columnist Winsor French. Author's Collection.

breakfast could be served with a foreign flavor in the Swedish Village, where the customer was served not one, but two cups of coffee, the one for dunking his pastry and the other to be drunk from the saucer, sweetened with a lump of sugar placed between the teeth and gums. One writer, incidentally, claimed to have discovered at least a dozen different doughnut outlets in the global village.

More conventional dining was available at Frank Monaco's Continental restaurant and bar, located on the lakefront and offering al fresco seating. Directly across a narrow side street was a Grapefruit Winery, described by Winsor French as "a lethal joint if ever there was one. . . . Everyone sat around on barrels, drinking outsized pitchers of grapefruit wine that I seem to remember cost all of a buck." He particularly recalled the "disastrous" results one night when bon vivant Lucius Beebe downed several pitchers on top of "his nightly quota of Martinis."

Wherever one chose to imbibe, it was sure to be within earshot of live music. "His food will be served to him amid Parisian or Neapolitan surroundings, with appropriate music and entertainment," noted a writer in the *Plain Dealer*. "A gypsy orchestra plays delightful music to patrons of the Hungarian cafe. A jovial and robust piano and song team invites the patrons to join in the rousing songs to be heard in Alt Heidelberg. Strolling musicians with violins, accordions and other string instruments keep Monaco's and Fortunato's in happy mood."

Continuous, changing entertainment on a larger scale could be enjoyed in the International Circle. On the first Sunday of the exposition in 1936, for example, the schedule called for performances of Slovenian peasant dances, a German beer-garden band, Russian Cossacks, Polish dancers, a Russian men's chorus, a Slovenian women's drill team, a Hungarian gypsy orchestra, and a Croatian chorus. It went on with practically no break from 1:00 to 10:00 P.M. "Some of the shows were on the amateur side, but they gave young people the chance to show their stuff," said restauranteur Herman Pirchner. "What they lacked in talent they made up in enthusiasm," which, of course, was the point. Announcer Jim Walsh, described by Mihal of the *News* as an "amiable grouch . . . always serious to a point of tragedy," introduced the acts. They began keeping a record of his moods at the Slovak tavern fronting the circle, with such notations as "Mr. Walsh smiled today at 5 min. after five.—Twice." An even bigger grouch was a policeman stationed on the circle, who one night stopped a noted concert pianist from playing a few impromptu chords on an unattended piano between acts. "That man gets $1,500 a night to play the piano," protested an indignant member in the musician's party. "Well," replied the unimpressed cop, "I get $45 a week to stop him."

Most of the participating nationalities organized special "days" at the exposition, with programs invariably culminating in the International

Circle. Slovak Day drew an estimated ten thousand of that nationality for a program of speeches, dances, and drills. Poles came from as far as Buffalo, Pittsburgh, and Detroit to see Florence Gorna of Cleveland's Warsawa neighborhood crowned queen of Polish Day. Italian Day featured a performance by the Giuseppe Verdi Singing Society. A mock Carpatho-Russian wedding reenacted by two residents of Lakewood's Birdtown neighborhood was a highlight of Russian Day.

When a west side couple decided to have a real wedding in Streets of the World, it became an international affair. Exposition guards cleared an aisle for the bride, who advanced to the center of International Circle between ranks of celebrants in Old World costumes. One of the strolling bands of the global village provided music. Gifts poured in from the surrounding shops: linen from Ireland, lace from Belgium, pottery from Italy, glassware from Czechoslovakia, jewelry from Hungary, silk from China.

European customs continued after the ceremony with a "Kiss the Bride" waltz, in which guests pinned a dollar to the bride's veil for the privilege of a kiss and a dance. The bridal party then retired to the Alt Heidelberg for the wedding supper, while wedding guests continued dancing and celebrating throughout Streets of the World for the rest of the night. As for the newlyweds, they took off for a honeymoon at Niagara Falls with a $100 check from the Great Lakes Exposition in their luggage.

Such events made Rychtarik's international village one of the most memorable attractions of the entire exposition. "It is a mark of the genuine appeal of the Streets of the World that long after the lights have dimmed and the crowd thinned in other portions of the Exposition, music, bright lights and laughter are still going strong there," observed John M. Johnston in the *Cleveland Press*. There were some initial complaints, from both patrons and concessionaires, over the quarter entrance fee on top of the fifty-cent admission to the outside exposition grounds. This was countered by a reminder that there had been an entrance fee to each individual foreign village in Chicago. Figures were later released showing that fully half the visitors to the Great Lakes Exposition made their ways to Streets of the World.

Outside opinion continued to stroke the egos of the Cleveland planners. "Your Streets of the World impress me very much," commented J. W. Conklin, a director of the Canadian National Exhibit. "They far surpass similar streets at world's fairs in the past few years—and I include the Chicago Fair." Even the Windy City concurred. "Looking back to Chicago's world's fair, it seems that, in respect to the foreign village stunt, Cleveland's show is ahead of Chicago's," commented a reporter for the *Chicago Daily News*.

■

Ethnic customs and color might dominate Streets of the World, but they weren't solely responsible for the area's popularity. Although Cleveland's French community was comparatively negligible (about one in a thousand), France was well represented in Streets. What was represented, authentic or not, was the popular perception of France as the country of prurient pleasures—in other words, the ooh-la-la factor. Here was the perfect spot for the Great Lakes version of Chicago's Sally Rand and San Diego's Zoro Gardens. "With French Casino as the focal point, the French village with its two thoroughfares, Montparnasse and Montmarte [*sic*], offers chiefly night life attractions to the Streets' visitor," observed Mihal of the *News*. "In a row side by side the nudist colony competes here with Olympia and Armorita [*sic*] and other exhibits of not too carefully draped female form."

That's not the way it was supposed to be, at least not in the planners' original vision. "No, we're going to use all of our experience not to develop anything that would react on the exposition as an objectionable feature," pledged Almon R. Shaffer in May. A thirty-year veteran of show business, Shaffer had worked on several projects with Lincoln Dickey, who appointed him as the exposition's associate director in charge of amusements and concessions. Part of his assignment was to hold the line against nudity and sex, and he owned that keeping them out "was a great job." He had already turned down several "risqué" applicants, including a nudists' village.

Shaffer's plans for a squeaky-clean exposition did not go unopposed. Winsor French reported in the *Press* having received a protest from Zorine, one of the nudists from the San Diego exposition the previous summer. She had "even bigger and better ideas" for Cleveland, but would now take her vision of the body beautiful to Rochester, New York, of all places. In the *Plain Dealer*, cartoonist James Donahey pictured a crestfallen young damsel behind a frilly oversized fan over the caption, "What, no fan dancers? Why, the very idea!" A real fan dancer weighed in with her reaction. "I think it is an insult to the art of dancing to assume such an arbitrary attitude," said Faith Bacon, who had appeared in the flesh, so to speak, at the Chicago and San Diego expos.

Shortly before opening day, another debate arose over the issue of "gigolos," male companions, which one expo nightclub planned to provide for unaccompanied women. The idea ran into the opposition of Charles Johnson, whose opinion as city dance hall inspector carried considerable authority. When the *Cleveland News* asked local women for their views, opinions were divided. "It's something different that ought to attract people," said one; "I don't think it would attract the right kind of people," said another. "That's a silly job for a man," thought a west side miss, "That sort of thing should be done by women." "I think it's a little far-fetched for Cleveland," thought an east side housewife. Such provincialism was decried by Winsor French, who pointed out that "Professional dancers, so called, have been flourishing for years in the deluxe restaurants of every great European city."

Inspector Johnson finally relented to the extent of allowing escorts under the rubric of "dance instructors." Identified by their white gloves, they would offer their services as dinner companions, dancing partners, and escorts through the grounds. Their salaries would be covered by the establishment, though they might accept tips from ladies gratified by their companionship. The main concession to conventional morality was a ban on extended relationships: agreeing to escort the same woman more than once would be grounds for dismissal.

Nudity too managed to make an immodest appearance at the Great Lakes Exposition. "They have forced it on us. The pressure has been so great no man could stand against it," confessed Shaffer in abject surrender. "I have tried to sell them on amazing scientific exhibits, on beautiful buildings and vistas, on jolly amusements like the anglers' paradise, on things of historical importance," he continued in a rueful it-might-have-been mood. "Some day such a show will be a success, but I'm afraid it won't be in my day. You've no notion how popular sex is with a lot of people." Indeed. "And so it appears," commented Loveland in the *Plain Dealer*, "that . . . the Cleveland exposition will not be a Sunday School picnic in every particular."

If San Diego had its Nudist Colony in Zoro Gardens, Streets of the World would be able to offer the Little French Nudist Colony. On his way to *Julius Caesar* at the Old Globe, *Plain Dealer* critic Ward Marsh was sidetracked into the peep show. He was ushered into a small room facing an even smaller window approximately twelve by eighteen inches in size. When a screen was removed from the window, he reported seeing "by trick lighting and reflecting processes, three girls attired for the bath or a day in a Nudists' camp. Their figures proportionately-reduced stand about four inches high." They didn't call it "little" for nothing. For twenty-five cents, viewers got a four-minute peek.

Nearby was a similar concession, Olympia, which featured a live model reclining in the attitude of Manet's nude painting of the same name. After several weeks, the girl's repose was disturbed by a pair of Cleveland policewomen at the behest of her parents. Manet had painted his model, Victorine Meurent, at nineteen years of age; it appeared that the expo version was no more than fourteen. The show's manager professed to be "amazed" at the news.

The only nudes to be seen at the Artists' Colony were apparently in the murals on the walls. Sponsored by the local artists of the Kokoon Club, it evoked the ambience of a Greenwich Village café with demonstrations of

Providing some of the risqué appeal of the French Quarter in Streets of the World was the Little French Nudist Colony. For a quarter, back-to-nature enthusiasts received a four-minute peep at live models through a window-and-mirror arrangement that reduced their undraped forms to Lilliputian dimensions. If nothing else, the full-sized models outside its entrance attracted a good deal of interest from passing crowds. *Cleveland Press* Collection.

printmaking and portrait sketching. One evening a patron who agreed to sit for a likeness was so pleased with the result that he handed the young artist a twenty-dollar bill with his compliments. In answer to his question, the sketcher learned that he had just limned the popular illustrator Maxfield Parrish.

"There are weird contrasts, to be sure," said one stroller through Streets of the World. "Just how the Nudist Colony got across from a Syrian gift shop is beyond explanation." Had he ventured farther into the Syrian Village, he needn't have been so puzzled. Amid the cafés and gift shops could be found the Syrian Temple of Dance, where spieler Roland Taylor extolled the virtues of its dancing girls. Joining the undulating harem a week into the summer was oriental dancer Princess Zulecka, "late of the San Diego fair and of the Century of Progress."

The hottest corner of the French Quarter, the cynosure of naughtiness, was the French Casino, a nightclub concession operated by Phil Gordon and Mike Speciale and unblushingly promoted by publicist Gardner F. Wilson. His preopening ads for its *Folies de Nuit* floor show promised

"Callipygian Beauties Treading Pavanes and Rigadoons in Diaphanous Garments That Will Be the Talk of All America!" It had readers running to their Webster's unabridged, if not to the French Casino.

Wilson had only begun to incite. Barely had the *Folies* opened when the ladies of the chorus were reportedly threatening to go on strike for the right to wear brassieres. Manager Speciale expressed concern that the weather was too hot for such encumbrances, but the modest mademoiselles weren't buying that. Their main concern was for the feelings of their parents, boyfriends, and hubbies, they claimed. One unnaturalized miss feared deportation to Russia if immigration authorities were to catch her au naturel. Whether they won the right to cover up went unreported; the curious would have to go see for themselves. While city authorities did nothing to interfere with the show inside, Mayor Harold Burton did order bras to be painted on the nude posters outside the Casino.

"The P.A.'s are having a field day," observed *Plain Dealer* columnist Phil Porter with indulgence. During that summer's heat wave, a pair of *Folies* chorines stripped down to two-piece bathing suits and jumped into a fountain right on Public Square to cool off. They were ordered out of the water by a cop and duly photographed. Then Mrs. Gayle Speciale went to court asking for an injunction ordering her workaholic husband to spend at least one night a week at home from the casino. Common Pleas judge Frank S. Day, expressing his sympathy, granted her an order constraining Mike to Sundays at home. "I personally am a home man," commented His Honor with a reasonably straight face. "Nothing, not even business, can keep me from my home." Speciale happened to be out of town on business, but there in support of Mrs. Speciale were a reporter, a photographer, and Gardner Wilson.

But Wilson's masterpiece, as it were, was a creation named Toto Leverne.

■

Her real name (so she said) was Trudye Mae Davidson, and she hailed from the left bank—of not the Seine, but Lake Michigan: Evanston, Illinois, to be precise. One account placed her birth in a Scottish village near Glasgow. Her résumé claimed appearances at the Folies-Bergères and the Lido. She said she had been an honor student at Northwestern and was a graduate of Chicago's Goodman School of Drama. Some or all of it may have been true, but it really didn't matter. The French Casino had engaged her to be Toto Leverne.

Toto (if we may drop the formalities) was the headliner of the *Folies de Nuit,* outranking the chorus and even the female impersonator. Advance publicity had it that her costume would consist of a dress composed of

Publicity such as this quarter-page newspaper ad established the French Casino as the most sensational show in Streets of the World, if not the entire Great Lakes Exposition. Despite its location at the very end of the amusement zone, those in search of "Callipygian Beauties" beat a path to its doors. "You've no notion how popular sex is with a lot of people," said Almon Shaffer, the expo's amusement director, after he lost the battle to keep nudity off the grounds. *Cleveland Plain Dealer*, June 21, 1936.

Some of the labor militancy of the 1930s even managed to infiltrate the French Casino. A dancer called Zuzzana is seen addressing her chorine sisters on strike for the right to cover up with brassieres. Cynics viewed it as just another example of publicist Gardner Wilson's efforts to keep the expo nightspot in the public eye. *Cleveland Press* Collection.

a mysterious material that would disappear when exposed to the lascivious rays of a certain-colored light. Her act received national exposure in *Time* magazine, which described "her bare body . . . displayed five times a day to the 1,000 pop-eyed customers of the French Casino." Getting into the role, Toto was quoted as saying, "I feel wicked as hell. I've never appeared this nude before, and my family don't know what to think."

According to later reviews, the chorus members were clad in the diaphanous dresses. Toto's costume consisted of a stuffed swan's neck, which she strategically maneuvered as she danced, before discarding it entirely. Behind its outer facade, most of the casino was apparently covered by a large canvas tent, which admitted so much rain one night that the swan's neck went soggily limp and Toto's exposed body glistened with rivulets of rainwater. Her tribulations were only beginning. During the July heat wave she went into her routine another night with gay abandon, then suddenly collapsed at the feet of Dudley Blossom Jr. and had to be treated at the infirmary for heat prostration.

Toto Leverne, featured dancer at the French Casino, demonstrated some of her moves for a select but appreciative audience. She appears to be clad in one of the "diaphanous garments" touted in pre-expo publicity, while her admirers model what the well-dressed man on Short Vincent Street wore in the 1930s. When Toto threw herself into the lake after receipt of a censorious letter, there was no shortage of volunteers to pull her out. *Cleveland Press* Collection.

A few days later she was back in the infirmary after jumping agitatedly into Lake Erie from a pier right in the middle of the midway. A young exposition guard fortunately was on the spot to plunge in and pull her out, minus half her clothes. Reporters and photographers also happened to be on the scene. It appeared that the cause of Toto's distress was a letter she had received from a woman who had read about her in *Time*. "Queen Victoria was sure she was going to heaven. Are YOU?" she wrote. Eyes cast modestly downward, the danseuse nevertheless vowed not to give in to Victorianism. "My dance is a thing of beauty; a thing for the higher-minded people, the intelligentsia," she insisted with quivering lips. "I can't abandon my nude number, I just can't."

Though Toto managed to keep out of the infirmary after that, she couldn't stay out of the headlines. Her performance was broken up the very next night by former Georgia congressman William D. Upshaw, who happened to be in town for the Townsend pension convention. Snatching up a tablecloth and smashing some bottles of booze, the onetime Prohibition candidate for president charged out to cover the unclad Toto, crying words to the effect of "God save American womanhood!" He had trouble remembering his line, however, and several retakes were necessary before Gardner Wilson was satisfied and handed Upshaw his $25 honorarium.

Toto had become the exposition's best-known personality, the toast of the amusement zone. She even appeared as a guest on a *Fibber McGee and Molly* broadcast from Radioland, but her most memorable contribution was an awkward pratfall when backing offstage. She was a little confused wearing so many clothes, she later explained. Toto also appeared in mufti for a daytime tour of the exposition grounds in the company of a *Press* reporter. "I never realized it was so big," she exclaimed. Taking a whirl on some rides, she admitted, "They scare the pants off me." She declined to try her luck with a weight-guesser, however, and also turned down a free long-distance call from Ohio Bell on the grounds that "the people I know aren't up yet."

And then, at the height of her celebrity, Toto left it all behind. She suddenly walked out of the *Folies de Nuit,* the Great Lakes Exposition, the whole town itself, reportedly carrying away her belongings "in a little tomato basket." That detail was supplied by Wilson, who was left to deliver her valediction. "I'm going to be married soon and I don't want all of Cleveland and Ohio to have looked at my body before my husband does," he said she said. According to Winsor French, however, her departure after several missed shows was not of her own choosing.

Anyway, it was only Trudye Davidson who was gone; "Toto Leverne" remained the property of the French Casino, and a new Toto promptly made her appearance. She was Madeline Gardner, one of the Public Square bathers of the previous month, and French described her as "the most undressed eyeful I ever have seen on land or sea." While the nightclub kept possession of Toto's name, however, it lost the rights to its own, when it was successfully sued by a French Casino, Inc., of New York City. Subsequently it carried on as the French Cafe.

Like a swallow to Capistrano (or a buzzard to Hinckley?), the original Toto—or Trudye Davidson, she must now be called—then returned to the revue to dance under her own name and more clothing. "The name Toto doesn't mean anything," she was quoted in a local paper. "It's the name Trudee [*sic*] Davidson that counts."

■

By whatever name, it was fitting that Toto/Trudye was on the scene for the final days of the exposition in which she had played so prominent a role. Those days would be eight more than originally scheduled due to the extension granted by the Great Lakes Exposition's executive committee, "in response to an insistent demand from public officials and business men of Cleveland and from many residents of the Great Lakes area who have not had an opportunity to visit the exposition."

Lincoln Dickey was determined to go out with not a whimper but a bang. He announced a "Festival of Light" to be produced on each of the last eight nights, heralded by fourteen gargantuan searchlights hurling 4 billion candlepowers' worth of beams against a screen of smoke laid by airplanes passing a thousand feet overhead. A nightly fireworks display of eight hundred shells, four hundred rockets, and two thousand Roman candles would add to the spectacle. Originally fired off at 9:30 P.M., the pyrotechnics spooked the horses in *Parade of the Years* so much that they had to be delayed thereafter for a later hour. On the final Thursday, appropriately costumed celebrants were granted free admission to join a Mardi Gras parade that snaked its way through the grounds to Streets of the World. Officials were also on the lookout in those final days for that eagerly anticipated four-millionth expo-goer.

A special celebration took place in Streets of the World that week to honor the hardiest bunch of troupers of all the ethnic acts in the International Circle. These were the Belgian Wooden Shoe Dancers, who were awarded an ovation and public party following their five-hundredth performance of the summer. Even Rudy Vallee had become part of their act, when he was spotted in the audience and brought onstage to join in the dance and receive the kisses of the females of the company. "In rain or shine or heat or cold the kloppety-klop of their cheerful shoes has kept going now 100 days," commented John Gourley, "so performers and concessionaires here thought this would be a good time to tell them we like the job they have been doing." Some of the credit may also have been due to John Vrombaut, the wooden shoe carver in the tiny Belgian Village.

Workers and performers throughout the grounds were preparing to say their farewells and go off in various directions. Those who had been detailed to work in civic and commercial exhibits would be returning to their regular assignments. Others, such as the jinrikisha pullers and Marine Theater swimmers, would be reporting to college campuses. Many of the Old Globe actors planned to look for gigs in New York; the Lincoln funeral choir from *Parade of the Years* would rejoin the Gilpin Players of Karamu House, the interracial theater on Cleveland's east side. The

Located in the center of Streets of the World, the International Circle served as a showcase for various ethnic traditions and acts. In the course of a typical day, five hundred or more spectators could watch everything from a female drill team to a Croatian chorus. During the summer of 1936, a hardy troupe of Belgian Wooden Shoe Dancers clogged five hundred performances on its stage. Cleveland Public Library.

barkers on the midway likely would hit the tanbark trail. The majority of local employees would simply return to their neighborhood homes.

Many, if not most, however, would be back on the lakefront the following summer. Exposition officials had been studying the possibility of reopening the show for a second season. On the "reasonable expectation" that half a million in additional capital could be raised, the executive committee voted in favor of a return engagement.

So the mood on the grounds for the closing on October 12 was more bittersweet than somber. "This is not a wake, after all, but a celebration," said a cheerful Linc Dickey. The only disappointment may have been the failure of that four-millionth patron to show up at the gate, but the expo had come close with an official total of 3,979,229. Some may have been kept away by the 40-degree weather—too bad some of that heat wave in July couldn't have been recycled. During the day Alf Landon, the Republican candidate for president, showed up to press some flesh. Exposition officials gathered that evening for closing ceremonies in front of the Firestone exhibit, where a bugler of the 11th U.S. Infantry sounded taps, the Singing Fountains were stilled, and the midway lights to the east dimmed.

"After the fireworks, the sound of hammers and packing began," wrote Loveland in the *Plain Dealer*. "The visitors took a last hot dog or drink, took a last look, gave a last cheer, and started home, conversing about what next year's exposition would be like." In an autumnal mood, Winsor French chose to dwell on some of the intangible perks of a summer on the lakefront. "It has, if you ask me, been a giddy, honky tonk summer," he wrote in the *Press*. "The town has accustomed itself to eating out of doors, burning the midnight oil with colors flying, and plying the Exposition midway until all hours."

DESIGNING MAN

"The town's busiest artist right now is Richard Rychtarik, scene designer, architect and painter," wrote Noel Francis in the *Cleveland News* early in 1936. "He is at work on designs for 'Streets of the World' exhibit for the Great Lakes Expo." Rychtarik actually was even busier, having his hand in designs for the expo's music shell and transportation pageant as well. Multitasking was nothing new for the Czech immigrant, who for the previous dozen years had been involved in teaching, art exhibitions, and stage designing for plays, opera, and ballet in Cleveland.

One of the buildings he designed for the Czech Village in Streets of the World was a reproduction of his grandfather's house in his native village, Chocen, in Bohemia. So many of his ancestors had been mayors of the town that they acquired the surname Rychtar—Czech for mayor or burgess. Collateral branches of the family were called Rychtarik, or "little mayor."

Waslav Richard Rychtarik was raised in Prague, where one of his earliest memories was of hanging over the railing of the highest balcony in the National Theatre. Ibsen's *Hedda Gabler* sent him into a screaming fit, but an adaptation of Verne's *Around the World in Eighty Days* inspired him to try a realistic staging for his friends at home, with real snow in place of painted icebergs for a polar scene.

"It was a great artistic success,—but it melted on our best carpet, and my father vigorously applauded a certain part of my anatomy," he wrote later. "This decided a reverse from stage realism."

No matter; he had the theater bug for good. Outside of school, he summarized his chief recreational activities as "Talked theatre, talked

music / Made theatre, made music / Dreamed theatre, dreamed music."*
At seventeen he ran away to Berlin to work for the legendary director
Max Reinhardt—moving scenery, mixing paint, and carrying beer for
the stagehands. He returned to Prague for formal studies in painting
and architecture.

Not even World War I could keep Rychtarik from making theater.
During his service in the army, he managed to design a portable stage
for the troops. After the war, he designed settings for Prague's National
Theatre, where *King Lear, Coriolanus,* and *Rosmersholm* were among his
stage credits. Operas such as Berg's *Lulu,* Strauss's *Elektra,* and Smetana's
Libuše were also seen against Rychtarik's scenery.

With the aid of an International Scholarship, the young architect
began shuttling to and from America in the early 1920s, furthering his
education and looking for assignments. In 1924 he boarded the SS *Le-
viathan* as an emigrant to the United States. Though his ultimate musical and theatrical dream was to design productions for the Metropolitan
Opera, his immediate destination was Cleveland, Ohio.

Holding down a day job as art director for a paint company, Rychtarik
became part of the city's lively cultural scene. Nine of his works in various mediums, from drawing to sculpture, were accepted for showing in
the Cleveland Museum of Art's annual May Show. He taught theater history and stage direction at Cleveland College, the downtown extension
school of Western Reserve University. He and his wife Charlotte corre-
sponded regularly with the Ohio-born poet Hart Crane. Rychtarik also
obtained a foothold in his first artistic love by designing some stage sets
for the Cleveland Play House.

When the Cleveland Orchestra began laying plans for its own concert
hall in University Circle, Rychtarik lobbied its founding manager, Adella
Prentiss Hughes, for the building of a dual-purpose facility suitable for
opera as well as concerts. She answered politely that while his suggestion
was "interesting," the orchestra was bent on a hall "dedicated to the sole
purpose of concert giving."**

A few years later, however, the Depression put a temporary end to the
annual Cleveland visits of the Metropolitan Opera. Artur Rodzinski, the
Cleveland Orchestra's new conductor, decided to fill the vacuum by staging operas in Severance Hall, and Rychtarik was engaged to design the
sets. Over four seasons in the midthirties, he applied his talent and vision

---

* Richard Rychtarik, Autobiographical Sketch, November 23, 1934, Cleveland
Orchestra Archives.

** Richard Rychtarik to Adella Prentiss Hughes, Dec. 12, 1928, Adella Prentiss Hughes
to Richard Rychtarik, Feb. 13, 1929, both in the Cleveland Orchestra Archives.

to such landmarks of the repertoire as Wagner's *Die Walküre*, Verdi's *Otello*, and Strauss's *Der Rosenkavalier.*

Working within the somewhat restricted confines of the Severance stage, Rychtarik rejected realism for more suggestive settings. Flats often did double duty, mounted on rollers with scenery painted on both sides to facilitate quick, smooth scene changes. The biggest challenge—and greatest opportunity—of the series came with the American premiere of Dmitri Shostakovich's modern shocker, *Lady Macbeth of Mtsensk.*

According to Rodzinski's widow, Halina, Rychtarik's *Lady Macbeth* set "conveyed the milieu of Russia circa 1840, but was spare and modern, and most importantly, functioned like an integral piece of a mechanism."* Even more important from the designer's point of view was the transfer, after two nights in Severance, of the entire production, sets and all, to New York for a single performance in the Metropolitan Opera House. "Today I still hope," he said at the time of his old ambition to design for the Met.

In the meantime, the Great Lakes Exposition afforded ample opportunity for Rychtarik to demonstrate his virtuosity. Besides his ten-acre tour de force in Streets of the World, he designed the scenery flats for Edward Hungerford's transportation pageant, *Parade of the Years.* He was also credited with the overall concept for the Sherwin-Williams music shell on the Mall. Another artist actually executed the statues on either side of the shell, but their placement evoked the sculpture groups flanking the stage of Smetana Hall in Rychtarik's Prague.

While Rychtarik managed to incorporate his grandfather's house into Streets of the World, the ultimate utilization of the Czech Village must have come as somewhat of a disappointment to its creator. Plans for including authentic Czech tenants and shops fell through, and the buildings instead were filled with a motley collection of generic photographers, shooting galleries, and novelty shops.

Another disappointment was the demise of opera at Severance Hall after the Met resumed its tours. Rychtarik teamed up with Boris Goldovsky, head of the Cleveland Institute of Music's opera department, to take up the slack with the formation of a Civic Opera Company. Their first production, not coincidentally, was the Czech national opera, Smetana's *The Bartered Bride.*

Then at last appeared the rainbow bridge to his operatic Valhalla: the Metropolitan Opera wanted Rychtarik as a set designer. He was then forty-six years old; his blond hair, receding from a broad forehead, was showing hints of gray. Slightly above average height, he carried but a

---

*Halina Rodzinski, *Our Two Lives* (New York: Charles Scribner's Sons, 1976), 116–17.

Scenic architect Richard Rychtarik left his mark all over the grounds of the Great Lakes Exposition, from the Sherwin-Williams music shell to his chef d'oeuvre, Streets of the World. The Czech native was already admired in Cleveland for his operatic sets at Severance Hall. Not long after the expo, he achieved his life's ambition of designing for the Metropolitan Opera. *Cleveland Press* Collection.

slight amount of excess flesh on his 178-pound frame. His blue, widely spaced eyes could sparkle when smiling or darken in concentration.

Rychtarik's first assignment at the Met was Gluck's rarely heard *Alceste*, followed by a production of Mozart's *The Magic Flute* conducted by Bruno Walter. His sets for the latter won the approval of the demanding Virgil Thomson in the *New York Herald Tribune:* "Though not strikingly original or powerful in themselves, they were dignified, fanciful, tasty . . . and the scene shifting, so often a dragger-out of this work, was as expeditious as anyone could wish."

One of his most successful and long-lived productions at the Met was a 1942 revival of Donizetti's *Lucia di Lammermoor.* "Certain conditions peculiar to opera must be kept constantly in mind," said a *Theatre Arts* magazine appraisal of his work. "For example, Mr. Rychtarik uses many levels in constructing a grand opera set; he has been accused, he says, of overdoing it. But a very practical consideration lies behind the device: the singers must be able to see the conductor."

Rychtarik continued to accept freelance assignments as a "scenic architect," as he preferred to style himself. He designed several operas for the Berkshire Festival in Tanglewood, including the American premiere of Britten's *Peter Grimes* under Leonard Bernstein in 1946. His sets for *Falstaff* were seen at La Scala in Italy, and for a *Don Giovanni* in San Francisco, he introduced slide projections to American opera.

In 1947 Rychtarik was appointed technical director at the Metropolitan, giving him the responsibility of coordinating all aspects of opera production, including scenery, costumes, lighting, properties, and carpentry. His career at the Met ended two years later, when Edward Johnson was succeeded as general manager by Rudolf Bing.

Rychtarik then moved into the new field of television, becoming chief scenic designer for the Columbia Broadcasting System. His television credits included seventeen episodes of *The Honeymooners,* though his work for *Studio One,* a drama series, was undoubtedly more compatible with his stage experience, as was an adaptation of *Jane Eyre.*

Retiring from CBS in 1964, Rychtarik lived in New York with his second wife, Trude (Gertrude), until his death in 1982 at the age of eighty-seven. Given the nature of his major work, little survives beyond images captured in photographs. There are some models of his stage sets in Severance Hall, and the Western Reserve Historical Society recently acquired a brass taboret he designed in 1928. Perhaps his greatest legacy, however, rested in the memories of the millions who explored his Streets of the World in 1936 and 1937.

Second Act: 1937

Gone were the smells of popcorn and hamburgers, the fortune-tellers, the "jungle noises" of Cliff Wilson's snake show, the girls of the French Casino . . . especially the girls.

"There are no girls in fetching costumes; no girls wearing trousers; no girls with sun-tanned backs; no girls of any description," mourned Roelif Loveland on a midwinter inspection of the Great Lakes Exposition grounds, a day or two after the arrival of 1937. "There are no hooch-dancers in Amourita. There isn't the least bit of hot-cha in the entire exposition grounds, and one is impressed with the sinister thought that the most important part of any exposition, great or small, is and ever shall be—gals."

Instead of gals, Loveland saw only ice in the streets, a couple of dozen expo police, and a guard dog who answered to the name of Johnny Expo. The guards' chief activity consisted of tracking down and expelling the tramps who seemed intent on reclaiming their old haunts on the one-time city dump. "The bums hop over the wire fence, and some of them are seeking shelter, and some of them have come to steal canvas, with which to pretty up their shelters elsewhere," reported Loveland. One interloper brazenly vaulted back inside only twenty minutes after being expelled, in exactly the same place he'd entered for his first offense. "What the hell you think I jumped over the fence the second time for?" he asked the exasperated guard. "What I want is to go to jail. It's clean and warm there."

Noticing a wisp of smoke rising from the chimney of the Firestone farmhouse one morning, guards discovered a young man nonchalantly frying up some bacon for breakfast. It turned out that he was a college student hired by Firestone to tend their exhibit during the off-season.

Evidently no one had bothered to notify the regular patrol. Another special caretaker was bedded down on Byrd's South Pole ship, anchored in the rapidly freezing waters of Lake Erie. As a former officer in the Russian navy, Captain Ralph von Suboff must have found Cleveland's winter comparatively balmy; his ship was no stranger to snow and ice.

Life went on outside the grounds that winter. Alf Landon, whose quest for the White House had begun at the Republican National Convention in Cleveland, went down to resounding defeat by Franklin Roosevelt in November. Father Charles Coughlin, who had vowed in Cleveland to quit the airwaves if his third-party candidate didn't garner 9 million votes, kept his word—for a few weeks, at any rate. William Lemke fell short of even 1 million; the Radio Priest delivered a farewell broadcast in November but was back on the air by January.

In Cleveland, the day shift at the huge General Motors Fisher Body plant on Coit Road failed to punch out on the afternoon of December 28, 1936. Unhappy over management's postponement of a scheduled grievance meeting, the workers shut down their machines and simply sat down at their posts. Women workers were directed to leave, as a core of union men remained to inaugurate the nation's first significant sit-down strike. It spread to GM's Flint plants a few days later and led to the historic recognition of the United Auto Workers union by the country's largest automaker. Rubberworkers in Akron emulated the autoworkers in February.

Not too far from the Coit Road plant, the upper torso of a woman was deposited by the waters of Lake Erie at the foot of East 156th Street on February 23, 1937. It had been dissected with evident skill, qualifying as victim no. 7 in the city's continuing torso-murder saga, despite its appearance so far from Kingsbury Run. The victim was never identified, nor was Safety Director Eliot Ness any closer to learning the identity of the killer.

On a lighter note, the Circle Theater at East 102nd Street and Euclid Avenue ushered in the new year with the *Folies de Nuit* revue from the French Casino, which had been the talk of the Great Lakes Expo in 1936. The show even boasted Toto Leverne, though this Toto's identity was undisclosed. "In case you go just for old time's sake, let us warn you that the gals are wearing more frou-froux and ruffles than they did last summer—probably a concession to the weather," cautioned the *Cleveland News*.

Appearing in the dead of winter, they may nevertheless have served as a reminder to Loveland to take heart—the expo and its gals would be back!

■

Planning in earnest for the 1937 season of the Great Lakes Exposition had begun in December, when Dudley Blossom collected $300,000 of the $.5 million capital needed to reboot. It was not accomplished without high-pressure tactics, according to a trustee assigned to secure the additional underwriting. Howard Dugan, manager of downtown's Hotel Statler, approached his prospects with the assertion that the executive committee intended to triple their previous pledge, but added his personal opinion that double would be sufficient. "So send me your check *right now* by messenger," he said in closing the deal. "I'll take it over to the committee myself this afternoon—and tell them DOUBLE is enough, before they can hold a meeting and triple the amount."*

Actually, the $500,000 goal was less than half of the $1 million raised to underwrite the opening year. It had been needed then, since the expo reported a $1.1 million deficit for 1936 because of underestimated construction expenses and overestimated attendance goals. The former had been caused by the necessity of completing the job in the challenging time frame of eighty days. The attendance shortfall was laid by implication at the feet of Clevelanders themselves, who had made up no more than an estimated 40 percent of expo visitors.

But the bottom line didn't tell the entire story. Accountant A. C. Ernst, one of the exposition's vice presidents, claimed that the event had brought $30 million of extra spending into Cleveland and predicted that another year would add $40 million more. Conventions alone had brought in $12 million of the former total, according to the Cleveland Convention and Visitors Bureau. "This money, earned in other communities, was spent here by the 312,245 convention delegates who attended the 176 conventions and meetings here," stated Mark Egan, the bureau's manager. "Today we are a happy city, with so many people with money to spend that it is next to impossible to get into a store to do Christmas shopping," added Dudley Blossom, the expo's general chairman.

There were also benefits that couldn't be measured in dollars and cents. Blossom pointed to the transformation of the lakefront, which "would have remained a dump for another 20 years," but for the exposition. "As it is, we have built something of lasting beauty, and we are going to make it better than ever," he said. In his report to the trustees,

---

*Quoted in Elmer Whaler, *Tested Sentences That Sell* (New York: Prentice-Hall, 1937), 61–62.

President Eben Crawford stressed the effect of the exposition on the city's reputation. Visitors had not only left their dollars here but carried favorable impressions of Cleveland back to their hometowns. "Hundreds of programs emanating from the exposition have been broadcast by the radio chains and by local stations," he observed. "Thousands upon thousands of columns of the most desirable news and comment . . . have been published in newspapers, trade journals, magazines, and other publications in the United States, in Canada, and in many countries throughout the world."

Exhibitors on the grounds, such as Firestone and Florida, had expressed an interest in signing on for another year. Downtown hoteliers had unanimously seconded the idea. A plant valued at an estimated $2.5 million was already in place, and a year's experience in operating it had been gained. As of December, Cleveland's was the only major exposition on the national calendar for 1937.

The *Cleveland Plain Dealer* editorially endorsed another year even before the close of the first: "For Cleveland's sake, for the sake of the Great Lakes area, for the sake of thousands scattered through many states who, for one reason or another, could not get to the exposition this year, we believe the enterprise should be improved and opened again next season. . . . The 1936 errors could be avoided and the 1936 experience capitalized." Its support was given conditionally, however, contingent upon improvement in three areas: greater emphasis on educational features, better publicity, and "a more rigid cost-accounting system."

■

While they might promise a better show in 1937, exposition officials could hardly advertise it as bigger. One of the most notable changes for the second season called for the retreat of the main entrance from St. Clair back to Lakeside Avenue. This was bound to please local drivers, who would thereby enjoy unimpeded use of Lakeside for the entire summer. No concessions were made for out-of-town drivers, who would still be expected to contend with Cleveland's singular left-hand turn. "As the Great Lakes Exposition opens Cleveland will be host to thousands of visitors who will be amused, amazed, confused and finally disgusted with the 'funny traffic customs' in your city," wrote a Toledo driver to the *Cleveland Press*. "The 'ring-around-rosie,' rotary, or outside left turn, takes first prize."

With a new main entrance situated north of Lakeside, the former Sherwin-Williams Plaza was stranded outside the grounds. So was Public

Hall, which would be devoted exclusively to the convention trade for the entire summer. The impressive 1936 entrance on St. Clair, with its seven monumental pylons, was left in place to serve as a kind of free, ceremonial approach to the new entrance. As for the Sherwin-Williams music shell, a truck turned up on Lakeside at the end of January to transport it to a new home. Trolley and high-tension wires were temporarily removed from East 4th to West 3rd Streets, clearing the way for the seventy-five-ton structure to be hauled to the lower exposition grounds.

Parked directly east of the bleacher section of Municipal Stadium, the relocated music shell would serve as the home of Sherwin-Williams Radioland. Squeezed out in the new arrangement was the modernistic Porcelain Enamel Building as well as the Great Lakes Symphony Orchestra, which was not reengaged for 1937. Another casualty from the previous year was the *Parade of the Years* pageant. "Easily the most beautiful and instructive show on the grounds, for all its excitement it failed to crawl into the black," mourned Winsor French in the *Press*. In its place north of the railroad tracks would be an ice show, Winterland.

Other changes in the lower exhibition area included rebranding the former Automotive Building as the Varied Industries Building. On the waterfront, the Byrd South Pole ship and the *Moses Cleaveland* were being sailed eastward to the amusement zone. Last year's Admiralty Club, the upper-class retreat on the *Cleaveland,* would be replaced by the equally exclusive Recess Club, installed in the upper two floors of the Horticulture Building. Next door at the former Marine Theater, what promised to be the exposition's most spectacular reinvention was also underway.

New attractions were also planned for the amusement zone, where the *Moses Cleaveland* would lower its gangplank as Herman Pirchner's Show Boat. Pirchner's Alpine Village would be doing business at its old stand, but over at the Old Globe Theatre, the Shakespearean players were being replaced by Tony Sarg's Marionettes. Ripley's "Believe It or Not" Odditorium was the new king of the midway, joined by such other newcomers as the Crystal Maze, Fun House, The Curse of a Nation, and Rigolarium.

Little change was projected in the popular Streets of the World attraction. Even after the rigors of a Cleveland winter, designer Richard Rychtarik was opposed to applying a coat of fresh paint to his weathered Old World facades. "Budt now it looks so ree-al!" he protested in his Czech accent. The only major transformation was taking place in the northeastern corner, where the former French Casino was becoming Billy Rose's Pioneer Palace. It wasn't the only finger the noted Broadway producer had in the Great Lakes expo pie; he had even bigger plans for the old Marine Theater. They had to be big, because as everyone knew,

Far less impressive than its predecessor's seven towering pylons, the main gate for the 1937 exposition was a utilitarian arrangement at the northern end of the Mall. It left the Sherwin-Williams Plaza outside the grounds, necessitating the relocation of its music shell to the lower grounds. While the Great Lakes Exposition lost a few acres, Clevelanders regained unimpeded use of Lakeside Avenue. *Cleveland Press* Collection.

Billy Rose didn't do anything small. As Loveland put it in the *Plain Dealer*, "We have heard so much about Billy Rose that it begins to tire—but you can take it from this reporter that the water show is going to be the gol darndest water show ever seen."

■

With far less to construct, and more time to do it, the buildup to opening day proceeded at a less hectic pace than the previous year. "The Exposition accomplished miracles of speedy construction last year, but there was a feeling that the drive to physical completion caused some weakening of the affair as a whole," observed the *Press* in March. "The underwriting, the advertising, the booking of special events, are more than a month ahead of where they were at this time in 1936." Young women "with figures to please the eye and faces which would give old men back their memories" were being auditioned for a new crew of Yeomanettes. Commercial artist Edward M. Eggleston was preparing publicity illustrations based on the swimsuit-clad figure of noted fashion model Edith Backus. Juan B. Larrinaga, creator of the "world's largest mural" for the San Diego Exposition, was executing a dozen large scenes for the theme exhibit of the 1937 Great Lakes Exposition: "The Making of a Nation."

Minus one major exception, preparations were under the general supervision of the same team which had gotten the 1936 show on the road. Eben Crawford having stepped down, his place as president would be filled by W. Trevor Holliday, president of Sohio. Linc Dickey would continue to handle day-to-day operations as general manager, assisted by Almon Shaffer and Peg Humphrey. A. N. Gonsior returned as construction chief. Prodding and cheering them all on was Dudley Blossom, general chairman, who drew on his musical gifts to write a new song for the occasion entitled "My Expo Rose":

> Give me a name for a rose,
> Billy Rose sounds good to me.
> Show me the Streets of the World,
> Peasant girls so fair to see,
> Lead me to cool Winterland,
> Skaters there are full of glee,
> Take me up high, in a blimp near the sky,
> the Exposition I must see.*

---

*"My Expo Rose," words and music by Dudley S. Blossom (Cleveland: Evan Georgeoff Music, 1937).

Under the watchful eye of Peg Willen Humphrey, muralist Juan B. Larrinaga applied finishing touches to a mining and petroleum panel for the 1937 theme exhibit, "The Making of a Nation." Larrinaga, who had executed the "world's largest mural" for San Diego's California Pacific International Exposition in 1935, painted twelve scenes of American life for the Great Lakes Exposition. Humphrey was the expo's associate director and Lincoln Dickey's Girl Friday. *Cleveland Press* Collection.

It was designated as Blossom's Opus 2, Opus 1 having been a University School song for the composer's alma mater. A local radio director described Opus 2 as "a fast fox trot, and a good job even for a professional." Whatever profits might accrue were earmarked for the exposition.

With opening day set a month earlier than the year before, workers began arriving at the end of May to set up shops in Streets of the World. John Gourley organized an afternoon tea for them to get reacquainted. Just south of Lake Shore Boulevard, a trailer camp was set aside to take advantage of the growing popularity of "homes on wheels." (Provision for future expansion may have been wishful thinking, as a mid-June census of the lot came up with no more than twenty-seven trailers.) Out on the lake, a concessionaire taking one of his swan boats for a shakedown cruise came up with an unpleasant catch—the lower half of torso victim no. 7.

A pair of outside events competed with the expo for the front page two days before opening. Steelworkers at Cleveland's Republic Steel plants set up pickets for the beginning of the Little Steel Strike. Coincidentally, Tom Girdler, Republic's president and an exposition trustee, had taken a gathering of the nation's most powerful steel executives through the 1936 expo's "Romance of Iron and Steel" theme exhibit the previous September. That Thursday also saw the arrival of the remains of John D. Rockefeller for burial at Lake View Cemetery. The oil baron had died in Florida at the age of ninety-seven, only a day after paying off the mortgage on his beloved Euclid Avenue Baptist Church.

■

Nothing occurred to steal the headlines from the reopening of the Great Lakes Exposition on Saturday, May 29, 1937. Two thousand people gathered at noon in the somewhat constricted space between Lakeside Avenue and the new main entrance. Compared with the seven imposing pylons still standing in splendid isolation back on St. Clair, the new portal was a modest, functional affair, distinguished by little more than a few spindly flagpoles.

Arriving with an escort, including Lincoln Dickey and Mayor Harold Burton, to perform the ceremonial honors was James Roosevelt, the eldest son of President Franklin Roosevelt. "As the official representative of the United States government, I do hereby declare the Great Lakes Exposition of 1937 duly opened," he proclaimed as he snipped the silk ribbon tied across the gates. Back in Washington, his father was scheduled to turn on the lights with the push of a button at 7:45 that evening.

Led by a seventeen-year-old Lakewood girl, expo-goers fanned out over the Court of the Great Lakes. They were the vanguard of a first-day crowd of 50,092, some 11,000 fewer than the previous year. Over the three-day holiday weekend, however, the 1937 version would attract 167,910 patrons, some 37,000 more than the first three days in 1936. There was little new to detain them on the diminished upper level: the Garfield cabin, the county building, wooden and brick model homes, and the Ohio Building stood relatively unchanged on their familiar sites. To catch some of the expo's vaunted new features, visitors had to take one of the two exterior stairways leading down into the Lakeside Exhibition Hall.

Dominating the underground space was the expo's new theme exhibit, "The Making of a Nation," which was built around a central rotunda designed to show off Larrinaga's murals. Four of them depicted the varied regions of the United States under the title *America the Beautiful;* the other eight illustrated such facets of American development as agriculture, transportation, science and invention, communication, and family and home. On the floor in the center was a relief map of the Great Lakes region, laid out in a fenced-off area fifty feet in diameter, with the area's major cities represented by scale models of their principal landmarks. An oversized construction of a compass, its pivot anchored in Cleveland, towered over the display. It was a three-dimensional reproduction of the official Great Lakes Exposition logo.

Radiating from the rotunda were complementary exhibits, such as a historical display of Lincolniana. Old Abe's favorite rocking chair was on loan from the Chicago Historical Society, as was the bed in which the assassinated president died. Also on view were Leonard Volk's life mask of Lincoln, a horseshoe from Lincoln's Old Bob, and a handbill from Ford's Theatre on the night Lincoln was shot. The exhibit was assembled under the supervision of Cleveland music dealer Anton L. Maresh, who provided many items from his personal collection.

Another section of "The Making of a Nation" featured a petroleum exhibit sponsored by Sohio. With models and dioramas, a young lecturer illustrated the drilling and refining of crude oil into gasoline. "Isn't it only a question of time when the supply will be exhausted?" a reporter quoted an onlooker. "We're finding more and more of it," answered the expert with a reassuring smile. Just in case, however, Dr. Charles G. Abbott of the Smithsonian Institution was on hand nearby to demonstrate his model of a solar engine. "Many scientists have pointed out that the world's supply of coal and oil could not last forever and that when it gave out man would have to turn to the sun for his source of power," commented David Dietz of the *Cleveland Press.* He thought Abbott's solar

Left: First to pass through the gates for the opening of the 1937 edition of the exposition was Lucy Ketring of suburban Lakewood. The seventeen-year-old Lakewood High student was escorted into the Court of the Great Lakes by Yeomanettes Irene Strong and Marjorie Herren. Behind them is the entrance to the Ohio Building. *Cleveland Press* Collection.

Below: Serving as a centerpiece for the 1937 theme exhibit, "The Making of a Nation," was a three-dimensional topographical map of the Great Lakes region. Large cities were represented within its fifty-foot diameter by models of their principal landmarks. The huge compass looming over the landscape was inspired by the logo of the Great Lakes Exposition. *Cleveland Press* Collection.

engine might someday make history, as did Alexander Bell's telephone at the 1876 Centennial Exposition in Philadelphia.

Displays such as these were intended to fulfill the pledge of expo officials to place more emphasis on education in its 1937 season. In the health section of the exhibit, the Camp Transparent Woman could be not only seen but seen through, revealing organs, blood vessels, and skeleton as clearly as if the viewer possessed Superman's x-ray vision. Constructed from cellhorn, a transparent substance, it was brought to the exposition through the efforts of the Academy of Medicine of Cleveland.

■

Across the Court of the Presidents bridge spanning the railroad tracks, the lower grounds sprinkled new attractions among the holdovers from the previous season. Blocking part of the prospect down Marine Plaza was Radioland, in the relocated Sherwin-Williams music shell. A new feature in the Western Reserve University Building was a demonstration of a lie detector by a recent psychology graduate. Little change was necessary in A. Donald Gray's Horticultural Gardens, one of the great successes of 1936.

Returnees in the Hall of Progress included the popular Ohio Bell Telephone exhibit, where visitors could listen to the sound of their own voices over the phone. Occupying a full quarter of the building again were the displays of the U.S. government, including the army's latest fighter plane with its seven machine guns. One new feature in the building was a television theater, where "television is demonstrated and explained to the public for the first time in Cleveland," according to Jay Taylor in the *News*. "If you have been inclined to regard television with tongue-in-cheek skepticism, a visit to Television Theater will change all that," asserted Jack Warfel in the *Press*.

What Clevelanders watched was generally nothing more exciting than expo-goers like themselves in the Varied Industries Building, across the Esplanade. A "Television City" had been set up there boasting $100,000 of equipment and 250,000 candlepower of lighting. This was in the former Automotive Building of the year before, a reminder of which was provided by a collection of horse-drawn carriages and early automobiles, illustrating the evolution of the latter from the former. Sohio also had a large exhibit in this building, with its own outside entrance marked by its name in towering three-dimensional capital letters.

Blossom Way featured the new Winterland on the old site of *Parade of the Years,* but Higbee Tower, the Firestone spread, and the sprawling Florida exhibit were all in their familiar locations. The last was even bigger than before, living up to its guidebook heading of "Mammoth Florida Exhibits." Having experienced a record-breaking tourist season the previous winter, with much of the increase from the Great Lakes area, the Sunshine State obviously considered its expo exposure as a good investment. Added to the columned manor house was a new Naturlarium featuring "a life-size Seminole Indian Village, a collection of rare Florida wild life and murals depicting the four most popular sports in Florida—swimming, fishing, golfing and hunting." Among the forty carloads of Floridiana shipped north was an entire grove of orange trees, to be transplanted on the shores of Lake Erie.

At the end of Blossom Way, the WPA's East 9th Street underpass still provided the main access to the amusement zone. There was a fresh frieze of cartoon cutouts overhead, replacing the circus parade of the previous year with the facades of Streets of the World.

■

Despite all the talk about change, the midway had essentially remained its honky-tonk self: noisy, gaudy, and crowded. Welcoming expo-goers just inside the entrance was Pirchner's popular Alpine Village restaurant and beer garden. Leading off the southern strip of concessions with its bubbling kettles and sweet smells was the maple sugar camp of W. S. Richards. Cliff Wilson was back at his old stand with his snakes and a new, unclassifiable monster named Tommy, described by one reporter as resembling "a turkey with elephantiasis, seen through the eyes of delirium tremens." Mammy's Cabin was gone, but its house specialty was available at a stand near the midway entrance with the equally downhome name of Chicken Roost.

Some of the other repeats from the first season included the pretzel and saltwater taffy stands, the shooting gallery, and the Skee Roll. The embryological specimens of the Bouquet of Life were back, as were the games and movie machines of the penny arcade. Old favorites reappearing in the rides section were the Ferris wheel, Flying Skooters, Loop-o-Planes, Tumble Bug, and pony track. New challenges for the more intrepid expo-goers included the Venetian Boat Swing, Octopus ride, and Rigolarium—the last described by the guidebook as "A European riding device with a special car accommodating two persons riding through a series of thrilling and surprising stunts. The laugh of the European Continent."

Even the fresh attractions may have been little more than cases of old wine in new bottles. In place of 13 Spook Street was a new "walk through" called the Crystal Maze, containing "hundreds of mirrors and illusions. Miles of Smiles." Carrying on in the tradition of the Front Page was an

Despite the presence of much-ballyhooed new attractions, the 1937 midway was essentially the same as its predecessor—loud, garish, and jammed shoulder-to-shoulder with thrill-seekers. Among its offerings were saltwater taffy, stomach-churning rides, and Ripley's "Believe It or Not" Odditorium. In a bow to family values, scantily-clad girls were in relatively short supply that year. *Cleveland Press* Collection.

International Crime Prevention Exhibit, in which actors demonstrated that "crime doesn't pay" by dramatizing some famous object lessons. The same moral was apparently inculcated by inanimate figures in a wax museum billed as The Curse of a Nation.

If anyone regretted the absence of John Hix's Strange As It Seems in the 1937 midway, Ripley's "Believe It or Not" Odditorium was present to satisfy the appetite for the abnormal. Inspired by Bob Ripley's popular syndicated newspaper feature, it included such live acts as a fingerless piano player, a man who drove nails into his skull, a woman who swallowed a twenty-two-inch lighted neon tube, and an armless woman who crocheted with her mouth. They were joined by Wenceslav Moguel, known as "El Fusilado" for his survival from the volley of a rebel Mexican firing squad in 1915. It left his face severely disfigured, missing a palate and jawbone. Perhaps the ultimate test of an audience's shock threshold, however, was provided by John Dunning, who could pull his wife around the stage in a wagon hooked only to his lower eyelids.

Dunning's act was often too much for the ladies in attendance, who were prone to keel over in a dead faint—possibly an even greater tribute than a standing ovation. The management was prepared for that response, with two nurses in attendance. They also had ready answers for any who might express sympathy for the performers. "I'll bet they make more money than you do," said one guide. Another offered the ingenious argument that the show was justified if only "because it makes normal people, or those with only slight handicaps, realize how lucky they are."

One thing missing, by design, from the midway in 1937 was nudity. Almon Shaffer, the exposition's director of amusements, was determined to hold the line against peep shows or "gyp joints" in the second year. "They've routed the few undesirable concessions that were on the Midway and in Streets of the World last year," noted one opening-day visitor with apparent approbation. True, the guidebook did mention a concession called The Fountain of Youth located near the end of the midway, describing it as "An illusion show with pretty girls—living tabloids of art in many scenes." No doubt it had some redeeming social or educational value.

North of the midway, the Coast Guard basin was much more crowded that year. Jostling the submarine S-49 and the paddleboat concession for dockage space was Byrd's South Pole ship, the *City of New York*. Berthed at the outer corner of the basin, its bow extending out into the lake, was the *Moses Cleaveland*.

As for Streets of the World, little change was needed or desired. William Kiefer apparently expanded his German Coffee Shop into a full-fledged German Restaurant, and journalist Zoltan Gombos appeared as proprietor of the Hungarian Cafe. Displaced from the western exhibition grounds, the sand sculptor set up his sandbox on the northern edge of Streets, overlooking the lake. One major new attraction in Streets was the exhibition in one of its chapels of the Crown of the Andes, a golden diadem fashioned for a statue of the Virgin in sixteenth-century Peru. Encrusted with a total of 453 emeralds, it was valued at $4.5 million. The biggest change, however, was found on the site of the former French Casino in the compound's northeastern corner. With nudity proscribed, the Casino had to go. In its place had appeared Billy Rose's Pioneer Palace, and Rose had assured expo officials that he could attract crowds without resorting to "vulgarity."

■

It was a cooler summer, in many ways, than that of '36. After the opening-day appearance of FDR's son, the nearest thing to a presidential visit was a stopover in July by his campaign manager, Postmaster General James A. Farley. After inspecting the new Main Post Office in the Terminal Tower

U.S. Postmaster General James A. Farley was one of the ranking visitors to the 1937 expo. One of the highlights of his tour was a review of the troops of the 11th Infantry, stationed on the grounds for the summer. Hat in hand, Farley was flanked by Captain Don Riley, commander of Company C, and Dr. Nicola Cerri, U.S. commissioner for the federal government's exhibit in the Hall of Progress. *Cleveland Press* Collection.

group, Farley arrived at the exposition to a nineteen-gun salute from Company C of the 11th Infantry. He was taken through the U.S. government exhibits in the Hall of Progress by Dr. Nicola Cerri, who had succeeded A. Harry Zychik as U.S. commissioner. Dudley Blossom bestowed the exhibition's Distinguished Service Medal on the visitor.

As before, a full calendar of special days had been planned to entice less distinguished guests to the expo. Goodyear Day in July brought an estimated thirty thousand employees of the Akron tire company. Classes were dismissed early to allow students and faculty to attend on Kent State University Day three weeks later. Wapakoneta, Tiffin, and Lakewood, Ohio; Baldwin-Wallace and Mount Union Colleges; Manx Societies; *Indianapolis Times* newsboys; chiropractors; and Cleveland merchant tailors all had their days in the sun or the rain, as the case might be. "Here can a man take his family to satisfy Jr., who wanted to go to Coney Island, N.Y., Sister, who was bent on Atlantic City, Mother, who meant to traipse all over Europe, Auntie, who would see Switzerland with its skating," summed up a Shepard correspondent in her local paper.

For Belle Vernon Day on July 11, the Telling-Belle Vernon Milk Company arranged to have its Sunday night NBC radio program broadcast from Radioland. That brought its star, tenor James Melton, to town for a five-day visit that garnered nearly as much publicity as that of Rudy Vallee the previous summer. Melton didn't bring his wife, a former Clevelander, but he did bring his Cleveland-made 1910 White touring car, which he had purchased for $195 and restored for an additional $1,900. He took Peg Humphrey, the expo's associate director for exhibits, out for a spin and photo op. Tickets for his broadcast were being distributed by Belle Vernon milkmen.

Streets of the World drummed up publicity with a series of contests through the *Cleveland News* to identify the largest families among the city's nationality groups, with winners to be rewarded with a day at the expo. Numbering seventeen, the Frank and Rose Jastrzebski family of Forman Avenue won the honors for the Poles. That record was surpassed the following week by the nineteen members of the Louis and Elvira Corsi clan of Garfield Heights. As the largest Italian family, they feasted on chicken à la cacciatore at the Trattoria Santa Lucia in Streets of the World's Riviera section.

A few miles outside the grounds, the Cleveland Museum of Art had organized another special exhibition which, though not officially part of the 1937 exposition, was at least partly intended for the benefit of its visitors. Perhaps taking his cue from the observation of *Time* magazine on the Twentieth Anniversary show, that the "only meagre part of Cleveland's show was the casual collection of U.S. painting," CMA director William Milliken had arranged as the sequel an Exhibition of American Painting from 1860 until today. Highlights of its 221 items in seven galleries were Albert Pinkham Ryder's *The Race Track* from the museum itself, Winslow Homer's *Snap the Whip* from Youngstown's Butler Art Institute, and John Sloan's *McSorley's Bar* from the Detroit Institute of Arts. Also featured was the work of such Cleveland School artists as Paul Travis, Charles Burchfield, Henry Keller, and William Sommer.

Outside events of the summer of '37 fell short of the excitement of the previous year. Two more torso-murder victims were discovered, both in the Flats (nos. 8 and 9), but no death masks were brought to the expo grounds for identification. In the absence of a national election, the summer's big story was the disappearance over the Pacific Ocean of aviatrix Amelia Earhart. There was no American Legion convention in town that September, but out at Cleveland Municipal Airport, thanks to the efforts of the WPA over the past year, the National Air Races would take off from what was called "the largest paved surface in the world." Cleveland had been hosting the event since 1929, when Earhart had competed in the Powder Puff Derby for women.

■

The exposition's second season had opened under the fairest of meteorological auspices. What was described as "perfect weather" brought out an attendance of 234,537 for the first seven days. Slightly below the first week's total in 1936, it was nevertheless higher than had been expected. But then, to plagiarize the title of a Louis Bromfield novel published that year, *The Rains Came*.

"It was horrible weather the first thirty days—rain, cold," recalled Herman Pirchner, skipper of the Show Boat. "Sometimes there were more people on stage than in the audience." While rainfall for 1936 had been 5.82 inches below average, U.S. weather forecaster Ralph C. Mize reported that as of June 1937 it had rained (or poured) 2.92 inches more than average in Cleveland. From the expo's opening day until the end of June, local *Billboard* correspondent Harlowe R. Hoyt reported only nine days without heavy rain. "And of those nine days one was cloudy," he added.

When the sun made a rare all-day appearance on the last Monday of June, it brought out twice the usual Monday crowd. "Result: Nearly 3,000 at Aquacade's first show; sell-out at Winterland twice; crowded Midway, crowded Streets of the World," reported Loveland in the *Plain Dealer*. Almon Shaffer thought that the belated arrival of the Crown of the Andes at the expo might have brought good luck. "This is the turning point," he predicted.

Shaffer would have made a poor weatherman. On the second day of July, snowflakes were spotted floating past the windows of exposition offices on the twentieth floor of the Terminal Tower. The expo feted its millionth visitor on July 5, thirty-eight days after opening; the 1936 version had reached that milestone in thirty-three days. It didn't record its second million until August 12—by then it was eighteen days behind the first year's pace.

Still, one might always hope for a change in the weather. After an unusually fair weekend, Lincoln Dickey walked over to the office of U.S. forecaster Mize in the Standard Building. In his pocket he packed a piece of metal, but it wasn't a pistol. "You helped us out when we needed it the most during the last week-end," said the fair's general manager with a possibly strained smile, "and as a mark of our appreciation I am privileged to present to you the Great Lakes Exposition Distinguished Service Medal."

Not everyone on the expo grounds had suffered equally from the weather. One new attraction on the lakefront was reported to be doing quite well; in fact, one might say that water was its element.

YODELING MAN

"The Great Lakes Exposition was the high and low point of my career." As the years rolled by, that bittersweet observation became a signature maxim for Herman Pirchner. For better or worse, the lakefront extravaganza retained pride of place in the memories of a centenarian.

It was a lifetime of numerous ups and downs, in which Pirchner made and lost several fortunes. In the public eye, he fell in and out of favor as a result of his business and entertainment ventures. His German heritage exposed him to changing attitudes toward the Fatherland.

He was born in the village of Hofgastein in the Tyrolean Alps of Austria, the son of an innkeeper with fifteen children. Though too young for service in World War I, he didn't escape the postwar hardships of the former Hapsburg Empire. Along with many of his siblings, Pirchner left Austria and arrived in Cleveland at the age of nineteen in 1926.

His first job was a prosaic position in a pretzel factory, but he and two of his brothers soon became involved in a more clandestine calling. Taking advantage of America's experiment with Prohibition in the 1920s, they began brewing illegal beer in the cellars of German social clubs. When the local mob demanded a piece of the action, Pirchner and crew decided to pursue other interests.

With the help of generous credit, Pirchner purchased a beer garden on Lake Shore Boulevard at East 185th Street, which he named the Alpine Shore Club. A speakeasy was located upstairs until the repeal of Prohibition in 1933, when Pirchner hired members of the Cleveland Orchestra for a celebratory concert. Believing Americans too inhibited socially, the gregarious proprietor set about to bring them out of their shells. "So we make everybody do something," he explained. "Sing a song maybe, do a little dance, or if they can't do that, just stand up and let us watch them swallow a glass of beer."

Far from ever forgetting where he came from, Pirchner made sure everyone else was aware of his origins. As William McDermott wrote in the *Plain Dealer*, "Herman himself, big and blond, would yodel among his friends and customers when the spirit of his native heath overcame him." In 1934 he opened his Alpine Village nightclub on Euclid Avenue in Playhouse Square, the heart of Cleveland's entertainment district. Following the same formula he had at his beer garden, the host greeted his guests in Austrian lederhosen and Tyrolean hat. He put in sixteen-hour days and became a millionaire by the age of thirty.

For the 1936 Great Lakes Exposition, Pirchner simply built a copy of the Alpine Village on the grounds and watched the customers pour in. Seeing his success, the expo's sponsors talked him into taking on an additional nightspot, the Show Boat, for the second season. Wining and dining him downtown at the posh Union Club, they intimated that the expo would back him against any loss.

"I was naive; it was the biggest mistake of my life," said Pirchner, who ended up in bankruptcy court after the exposition closed. About the only consolation he got out of that second season was finally setting a new stein-carrying record at the Alpine Village, where his initial attempt the previous year had ended in a shower of spilt suds.

According to the account carried by United Press International, Pirchner painstakingly arranged his pilsner pyramid atop a base of fourteen seidels with their handles aligned for his fingerhold. Twenty-six more seidels and fifteen shells were piled on in three more decks, to a total of fifty-five steins weighing 112 pounds. He lugged them a distance of forty feet to set what he claimed to be a new American and European record, the old one having been set by one Herman Pirchner. "I vunce studied cheometry," UPI quoted him, regarding the secret of his prowess.

Pirchner returned to work on a new fortune at his Playhouse Square Alpine Village and at another operation he had opened near Public Square, Herman Pirchner's Hofbrau. One other thing he had acquired from the Great Lakes Exposition was a wife, a singer named Constance Stoll. He married her, purchased a farm in Geauga County for his eventual retirement, and fathered two sons.

World War II posed some delicate problems for the Austrian immigrant. He went on record as favoring Germany's takeover of Austria in 1938 but was quick to add that his opinion was formed long before the rise of Hitler and that if the allies had permitted the union in 1919, "there would be no Nazi Germany today, but a great German democratic commonwealth." Then Japan embarrassed him on December 7, 1941, by bombing Pearl Harbor when the Alpine Village happened to be featuring a revue based on *The Mikado*. Suddenly Japan was no laughing matter, and Pirchner closed the show within two days.

After America went to war, the *Cleveland Press* received a letter purporting to expose "another traitor who should be properly dealt with . . . that

Herman Pirchner doffed his customary Alpine garb in favor of formal attire for New Year's Eve at the Alpine Village. Though he claimed to have lost a fortune in the 1937 Great Lakes Exposition, he gained it back in his Playhouse Square nightclub and other ventures. He often made himself part of the act, yodeling with the band or presenting a newlywed bride with a bottle of champagne and a rolling pin. *Cleveland Press* Collection.

well known nazi Herman Pirchner." Signed "A real American Father," it was quietly consigned, unprinted, to the paper's morgue. Pirchner's brother Karl actually spent part of the war in a Nazi concentration camp. Herman was drafted into the U.S. Army, though he probably made a greater contribution to the war effort by teaming with musician Mickey Katz to sell nearly half a million dollars worth of war bonds.

Home from the war, Pirchner resumed his pursuit of gemütlichkeit on Playhouse Square. Entertainers such as Cab Calloway, Sophie Tucker, and Artie Shaw shared the spotlight with visiting celebrities such as General Dwight D. Eisenhower. Mein host was generally part of the show with his Bavarian getup and stein-hefting exploits. Part of his routine was presenting new brides with gift packages consisting of a bottle of champagne and a rolling pin.

Floor shows at the Village often featured trimmed-down and sometimes unauthorized versions of popular Broadway shows. John Price, who later founded Musicarnival, liked to tell how he pirated the tunes of *Guys and Dolls* for Pirchner while working in New York. Broadway producer George Abbott once filed suit against Pirchner over his use of material from *Damn Yankees*.

Pirchner didn't confine his penchant for publicity to Playhouse Square. He hired the Cleveland Orchestra a second time, at his own expense, to give a benefit concert in Public Hall for European war orphans and widows. He was impresario for the appearance of Agnes Moorhead, Charles Boyer, Cedric Hardwick, and Charles Laughton in a reading of the "Don Juan in Hell" act from Shaw's *Man and Superman* at Music Hall. He even crashed the Grotto Circus on a dare in 1950, when his friend Carl Wallenda carried him on his back along a fifty-foot-high tightrope. He got across without mishap, then stumbled going into the ring to take his bow.

It was probably the decline of downtown that did Pirchner in. He faced bankruptcy again in 1957 but managed to reopen the nightclub with help from supporters and the sale of cows from his farm. Four years later, he gave up the ghost for good and sold the Alpine Village.

Finally out of show business, Pirchner opened a gourmet food shop at Severance Center in Cleveland Heights. He operated it for fifteen years with the help of his second wife, Maria, his first marriage having ended in divorce.

Even in retirement, Pirchner couldn't stay away entirely from Playhouse Square. He maintained an office in the Hanna Building into the 1990s, its walls covered with mementos of the Great Lakes Exposition and other ventures. By the time of his death in 2009, at the age of 101, he had survived the sinking of his expo Show Boat by nearly three-quarters of a century.

Broadway
on Lake Erie

8

Although they both spent several days crossing the Atlantic on the SS *Manhattan* in the summer of 1936 as members of the U.S. Olympic team, it is doubtful that Jesse Owens and Eleanor Holm saw much of each other. For one thing, he was black, she was white, and this was the 1930s. For another, he was a track and field man, she a swimmer. For yet another, he was in training and she wasn't—at least not by Avery Brundage's standards.

In her devil-may-care moods, Holm liked to tell reporters, "I train on champagne and cigarettes." She soon fell in with a group of shipboard newsmen and proceeded to train on her sport drink of choice, earning herself a reprimand from members of the U.S. Olympic Committee. She sloughed it off and continued partying, by one account running into an Olympic chaperone while being carried back to her stateroom. It was the final straw for the straitlaced committee head, Mr. Brundage, who informed a group of reporters—including some of her drinking companions—that Eleanor Holm was no longer a member of the team. Many of her teammates signed a petition urging her reinstatement, to no avail.

So Owens went on to Berlin to bring home the gold, and Holm merely went home to consider her options—which were far from negligible. She already was an Olympic champion, having won the 100-yard backstroke in the 1932 Los Angeles games. Swimming since the age of ten, she had set some twenty-eight national marks by the time she graduated from high school. Her looks were equal to her talent, with a trim athletic figure topped by attractive chestnut hair over a cover-girl smile. She had married bandleader Art Jarrett and had begun singing with his act; she also had a movie contract with Warner Bros. Now that her Berlin dreams had been dashed, she was pondering whether to renounce her amateur swimming status and go professional all the way, when her agent got a call from Billy Rose.

Billy Rose—the Bantam Barnum of Broadway! With the demise of Ziegfeld and the decline of Reinhardt, he was arguably the greatest producer in the land in 1936. Small only in stature (five feet, three inches), he seemed to be trying to overcompensate his entire life. He had been a high school shorthand champion and secretary to Bernard Baruch during World War I. He then turned songwriter, producing with collaborators such hits as "Barnie Google" and "That Old Gang of Mine." When he married America's best-known comedienne, however, he was annoyed to discover that the world knew him as "Mr. Fanny Brice."

Rose decided to make his own name as a producer. He opened the Billy Rose Music Hall on Broadway, then took over the old Hippodrome for a colossal musical starring Jimmy Durante and an elephant, which fully lived up to its title of *Jumbo*. In 1936 he was hired by a group of Texans who wanted to put on an exposition in Fort Worth to compete with the Texas Centennial Exposition in nearby Dallas.

Trumpeting the slogan "Dallas for Education, Fort Worth for Entertainment" all over the state, Rose soon proved that he was their man. He built an al fresco nightclub, the Casa Mañana, with a huge stage, elaborate floor show, and seating for thousands of diners. He staged a Wild West show and constructed an entire frontier town, featuring a plebeian nightclub called the Pioneer Palace. Just for good measure, he also revived his production of *Jumbo* on the grounds. Clearly on a roll and looking for new fields to conquer, Billy Rose turned his gaze northward to the Great Lakes Exposition.

■

As with many legendary shows, the story of the Aquacade's origins comes in multiple versions. In what became the official Billy Rose version, he had come to Cleveland in February 1937, to tour the shuttered expo grounds with Lincoln Dickey. Noticing a crowd on the lakefront, however, he came upon a pair of girls swimming in the lake to the tune of the "Blue Danube Waltz" on a phonograph. "As I watched them, I began to multiply, and the more I multiplied, the more excited I became," he recalled a decade later. He turned to Dickey and said, "If a water ballet looks that good with two girls, imagine what it would be like with two hundred. If it's okay with you and your committee, I'd like to produce a water show for your fair." When Dickey asked what he'd call it, Rose spotted a penny arcade across the midway and announced, "Watercade, or, if you want to get fancy, Aquacade."

It's a jim-dandy story, if one overlooks the fact that the expo's Marine Theater was nowhere near the midway, let alone the even slimmer chance of finding anyone other than ice fishermen on Lake Erie in February.

Another version told by Jean Skelly, the young woman working in the exposition's publicity office, centers on Eleanor Holm. She recalled being assigned between seasons to meet Holm, who was appearing with her husband's band at the Palace Theatre on Playhouse Square. "It was a cold night early in winter—she was a small girl, sort of lost in a big fur coat," said Skelly. She and a coworker escorted Holm to the Hotel Allerton, around the corner on East 13th Street. There was a swimming pool in the hotel, where a coach named Floyd Zimmerman was putting some of the young swimmers from the expo's Marine Theater through their routines. "Holm got excited and got in touch with Billy Rose," said Skelly. "Rose came to town and got the idea for the Aquacade."

It's true that Eleanor Holm and Arthur Jarrett headlined the stage show at the Palace in the second week of January 1937, with Eleanor billed as "The International Swimming Star who Made the Olympics Famous!" Billy Rose had come to town even earlier, however, and he already had the germ of the idea, if not yet the name, for the Aquacade. He had made a well-publicized appearance at the Great Lakes Exposition the day before its closing in 1936. That's when he toured the grounds with Dickey, looking over the possibilities for 1937. William McDermott, the *Plain Dealer* critic, spotted the pair downtown that night at the Mayfair Casino, where "you could see that something grandiose was fermenting in his [Rose's] mind and Dickey was seeing to it that it had to do with the Cleveland exposition."

Rose took in the *Parade of the Years* and pronounced it "crammed with showmanship," but that was someone else's show. He was also taken to the Marine Theater, where the show went on despite the near forty-degree fall temperature. "The coldest act was when to the dreamy music of the Blue Danube, a group of girls floated in a circle with their icy toes and noses sticking out of the water," according to the *Plain Dealer*. (Not quite February, but close enough.) "I'm crazy about it," Rose told Dickey of the show. Undoubtedly he was reminded of the finale of his Casa Mañana revue in Fort Worth, in which the stage receded from the audience to disclose a lagoon floating gondolas laden with chorines. Here was something to which he could apply the Rose magic. Rose proposed to not only put on a new water show but install a Cleveland version of his Pioneer Palace for the 1937 Great Lakes Exposition. All it would take was what Fort Worth had paid for his services: $100,000—a grand a day for one hundred days. Exposition officials signed him up early in February.

Once on board, Rose immediately moved to close the deal with Eleanor Holm as his star attraction. He was probably the one who had tipped her off to go see the swimmers at the Allerton, in order to whet her appetite. Her hopes of reinstatement by the Amateur Athletic Union being slim to nil, she "decided to cash in" on February 23. Rose provided the cash to the tune of $30,000 for the summer. With a high-profile female lead in the fold, Rose felt he could attract a male costar capable of sharing the spotlight. A few weeks later he reeled in his "Aquadonis Number One," none other than Johnny Weissmuller. A champion Olympic swimmer in his own right, Weissmuller was familiar to moviegoers for his portrayal of Tarzan in the Metro-Goldwyn-Mayer picture series.

■

Next on Rose's to-do list was lining up one of the largest chorus lines in history and building a theater in which it could swim as well as dance. As far as the chorus went, Rose had promised no nudity or vulgarity. "You see," he expounded to the local press, "gals should be beautiful, smartly dressed. They should never be nude or offensive." But bathing suits, of course, would be de rigueur for a water spectacle, and, of course, revealing to a certain point. The producer said he was looking for a hundred "aquafemmes" who were attractive and able to swim, plus thirty-six dancers and another three dozen "show girls, 5 feet 6 inches and upward." Girls from Greater Cleveland would get first crack at the openings before Rose cast his net over the rest of the Great Lakes.

Since Rose was much more knowledgeable about chorus girls than mermaids, he would rely heavily on the expertise of Floyd Zimmerman, the choreographer of the '36 expo's Marine Theater. Zimmerman's day job was swimming instructor at the Allerton Hotel pool, which he appropriated for the holding of Aquacade auditions. Several hundred local girls showed up for the first tryouts in mid-February. Rose, every inch the producer in his pearl-gray fedora, screened them for looks before sending them on to Zimmerman for their swimming tests. Also looking on in what was described as an "unofficial capacity" were Safety Director Eliot Ness and an assistant. Rose was joined in later sessions by Eleanor Holm, as much for photo-ops as for opinions.

One of the first to pass the preliminary test was a nineteen-year-old Lakewood girl, who then failed the swimming trial when a recent appendicitis incision caused her to double up in pain. "Too bad," said a sympathetic Rose as he helped her out of the pool, "You are lovely to look at." The great man's compliment, she said, made up for her disappointment. At least nine swimmers who made it to the Aquacade program were from Lakewood, which Zimmerman happened to call home, too. Many were veterans of his Marine Theater. Besides the aquabelles,

Several hundred local girls showed up early in 1937 to audition for Billy Rose's Aquacade. Producer Rose, though vertically challenged himself, liked his chorus lines tall and leggy. "I never get jealous of Billy," said his wife, comedienne Fanny Brice. "Beautiful girls are his business." *Cleveland Press* Collection.

Rose was also looking for two dozen Adonis-like male swimmers. "No little fellows," specified the Bantam Barnum. "The taller the better."

Rose's specifications for his aquatic stage were every bit as grandiose as those for his chorus. It would be 128 feet wide and 80 feet deep, flanked by two 65-foot-tall diving towers on either side with dressing rooms in the rear. Two 132-foot barges underneath would keep it afloat. Gear tracks on the bed of the lake and a series of fifty-horsepower motors would enable the pool between stage and audience to be opened for performances and closed for dancing between shows. The 1,800-ton stage was built in the Wells Construction Company's plant on West 49th Street and then towed to the lakefront site of the former Marine Theater. It took six tugboats to maneuver it through the harbor breakwater.

Preparing the site and building the rest of the theater was the responsibility of construction chief A. N. Gonsior, who took everything, including a six-week delay of steel delivery, in stride. "Building a thing like this is a tremendous task in organization," he said. "We're trying to do something here that has never been done before." It represented an outlay of $600,000, with the expo footing the bill. Even the "curtain" was unique, consisting of a 40-foot-high wall of water sprayed at a rate of twelve hundred gallons a minute by a row of two hundred nozzles across a span of 134 feet. It was blazoned by colored lights and lowered, not raised, for performances.

There was seating for an audience of five thousand, with tables for dining in front and grandstand seating in the rear. Architect Anthony Thormin designed a solid, functional exterior, embellished with broad horizontal stripes that anticipated the future Marcel Breuer addition to the Cleveland Museum of Art. Large six-foot-tall letters above the entrance proclaimed "BILLY ROSE'S AQUACADE."

■

This being a Billy Rose production, the hype had to be even bigger than the show. Asked just how big his new show was going to be, Rose customarily replied that it would have Lake Erie for a stage and Canada as a backdrop. "I got claustrophobia," he told a *Cleveland News* reporter, "Got to have big spaces." Aiding him was veteran publicist Richard Maney, who told a *Plain Dealer* columnist, "You have my word for it, Mr. McDermott, that Rose will either tame Lake Erie or he'll fix it so no one else will ever be able to do anything with it. If the waves don't recede at the rise of his hand, the skies clear at the arch of his eyebrows, someone—Erie for all I know—will be scolded into submission." Getting down, or building up, to specifics, in the *New York Herald Tribune* Maney wrote that the Aquacade stage "will dwarf the proportions of an airplane carrier," and Rose "will set up a shindig employing mermaids and mermen in numbers that, to the lay mind, seem outrageous. On the lake, under the lake and above the lake his nautical legions will carry on in extravagant fashion."

"What is it?" was the recurring question in a brochure that probably displayed the combined talents of Maney and Rose:

> IS IT A THEATRE? No! Though it presents a cast of world-famous stage personalities, directed by JOHN MURRAY ANDERSON, on the largest stage in the world.
>
> IS IT A RESTAURANT? No! Though you can dine sumptuously (and reasonably), table d'hote or a la carte, with the cuisine directed by an internationally-known chef.
>
> IS IT A NIGHT CLUB? No! Though you can dance under the stars, on a fabulous floating stage, to the music of America's best-known orchestras.

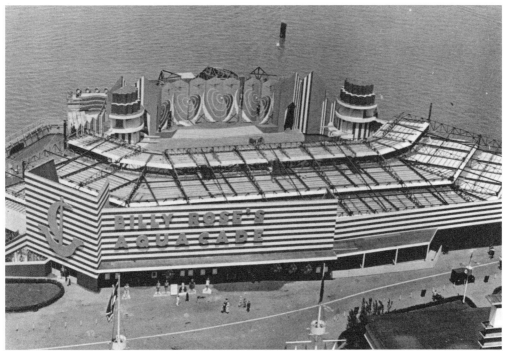

"Broadway on Lake Erie" was how Billy Rose summarized his Aquacade. Five thousand spectators and diners could be accommodated beneath its corrugated-iron roof. Its eighteen-hundred-ton stage could be moved out into the lake to form a lagoon for the swimming acts, then brought back to shore to provide a floor for after-show dancing. Cleveland Public Library.

IS IT A WATER SHOW? No! Though it stars JOHNNY (TARZAN) WEISSMULLER, ELEANOR HOLM JARRETT . . . and 100 (count 'em) beautiful Aquabelles.

And so on down the line. It wasn't an operetta, though it had a score by Dana Suesse and sets by Albert Johnson. Nor was it a musical comedy, nor a fashion show, nor a girl show, "Though it presents—artistically to be sure—500 of the most glamorous Aquafemmes on which the eyes have ever feasted."

In summation, it was "Billy Rose's AQUACADE—the newest thing in American entertainment—a $10 show scaled down to fit the purse of the times." It was, in distinctive red letters, "Broadway on Lake Erie."

Probably Rose's proudest achievement was coining the term "aquacade," which he registered as a trademark. He went on to exercise his proprietary rights by peppering the program with an entire vocabulary of aquajargon, including not only aquabelles and aquafemmes but aquagals, aquadolls, aquadonis, aquadudes, and aquabeaux, all under the direction of Archie

Bleyer, the aquaductor. One exception to the aquarule was a group of lady-go-divers. Understandably, the general public was a bit slow to learn the new language. Eleanor Clarage reported hearing such variations on the show's name as "the Aquade, the Aquarium, the Aquaduct, the Aquadock, and the Cavalcade."

Rose's Aquacade program bio was subheaded "a saga in superlatives," with no apparent sense of self-parody. "By any set of standards the Aquacade must win the *sui generis* classification. To say that it is a blend of the international water Olympics, the Ziegfeld Follies and the Roman Circus is skirmishing with understatement," it read. "Billy Rose plays big—he is a painter of ideas whose canvas is the illimitable heavens, who splashes his colors with the immense sweep of the rainbow, whose feet are on the pavement while his head is sniffing in the clouds."

■

Those who knew him had somewhat lower estimates of the Rose persona. "I remember Rose very well in our offices between seasons," said Jean Skelly. "He was an unmitigated jerk and a cheapskate and a mooch. He would come to bum cigarettes; I was glad I didn't smoke." In an open letter in the *Plain Dealer* to Grover Whalen on the eve of the New York World's Fair in 1939, Roelif Loveland said, "We note that your fair has Billy Rose's Aquacade. . . . Does Billy Rose still bum cigarettes?" Another reporter, Bob Considine, related a story much later about restauranteur Toots Shor's reaction to a rumor that the mob was planning to kidnap Rose. "Who would they contact?" he asked incredulously.

Despite his less than sterling reputation, Rose obviously knew how to pull a big show together. Since Fort Worth also decided to reopen for a second season, the producer spent much of the spring shuttling back and forth on the airways between Ohio and Texas. He was also cowriting lyrics for the Aquacade songs to music by Dana Suesse, a twenty-four-year-old woman called the "Louisiana Liszt."

A thousand details had to be handled. Rose sent the "Louisiana Liszt" back to her piano with a dismissive, "The music for that finale isn't what I want." Popular bands such as those of Wayne King, Xavier Cugat, Ted Weems, and Bob Crosby were engaged for fortnightly gigs to supply music for the between-shows dancing. Chef Louis Pierron was placed in charge of a kitchen, employing twenty chefs and fifteen dishwashers. Their culinary creations would be served and cleared by 350 waiters and busboys under the direction of maître d'hôtel Max Snyder. Nothing escaped the attention of Rose, who was even heard criticizing the backstrokes of his swimmers.

Most of the details, of course, were ironed out by Rose's professional staff. Before the aquastage was in place, Bob Alton rehearsed his chorus line in the Rainbow Room of the Carter Hotel. "Get some style girls," he admonished, "You look like beach combers." Floyd Zimmerman and John Murray Anderson plotted the swimming routines on the floor of the Allerton's ballroom, then put the swimmers through their moves in the pools of the Allerton and a YWCA. From the first day of rehearsals, Anderson always appeared in the same shabby suit, which he refused to change out of superstition (perhaps as a palliative for the ten black cats said to have the run of his New York apartment).

A week before opening, the stage was in place for final rehearsals. Anderson later claimed that during one run-through, the movement of the floating stage on its underwater tracks dislodged a dead cow, which made an unwelcome stage appearance. Besides the swimmers and the cow, he also had to coordinate the movements of three motor-driven miniature battleships which made their entrance in the final scene. Weissmuller didn't put in an appearance until that final week, then, with Holm, submitted to inoculations against the less-than-pristine Erie waters.

There was such a great demand for opening-night table reservations that a special telephone bureau was installed to take the calls. Admission for the two evening shows was one dollar on weekdays, a buck and a half on Saturdays; the charge for three weekly matinees was only seventy-five cents. A trainload of New Yorkers was reported to be en route to the opening on Saturday, May 29, 1937. It was a close call because of the production's unique technical equipment, but not even a water temperature of fifty-seven degrees would keep the show from going on. Shortly before 8:30 P.M., John Murray Anderson donned a new suit and consigned his rehearsal outfit to the trash.

■

Technical director Canton Winckler's forty-foot water curtain slowly descended into the lake to reveal seventy-five aquagals, aquafemmes, and aquadudes in white swimsuits poised on the edge of the stage across the lagoon. They stood at attention for a moment before, one at a time at quarter-second intervals, diving into the water with Rockette-like precision. The opening routine was set on a California beach and executed to a tune entitled "We Rule the Waves." A few minutes later, a fanfare heralded an announcement: "Ladies and gentlemen, the backstroke champion of the world, Miss Eleanor Holm."

She advanced to center stage clad in cape and slippers of silver sequins, to the strains of a song called "Happy Birthday to Love":

Though a year has passed, your fascination,
Has increased my love a thousand fold.—
Just a year ago today,
Luckily you came my way—*

Just a year previously, coincidentally, Eleanor had sipped that fateful glass of champagne. Majestically, she removed her silver slippers and let the mantle drop from her shoulders. Standing now in a one-piece swimsuit, she meticulously tucked her auburn locks into a bathing cap before moving to the edge of the stage and entering Lake Erie to waves of thunderous applause.

There was no plot to the revue, only a series of four themed scenes changed with the aid of a revolving stage. Set in the Coney Island of 1905, the second scene featured such turn-of-the-century musical standards as "In the Good Old Summertime" and "By the Beautiful Sea." Here Johnny Weissmuller had his introduction, making his entrance with his inimitable "Tarzan" yell. Featured also in the scene were diving clown Stubby Krueger and Aileen Riggin, a former Olympic diving champion. Action returned to the present on "A Beach in Florida" for the next scene, in which Holm and Weissmuller finally appeared together, along with aquabelles and aquabeaux. For many who witnessed it, their aquatic duet swum to the tune of "Strangers in the Dark" remained the show's most memorable moment.

For the grand finale, the action shifted to "The Shores of Lake Erie" for a futuristic fantasy headed "It Can't Happen Here," loosely suggested by Sinclair Lewis's antifascist novel of the same title. It depicted a symbolic struggle among Men in Black and Men in Brown (both played by ladies of the chorus) and Men (real men) in Red, to the accompaniment of a title song sung by Bob Lawrence. It was all a bit confusing for most viewers except for the ending, in which the forces of darkness were evidently subdued and a figure suggestive of Miss Liberty rose slowly above a long unfolding train of rhinestones to tower triumphantly above the huge cast, while Anderson's fleet of battleships disported busily in the waters below.

It was all done in about an hour, but no one appeared to notice, let alone protest. The Aquacade was one of those rare shows that appeared to surpass its hype. Elmore Bacon in the *News* summed it up in four words: "Tremendous. Gorgeous. Colossal. Magnificent." It was, he said, "like

---

*"Happy Birthday to Love," words and music by Billy Rose, Stanley Joseloff, Dana Suesse, Rudolph Bertram, and Fenyes Szaboles (New York: Crawford Music, 1937).

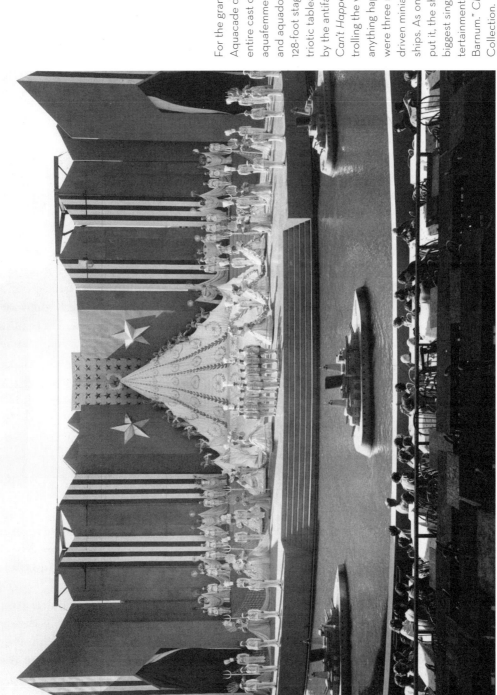

For the grand finale, the Aquacade deployed its entire cast of aquabelles, aquafemmes, aquadudes, and aquadolls across a 128-foot stage for a patriotic tableau suggested by the antifascist novel *It Can't Happen Here*. Patrolling the waters against anything happening here were three mechanically driven miniature battleships. As one local critic put it, the show was "the biggest single piece of entertainment on earth since Barnum." *Cleveland Press Collection.*

watching a four-ring circus. The stage is so wide and so many entertainers are performing that it keeps you busy focusing your eyes." He also noted without complaint, "The Aquafemmes lean considerably toward the Aquanude in that last stanza." To the *Plain Dealer's* W. Ward Marsh, it "proved to be the greatest aquaspectacle ever staged in these or, I dare say, any other parts . . . the biggest single piece of entertainment on earth since Barnum." Weissmuller, he marveled, "literally shoots through the water rather than swims, so great is his speed." While Charles Schneider of the *Press* thought the show's finale dull and drawn-out, his overall impression rivaled those of his colleagues for superlatives. "Broadway's Billy has really done himself and Cleveland proud," he wrote. "The pint-sized Napoleon of show business has made Lake Erie lie down, roll over and say uncle."

Even the seasoned New York critics were impressed. "We thought the great state of Texas gave Mr. Rose the needed scope for his imagination. How could we know that he was going to dig up Lake Erie?" wrote Hearst columnist Damon Runyon. "It is a brilliantly pleasing show, bringing Broadway to Lake Erie, and it provides a fitting climax this summer to the second year of the Great Lakes Exposition," said Malcolm Johnson in the *New York Sun*. "The whole crazy and glittering shebang is, in a word, an eyepopper, and Mr. Rose has again delivered the goods, by the vanload," wrote Lucius Beebe for the *New York Herald Tribune*. That the ballet at times outshone the stars, Beebe found "the more remarkable because all but ten of its 175 members were recruited from the vicinage of Cleveland." Syndicated critic Ira Wolfert also singled out the "Lake Erie belles who are not only architectural triumphs, but wheel and prance through the water with electric precision." In the context of the 1930s, Floyd Zimmerman's marine ballets were the aquatic equivalent of a Busby Berkeley movie musical.

■

Her maiden voyage a resounding success, the Aquacade settled down into its summer-long cruise. Not even the rain-plagued days of early in the run could dampen its show-must-go-on spirit. Director Anderson quickly improvised a "rain show," in which the more vulnerable costumes of the stage routines were replaced by bathing gear similar to that worn by those in the lagoon. "If Noah'd been in this show he'd have started building another ark long ago," cracked one chorine, while another observed that she was starting to get webbed feet from dancing in the rain. Audiences could view their tribulations in the relative comfort provided by a forty-thousand-square-foot corrugated-iron roof over the dining and seating areas.

Actually, the water coming from above didn't bother the cast so much as that into which they had to dive. "How black it looks. How dirty," noted a female reporter who joined the chorus line for a night. Filming for a newsreel one afternoon had to be delayed while swimmers with nets dragged the lagoon for driftwood and other flotsam, including a belly-up fish floating in the sun. Weissmuller, still smarting from his precautionary typhoid fever inoculation, asserted that they "ought to give the lake the shots." They did, in a way; but when they laced the lake with chlorine, the chorines complained that it was ruining their complexions.

As summer sailed into fall, the swimmers' chief gripe became the rapidly cooling lake. Roelif Loveland described the aquabelles coming backstage squealing with "ohs" and "ahs," while their aquabeaux were "considerably more voluble . . . hollering things never taught in Sunday School, all of which had a very definite bearing on the weather." Along with the rest of the cast, Holm passed on champagne in favor of steaming cups of coffee. When she was finally sidelined with a combination of laryngitis and exhaustion, Aileen Riggin rose from a sickbed herself to take her place. This gave Cleveland Heights High graduate Betty Jackman the opportunity to step out of the chorus and perform Riggin's diving numbers. Riggin was also busy training replacements for those aquabelles returning to school in September.

Standing-room crowds did their part to raise the temperature on the lakefront. "Probably the biggest crowds of the year attended Mr. Rose's Aquacade over this week-end," observed the *News* the first week in September, "and we make that occasion for the remark that few institutions will advertise this city for years to come as has the Aquacade. It was the spark of the expo this summer." Lincoln Dickey acknowledged as much two weeks later, when he presented the entire cast with the "bronze classification" of the Great Lakes Exposition Distinguished Service Medal.

Some of the Aquacade's most memorable moments took place offstage, many of them provided by its "Aquadonis Number One." Weissmuller's "Tarzan" yell was heard all over town. He practiced it backstage, first standing on his head to get his throat in the proper shape, but the airless confines of the tiny bathhouse made him dizzy. Taken on a golf outing in Kirtland, he found himself in his proper element. He let loose with a blood-curdling jungle cry that not only thrilled the caddies but turned the heads of a nearby herd of grazing cows.

For all his machismo, however, Weissmuller admitted to reporters that his household was ruled by his wife, Lupe Velez, a tempestuous Mexican actress who soon joined her husband in Cleveland. "Lupe would fly in when Johnny wasn't expecting her," recalled Herman Pirchner. "Johnny was a little flirtatious." The pair settled down in a suite at the Alcazar Hotel in Cleveland Heights, though it wasn't to what could be called domestic tranquility. Jean Skelly remembered seeing "Lupe Velez in all her fury chasing Johnny all around the apartment. I was young and observant," she added. "I learnt all about the seamy side of show biz."

Yet in her own way, Lupe took good care of Johnny. The hotel manager recalled seeing her returning from the market across the street with two live chickens to cook for him. On another occasion Lupe was frying steak in the kitchen while Weissmuller talked with a reporter and snitched chocolates in the living room. "Look, you double-crosser! Stop!" stormed Lupe as she charged in and grabbed the sweets. "You tol' me you wait. Always candy, then no spinach. I quit! I mean it! I'm serious thees time, I swear!"

At moments like that, Tarzan must have missed his movie Jane. Lupe shuttled between Cleveland and Hollywood all summer. She returned in September to nurse him through a chlorine-induced infection and protect him from other dangers. She went along with him in a surf boat towed by a blimp as a publicity stunt, but testing the waters at the Aquacade proved too much. "Look! Ees still filthy!" she shrieked. "I tell Billy Rose and Mr. Dickey it just ees no go. I take Johnny home."

She didn't, of course, and Johnny stayed the summer. His costar, meanwhile, seemed content at first to avoid the offstage limelight. Much of her leisure time was spent at the gentleman's farm of Leonard Hanna in the far eastern suburbs. She would drive out with other aquabelles such as Aileen Riggin and Polly Rose, Billy's sister, for gourmet lunches and recreational swimming in Hanna's unpolluted pool. One of her main complaints was about the "damned Lake Erie minnows" that tended to get lodged in her bathing suit during performances. She credited her attempts to outswim them with at least keeping her weight under control. If it wasn't the minnows, then it was the Three Stooges. Appearing at the Palace one week in July in a "Revue de la Nutts," Larry, Curly, and Moe crashed the show at the Aquacade, disrupting Ted Weems's band and sending Holm into hysterics.

Eleanor Holm Jarrett was soon to steal the extracurricular spotlight from Tarzan—but that's a story in itself.

■

The Aquacade may have gotten the lion's share of ink, but it was far from the only show on the lakefront. Unless one were a devotee of nudity or Shakespeare, entertainment was one area in which the 1937 exposition really was better than the first year. One of the prime attractions outside the Aquacade was another Billy Rose enterprise, the Pioneer Palace. It was a largely faithful replica of Rose's operation of the same name in the Texas exposition.

Entry to Pioneer Palace was free, patrons already having laid down two bits to gain access to Streets of the World. (Rose's taproom was designated as the American representative in the global village.) They entered through swinging doors into the ambience of an Old West saloon, its unpainted board walls adorned with cattle brands and six-shooters. Extending entirely across one end of the hall was a long bar manned by bartenders with slicked-down cowlicks across their foreheads. Rose's profits would come out of food and drinks; the cover charge was only a quarter.

Mirrors above the bar moved away to expose a stage for the floor show, which was largely vaudevillian. A chorus line in Gay Nineties costumes backed Lulu Bates, who belted out songs of the same period. Above the pianist in the pit was a sign imploring "Don't Shoot the Professor. He's Doing the Best He Can." Others giving their all included a Swiss bell ringer and a pair of girls who tapped out tunes on variously filled whiskey bottles. One performer who literally gave his last full measure was a fire-eater named Dan Nagyfy, a veteran from Rose's *Jumbo* and Fort Worth shows. Chemicals used in his act finally caught up with the sixty-one-year-old trouper, who was stricken with poisoning and taken to St. Luke's Hospital, where he died a few weeks later. His replacement didn't have much better luck, being sent to the expo infirmary with face and hand burns after only three days on the job.

Where Toto Laverne had once been the sensation of the French Casino, the toast of the Pioneer Palace was an act billed variously as the Beef Trust or the Rosebuds, another encore from Rose's nightclub and Fort Worth emporium. Toto had bared her flesh; these six dancers simply *bore* their flesh, ranging from 250 to 377 pounds apiece. Costumed in short babydoll dresses, they were unexpectedly nimble of step, if taxing on the boards. Performers' feelings aside, Rose justified the act by claiming that it made "every woman in the audience feel slim."

Next to the two Rose properties, the most enticing show on the grounds was Winterland, the ice extravaganza set up on the site of the previous year's transportation pageant. Though Lucius Beebe joined Winsor French in regretting the absence of *Parade of the Years,* "since last summer it was the most exciting single attraction of the show," expo officials were hopeful of profiting from the contemporary interest in skating epitomized by Sonja Henie in the movies. Winterland's producers in fact had sought to sign the Norwegian star as their featured performer but settled in the end for Evelyn Chandler, billed as the "Queen of America's Figure Skaters."

Chandler and a supporting cast of fifty skaters were provided with four thousand square feet of artificial ice on which to execute their spins and axels. Seventeen thousand dollars worth of equipment and three hundred gallons of water per minute went into its manufacture. It was kept in skating trim with 28,750 square yards of canvas pitched overhead in a double-layered tent to provide insulation against the summer sun. On the inside of the inner tent was painted a blue sky with twinkling stars, while massive faux icebergs bordered the skating rink. Among the special effects were whistling winds and a snowstorm. There was seating for three thousand spectators, whose admission was forty cents for adults, a quarter for children.

Though described as "merely an ice-skating exhibition," Winterland was nevertheless rated as "one of the most popular and most entertaining shows on the grounds" by critic William S. Cunningham. "There is a little fantasy written around the performance, something about an Ice King who falls in love with the Lady of Spring," he wrote. "But you needn't worry about that." Jean Skelly remembered it as "a really good ice show, the forerunner of the ice shows that later came to the Arena."

■

Less ostentatious shows were open on the midway, of which Tony Sarg's Marionettes was the most conspicuous. Certainly they had the most impressive stage, being quartered in the freestanding Tudor structure occupied during the previous summer by the Shakespearean troupe of the Old Globe Theatre, with no more outward sign of change than a new signboard. A human barker outside dubbed "Waxo" lured patrons by imitating the jerking movements and unnatural expressions of a marionette. Inside, where live actors had once presented "tabloid" versions of *Julius Caesar* and *As You Like It,* a cast of 120 different puppets enacted such shows as *Alice in Wonderland, Rip Van Winkle, Hansel and Gretel, Uncle Remus' Stories,* and the *Adventures of Sinbad the Sailor.*

Characters measured an average of two feet in height and were each manipulated with nine strings pulled by half a dozen puppeteers concealed above. Two operators and more than the usual number of strings were required to produce the bumps and grinds of a dancer called Fatima, probably in the Sinbad show. There was a touch of irony in the *Alice in Wonderland* playlet, which was introduced by one of the puppeteers costumed as Alice. She was actually an actress named Elsie Dvorak, who had played Shakespearean roles in the Old Globes at Chicago and Dallas.

As the season progressed, *The Mikado* and *Faust, the Wicked Magician* were added to the repertoire. Admission to the hourly shows was a quarter for adults, fifteen cents for children.

In the middle of the midway's southern strip was a plain facade designated Town Hall, behind which was presented a different kind of drama— or "drammer," as it was fancifully subtitled by Roelif Loveland. This was

Filling the space on Blossom Way formerly occupied by a transportation pageant, Winterland was another newcomer to the 1937 Great Lakes Exposition. Starring figure skater Evelyn Chandler, it was the forerunner of such spectacles as Ice Follies and Ice Capades. Its four thousand square feet of artificial ice were kept in frozen trim by an insulated tent. *Cleveland Press* Collection.

the nineteenth-century melodrama *The Drunkard,* written to dramatize the evils of alcohol and the virtues of temperance. From their booth in the Hall of Progress, members of the Women's Christian Temperance Union dismissed W. H. Smith's play as an "outmoded weapon" in their more scientific crusade against drinking. The Cleveland Play House had revived it in 1934 as a period piece. At the Great Lakes Exposition of 1937, a troupe imported from Los Angeles played it strictly for laughs.

"The crowd last night howled, wept and suffered with the actors, and despite the moral clearly evident, drank numerous bottles of beer," reported Loveland in the *Plain Dealer.* Just in case the audience didn't get the point, a black-whiskered plant circulated among them, heckling the actors. According to the *Plain Dealer*'s Eleanor Clarage, a "Teutonic gentleman" one night still didn't get it, rising at the end of the first act to indignantly harangue the audience: "Shame on you peoples for making fun of these peoples," he reportedly lectured, "they're doing the best they know how." (One can't entirely rule out the possibility, of course, that he, too, was just a plant.)

Located amid the rides of the amusement zone was a free Children's Theatre, sponsored by the May Company department store. There members of the Cleveland Play House, under the direction of Esther Mullin, enacted such stories as "Red Riding Hood" and "The Mad Hatter's Tea Party," thrice daily. A free children's playground was also available next to the blue-and-white tent of the May Company Pavilion.

Those in search of more serious drama might have found it at the extreme western end of the Horticultural Gardens in the form of a Greek play, *Aeolic Fragment*. Presented in a natural setting under the direction of Hope Holmes of Hudson, Ohio, it was described as "a triangle-love tale," performed to the accompaniment of a flute and a harp. It's unlikely that it took much business away from the Aquacade.

■

Herman Pirchner was not a happy camper that summer of 1937. He had threatened to pull his Alpine Village off the midway even before the expo reopened, saying that it was asking for too high a cut from his profits. Officials responded that they had offered him the same deal as in the first year, when their cut had been 10 percent of gross receipts. Obviously, their differences were ironed out, because Pirchner not only reopened the Village in 1937 but took over operation of the Show Boat nightclub on the relocated *Moses Cleaveland*. Possibly this was intended as a deal sweetener; it turned out to be more like an albatross.

While the Alpine Village was as popular as ever at the head of the midway, the Show Boat at times resembled a ghost ship. One cause certainly had to be the inclement weather, which kept attendance down throughout the grounds for the first few weeks. Another may have had to do with that old real estate mantra: "location, location, location." Anchored in an out-of-the-way corner of the midway, the *Cleaveland*'s nearest neighbors were the kiddie rides of the amusement zone. The exclusive Admiralty Club had abandoned ship for new quarters next to the Aquacade. In its place on the top deck, Pirchner installed the El Dorado Club, but the city's high society was now over at the Recess Club. Pondering his poor hand in the middle of August, Pirchner decided that the time had come to play a wild card: the Show Boat would challenge the expo's ban on nudity.

Amusement czar Almon Shaffer had thus far upheld his pledge to keep the 1937 exposition safe for "the kiddies and grandparents." Officials claimed that the girlie shows weren't missed, although not everyone concurred. "Since the days of Little Egypt, semi-nudes, near-nudes, and just plain nudes have been the mainstays of world fairs," pointed out the *Akron Beacon Journal* on the eve of opening day. "If the Cleveland exposition wishes a black showing in its ledgers, it should know by now that no nudes is bad nudes."

Certainly Herman Pirchner wouldn't argue with that conclusion. He announced that he had signed fan dancer Faith ("Sizzling") Bacon to head a new revue at the Show Boat. "Miss Bacon will be nude. Completely nude," he added defiantly. When Lincoln Dickey threatened to stop the show, Pirchner countered that he couldn't, because the Show Boat wasn't on the exposition grounds: "It's in the lake and I can make my own rules." According to Philip Porter in the *Plain Dealer,* officials feared Pirchner "might detract attention from the Aquacade, where the big money of the Expo is invested, and which is now clicking like nobody's business." Pirchner was not without his supporters, who pointed out that "he was the only Clevelander who had big money in an Expo show and ought to have more consideration, etc."

Round one went to Pirchner, who threatened to close up shop if the show couldn't go on. On it went, billed in newspaper ads as "The One and Only Nude on the Exposition Grounds." Pictured in her "Leda and the Swan" pose, Ms. Bacon managed to look enticingly blond, sloe-eyed, callipygian, yet somehow innocent. In her twenty-six years she had appeared in the Shuberts' *Artists and Models, Earl Carroll's Vanities,* and with Maurice Chevalier in the Casino de Paris. Nonetheless, she cultivated an image of offstage wholesomeness in her interviews with local reporters. She neither smoked nor drank, danced mainly to support a tubercular sister, and had a suppressed desire to become an obstetrician.

Deciding, undoubtedly in the line of duty, to see her act for himself, Almon Shaffer delivered a somewhat circumspect verdict. "She's a very talented dancer. I don't find it objectionable myself," he ventured. "Maybe the rest of the officials had better see it first, though, before we say anything." Ward Marsh, who always seemed to draw such assignments for the *Plain Dealer,* had trouble deciding whether Ms. Bacon was "absolutely nude," but he was sure "she has little to worry the censor or the critic." Decades later, even Pirchner wasn't sure. "Her performance was actually very artistic," he said. "It was kind of an illusion; you couldn't tell. I never really knew."

In the end Lincoln Dickey had the last word, and it was based on financial rather than artistic considerations. Examining the books for Show Boat, he concluded that "nudity doesn't pay." Pirchner protested that Bacon had increased his business by 50 percent, but he evidently failed to make his case. At the conclusion of her two-week contract, Bacon's show was closed just before Labor Day.

In an effort to recoup his losses during the second season, Herman Pirchner challenged the expo's ban on nudity by engaging fan dancer Faith Bacon for an appearance at his Show Boat nightclub. "Miss Bacon will be nude. Completely nude," he affirmed, but neither he nor others who witnessed her act were ever really sure. Opinion was equally inconclusive as to whether her performance helped his bottom line. *Cleveland Press* Collection.

■

Originally scheduled to close on Labor Day, September 6, the 1937 Great Lakes Exposition, like its predecessor, was granted a reprieve. Early in August Dudley Blossom announced a three-week extension to its run, stating that the show would now "close positively" on September 26. The decision, he said, was made in response to "insistent and wide-spread demand from public officials, exhibitors and concessionaires and from the indications in many letters to exposition officials that people all over the nation are hopeful that they can visit the exposition during September."

More candidly, W. T. Holliday, the expo's president, observed that attendance had picked up since the return of good weather, and that the 1936 expo had finished much stronger at the gate than when it opened. "Probably no exposition in the world was greeted with an unfriendlier brand of weather than the '37 Exposition," asserted an editorial in the *Press*. "Not until just recently have we had anything resembling a 'break' for those genuinely interested in seeing the show."

As if to jump-start a final surge in attendance, Saturday, August 14, was declared Jubilee Day. Special tickets were placed on sale for fifty cents, granting admission not only to the grounds but to the Horticultural Gardens and Streets of the World as well—a $1 value. Among the special events scheduled were amateur boxing matches, Gene and Glenn programs in Radioland, and a bathing beauty contest in Streets. Clevelanders and out-of-towners responded with a record attendance for the year, 105,819. Despite cool temperatures, the second week in September brought the year's highest weekly gate at 304,105, some 35,000 more than the nearest runner-up.

Amid the accustomed sights were signs of the approaching end. Concessionaires in Streets of the World staged a "Carnival of Bargains," cutting prices of all remaining goods nearly in half. The White Sewing Machine Company advertised "Big price slashes for quick disposal" on the forty-three demonstration models from its exhibit in the Hall of Progress. Unnoticed by the average expo-goer was the arrival of A. N. Gonsior, the man who had built the exposition, there to supervise its demolition. At an Aquacade benefit for the Showmen's League of America, Lincoln Dickey presented a loving cup to Billy Rose, who responded with uncharacteristic humility. "Aquacade would never have seen the light of day without the aid of Dickey, for he helped a dream come true," said the producer. Rose and Dickey, as it turned out, were not finished collaborating.

Dickey told Jack Warfel of the *Press* a week before closing that Aquacade was one of the three most significant contributions of the Great Lakes Exposition. Because of it, he said the marine show would be "an indispensable part of all future expositions." Another was the Florida exhibit, which he considered "the greatest state exhibit ever shown." Finally, there was Dr. Charles Abbott's solar boiler from the Making of a Nation theme exhibit. "Dr. Abbot's [*sic*] boiler will be to the Great Lakes Exposition what the introduction of electricity was to the World's Columbian Exposition of Chicago in 1893," predicted the expo's general manager.

A highly creditable crowd of 81,359 passed through the turnstiles on the final day, bringing the year's total attendance to 3,518,740. It was almost half a million short of the first year, and far lower than the once-anticipated 5 million, but gratifying nonetheless, given the weather woes of early summer. Thousands of that final crowd gathered at the Radioland shell at 9:15 that evening to witness the closing ceremonies. Mayor Burton, Blossom, and Holliday took their final bows, and Dickey handed out Distinguished Service Medals ("gold classification") to, among others, Peg Humphrey, Almon Shaffer, and A. N. Gonsior. The official exposition flag was lowered and presented to Blossom, after which a bugler sounded taps, which was echoed by another from the roof of the Firestone Building at the other end of the Esplanade. As the lights dimmed around 10:10, a quartet sang "Auld Lang Syne."

Officially it was over, although there were fireworks to follow, including a final bombardment to use up all the summer's leftover rockets. In the midway and Streets of the World, they planned to keep the lights burning till sunrise.

On the morning of closing day, the *Plain Dealer* had listed the intangible benefits of the expo, including "the goodwill of more neighbors, a reversal of the deplorable Cleveland habit of turning our back upon our greatest natural asset, the lake; the changing of an important sector of that lake front from dust bin to beauty spot, and finally the spiritual value of having put across a vast civic enterprise." Winsor French wrote a more personal postmortem the following day in the *Press:* "Cleveland, I think, is going to miss the Exposition far more than it realizes," he said. "If nothing else, it at least convinced some of the more conservative that home is not always the most amusing place to be."

AQUASCANDAL!

When Eleanor Holm agreed to star in Billy Rose's Aquacade, her husband, Art Jarrett, reportedly turned down an offer to appear as bandleader in the same show, fearing he'd be upstaged by his wife. When Fanny Brice was in Cleveland a few weeks before the opening of the

Aquacade, she was asked if she ever got jealous of the girls in her husband's productions. "Jealous? I never get jealous of Billy," she replied. "Beautiful girls are his business."

Though it's highly unlikely that Brice and Jarrett ever got together after the Great Lakes Exposition for a meal of fricasseed crow, such a repast might have been called for in view of the soap opera that unfolded on the shores of Lake Erie in the summer of 1937.

While Jarrett went off to lead his band at the Texas Centennial Exposition in Dallas, Brice went to make a movie in Hollywood. Eleanor and Billy, their respective spouses, were accordingly left to their own devices in Cleveland. They didn't pursue them alone for long.

According to Winsor French, Jarrett was calling his wife nightly from the Lone Star State. Rose was generally on the scene in Cleveland, however, and when called away for business himself, he bombarded his star with several telegrams a day. Herman Pirchner remembered "the tremendous effort Billy Rose put into wooing Eleanor Holm" in Pirchner's El Dorado retreat atop the expo's Show Boat: "He was really in love with her."

Rose later claimed to remember "the exact moment" he fell in love with Holm: "It was 8:56 on the opening night of the Cleveland Aquacade in 1937." That was the moment when his leading Aquabelle made her first dramatic splash in the waters of Erie. According to more than one biographer, however, his interest had been stirred since the moment he had signed her up in February. Possibly stature played a role, too: Fanny Brice was four inches taller than the Bantam Barnum, and Eleanor Holm an inch shorter.

In addition to trysting in the El Dorado, Rose was also seen at the Lake Shore Hotel in Lakewood, where Holm shared a suite with her Aquacade costar Aileen Riggin. Word got back to Fanny Brice, who had returned to New York. This was in flagrant violation of Number 4 in the "ten attributes of a perfect husband" she had playfully given out to the press a few months previously: "He should have the technique not to let the woman he loves find it out when he steps out—as all men will." Dropping her comic persona, she picked up the phone and called Eleanor, identifying herself as "Mrs. Rose looking for Mr. Rose" and then slamming down the receiver.

Arthur Jarrett soon got his own wakeup call, but this one was from Eleanor Holm Jarrett. Answering the phone in Dallas at 5:30 A.M., he was greeted by his wife with the words, "Art, I want a divorce." Jarrett went to the press with his story, and the press went to Holm for hers, in which she admitted that they had been discussing the possibility of a divorce due to their separate careers. "And maybe we'll be lucky enough to work to-gether some time and there won't be any divorce at all," she backstroked a bit awkwardly.

According to the *Cleveland Press,* however, Eleanor had removed her wedding ring several weeks previously in favor of a new and bodacious five-carat diamond given her by Rose. Holm indignantly denied this, claiming she had bought the $1,800 bauble more than a year ago "with my own hard-earned money." Rose had nothing to do with either her request or her ring, she said. "My goodness, Rose's married—happily married." Members of the Aquacade cast believed her version about the ring, at any rate. According to the *Plain Dealer*'s Phil Porter, they were willing to "bet you 3 to 1 that Billy didn't pay for it, because he continually bums cigarettes from them and has never been seen carrying a pack of his own."

Rose himself denied ever giving Holm a diamond and verified her de-scription of his marriage. "I have been happily married for eight years," he said. "I have no intention of asking for a divorce." In the press, Fanny Brice reassumed her comic persona. "I certainly would feel unflattered if just a swimmer got him," she cracked. "Probably she can beat me in the water—but that's all." Jarrett, who had been leery of being upstaged by his wife and now saw their story on the front pages of every paper from the *Youngstown Vindicator* to the *New York Daily News,* suddenly de-cided that any further comment on the affair "would be very ungallant on my part."

Once the first flurry of rumors had settled, observers began to won-der whether any legs were being pulled. "I believe it is just a publicity stunt," commented Eleanor's mother, Charlotte Holm, saying she had been told so by her daughter. "Miss Holm wasn't answering the telephone or seeing any callers at her Lake Shore Hotel suite," stated the *Press* the day after the story broke. "She was, however, seeing larger crowds at Mr. Rose's Aquacade at the Great Lakes Exposition and hearing more ap-plause for her singing and swimming."

Capacity crowds were reported the very evening after the first story and for both the matinee and evening performances on the following day. "The sequence of events may lead the cynical to see . . . that while the technique of press agentry may have changed somewhat since Anna Held took her milk baths, the objective is the same," observed the *Plain Dealer* in an editorial headed "Box Office Romance," concluding, "In this instance it would appear that the objective has been attained."

Even after the publicity cooled down, attendance at the Aquacade continued to surge. Because of the inclement weather of June, as well as slow word-of-mouth about the show's merits, the Aquacade's weekly

Seen in a rare moment of relaxation was Billy Rose with his two Aquacade costars, Eleanor Holm and Johnny Weissmuller. If Johnny looked like the odd man out, it's because he was. Rose and Holm became an "item," while Weissmuller was kept on a short leash by his temperamental wife, Lupe Velez. *Cleveland Press* Collection.

receipts averaged only from $7,000 to $13,000 early in the run, reported the *Plain Dealer*'s William McDermott. The week of the Rose-Holm gossip, however, produced a sudden spike of an extra $10,000 at the gate. During August receipts continued to climb, from $38,570 to $46,765, with $50,000 expected for the week of Labor Day. Asked for his interpretation of this phenomenon, Rose, for a change, affected coyness. "I never try to keep my name out of the newspapers," said he.

Cynics such as Porter had advised waiting until after the close of the exposition before putting any stock in divorce rumors. Two months after the show, they were the ones dining on crow when it turned out that there had been real fire behind the smokescreen of stories all along. Billy Rose announced his intention to marry Eleanor Holm as soon as they both could obtain divorces. While awaiting the decision of the courts, the pair took off together for California.

"It's just an instance of four bullheaded careers clashing," Rose had explained. "Miss Brice wants her career. Arthur Jarrett wants his. Miss Holm is willing to give up hers for me. I don't know why, but she is and that's that."

"Don't speak ill of Billy Rose. He's the man I love," expo worker Jean Skelly recalled hearing from Holm. According to Pirchner, who watched their courtship blossom in his club, "She said he wasn't going to do to me what he did to Fanny Brice, but she eventually married him."

When Rose launched a new Aquacade at the New York World's Fair in 1939, Eleanor Holm was "Aquabelle Number One" in the program and Mrs. Billy Rose in private life.

9

Lakefront Legacy

On a gray December afternoon in 1941, workers gathered at the northern windows of downtown office buildings to stare at thick clouds of black smoke rising from Cleveland's lakefront. Just beyond the northeastern corner of Municipal Stadium, the Horticultural Building of the Great Lakes Exposition was enveloped in flames. Firemen struggled vainly to quench the three-alarm blaze, which quickly consumed the structure's plywood shell and left only its steel skeleton standing against the horizon.

True, the building had become an eyesore in the view of many, and plans were already in place to raze it and salvage its steel. That wasn't part of the original idea, however. The building and gardens, along with the WPA-built East 9th Street underpass, were intended as three permanent gifts to the city for its support of the exposition. "The permanent horticultural building and the gardens, showing how the lake front can be improved and landscaped, will be a lesson the city will take to its heart long after the exposition has become a memory," the *Cleveland Plain Dealer* had predicted on the eve of opening day in 1936. Now, only five years later, the last of the two hundred or so buildings put up for the lakefront show was a pile of smoldering ashes.

Most of it, of course, had been only temporary and had come down by design. Before they could be cleared from the Mall, the seven stately pylons from the original entrance on St. Clair Avenue were ignominiously plastered with signs such as "Let's Go Ahead with Burton" for the fall election. Flagpoles and lighting fixtures from the lower exhibition area were destined for resurrection on the grounds of the Palisades Amusement Park in New Jersey. Those spiffy nautical outfits of the Yeomanettes, along with the uniforms of the exposition police, were reportedly slated to be shipped to Ethiopia, possibly for the garnishment of Mussolini's occupation forces.

Most of the temporary buildings put up for the Great Lakes Exposition were dismantled or razed shortly after the end of the second season. Within months, much of the downtown lakefront resembled the wasteland that had prevailed prior to the visions of expo planners. As if to underline the irony, remains of the last two torso-murder victims were discovered amid the rubble. Cleveland Public Library.

Demolition began in Streets of the World and proceeded westward. Spared for a couple of years were the sprawling Hall of Progress and the Varied Industries Building, which would be occupied by the World's Poultry Congress in 1939. Soon much of the lakefront was beginning to resemble the wasteland it had been prior to the exposition. As if to add insult to injury, the last two torso-murder victims were discovered in the summer of 1938 in a pile of refuse near the 9th Street underpass. Eliot Ness never brought the killer to justice, though he became personally convinced that the butcher was finally out of circulation behind the gates of a mental institution.

■

The flaming exit of the Horticultural Building pretty much prefigured the end of the exposition's planned legacy. Before long the East 9th pedestrian underpass was replaced by a traffic underpass for the westward extension of Lake Shore Boulevard. That left only the Horticultural Gardens, which endured for several more decades north of Municipal Stadium. Not long after the untimely death of their creator, they were renamed the Donald Gray Gardens in his memory.

They weren't nearly as impressive as the horticultural display that had overwhelmed visitors to the Great Lakes Exposition. Their original expanse of three and a half acres had been whittled down by the inroads of stadium and port activities. No longer did they descend to the edge of the water, as landfill for the facilities of the Port of Cleveland later separated them from the lakefront. The formal nationality and period gardens had been abandoned, though the naturalistic shaded slopes leading to the pergola-bordered walk on top remained. Ironically, among those who benefited most from the rustic downtown retreat were the hoboes who had been displaced from the old city dump from which the exposition had risen.

During the day at least, others would find their way to the Donald Gray Gardens. Growing up on the west side in the 1970s, Matt Franko was far too young to remember the expo but became quite familiar with its gardens. His parents, following their marriage in St. Augustine Church in Tremont, had sought out the gardens as a background for their wedding pictures. "After church [at St. Malachi] on Sundays we would go to play in the gardens—me and my two brothers and two sisters," says Franko.

Despite the overgrown shrubbery and crumbling reinforcement walls, the Frankos still found the grounds beautiful. "It seemed more like ruins to me. We were the only ones in the gardens," he recalls. "We would play tag all through there. There was a big statue of a woman—we all would go sit on it and have our pictures taken. . . . The fountain was working once in a great while—but other times not."

As the century neared its close, the Donald Gray Gardens enjoyed a modest revival as a haven for birdwatchers. As the northernmost spot of greenery on the downtown lakefront, they offered a convenient alighting place for migrating avian flights on their trips between Canada and points south. One nature lover in the 1990s reported spotting whippoorwills, red-breasted nuthatches, yellow-bellied sapsuckers, black-crowned herons, and even a bald eagle on the premises. When plans were made to replace Municipal Stadium with a new football stadium for the return of the Cleveland Browns in 1999, naturalists became the foremost advocates of preserving the gardens. The Browns won that one (if little else since), and the Donald Gray Gardens went the way of the rest of the Great Lakes Exposition.

Not even the Golden Book of Cleveland managed to survive the expo's demise. More than half a million visitors had signed the gigantic register near the main entrance in the first seven weeks, but little was heard of it afterward. It couldn't have been easy to mislay a five-by-seven (*feet*, not inches), two-and-a-half-ton tome, but somehow it happened. Its promoter had expressed his intention to donate it to a "Historical

Intended as the principal permanent legacy of the Great Lakes Exposition were the Horticultural Building and its adjoining Horticultural Gardens. Four years after the expo closed, the building was a pile of ashes following a three-alarm fire. That left the Donald Gray Gardens, renamed after their creator, which endured in somewhat reduced splendor north of Municipal Stadium for sixty years, until they were obliterated along with the old stadium. *Cleveland Press* Collection.

Museum" following the expo, but there is no record of its acquisition by the Western Reserve Historical Society, which would have been the logical repository.

Erick Trickey, an editor at *Cleveland Magazine,* tried to track it down as a follow-up to an anniversary piece on the exposition. A former Clevelander called from California to say that he remembered his parents finding it in the garage of a home they had moved into in Bratenahl right after World War II. Several years later, his father sold it for $200 to a doctor who said he was relocating to Arizona. It took several men the better part of an hour, and some of their most colorful vocabulary, to maneuver the crate-encased book onto a flatbed truck. From that suburban driveway, the Golden Book of Cleveland, like the hero of a western movie, presumably disappeared into the setting sun.

Some of the exposition's principal actors proved scarcely more enduring than its landmarks. Hardly a year had passed since closing day when the event's lead mover and shaker, Dudley S. Blossom, was dead at the age of fifty-nine on October 8, 1938. Between the two seasons, the Chamber of Commerce had presented him with its Cleveland Medal for Public Service. Among his numerous civic, cultural, and charitable interests, however, the Cleveland Orchestra had probably been closest to his heart. "He has been founder, donor, executive and godfather for the Musical Arts Association, which put the Cleveland Orchestra on an endowed basis and helped create Severance Hall," the *Plain Dealer* had once observed. In recognition of his support and that of other family members, the orchestra in 1968 named its new summer venue Blossom Music Center. If Blossom ever returned in spirit to check it out, it may have reminded him of the Sherwin-Williams music shell from the 1936 Great Lakes Exposition.

While Blossom had lined up the backing, Lincoln Dickey as general manager had made the Great Lakes Exposition a reality. Evidently, he paid no heed to a graphology expert who visited the expo in 1937 and analyzed his handwriting. She found him "extremely energetic, eager, vital, enthusiastic" but left him with a warning: "You just cannot keep up the pace at which you are going." Regardless, Dickey went on after the expo to become Billy Rose's right-hand man for the Aquacade at the New York World's Fair and San Francisco's Golden Gate Exposition in 1939 and 1940. He died from a heart attack on the eve of the New York fair's last day, two years later and three years younger than Blossom.

A. Donald Gray was also gone by 1939, as noted elsewhere; Richard Rychtarik, while destined for a more than normal lifespan, had left Cleveland in 1940 for New York. Even Herman Pirchner, who gained less from the exposition than most of the other major players but survived for seven more decades as its principal embodiment, has finally rejoined the old expo gang.

Billy Rose and Eleanor Holm enjoyed more than a decade of what seemed wedded bliss, then went through an acrimonious divorce action inevitably tagged by the tabloids as the "War of the Roses." Rose turned his inextinguishable energies from show business to the stock market, amassing a nest egg of an estimated $30 million by the time of his death in 1966. Holm outlasted him by nearly four decades, basking in the Miami sun as the wife of a former oil executive. "She was about 90," said wire reports of her death in 2004. Another former expo sensation, Trudye Mae Davidson (aka Toto Leverne) had died in Florida in 1988 as Mrs. Gertrude Forsythe.

The ranks of the expo's several thousand minor players inexorably thinned through the years. One of several young women who dressed as peasant girls and danced in Streets of the World was Gwendolyn Taylor. She remained active in local musicales and little-theater groups until her death at eighty-five. Banjo- and guitar-playing Frank Vadnal, who performed with his siblings in the Slovenian Village of Streets, was inducted into the Cleveland-Style Polka Hall of Fame two years before his death in 1995. Until her death in 2001, Betty Jackman Speacht treasured her moments in the Aquacade spotlight with Holm and Weissmuller. "Johnny was dear. He was sweet," she remembered some sixty years later, safe from the wrath of Lupe Velez.

■

Despite the destruction of its physical footprint, the Great Lakes Exposition managed to leave an extensive indirect legacy, both anticipated and unforeseen. Financially, its major backers never suggested that it wasn't worth the outlay, though the original $1 million underwriting in 1936 was never recovered. Those who had anteed up the additional half million to extend the show a second year were repaid no more than fifty cents on the dollar. It was revealed also that in both years "a small group of public-minded citizens" had provided emergency loans totaling some $400,000 to help the expo over some slack periods, which had been repaid in full.

Whatever monetary profits might have come out of the exposition had to be measured in terms of the spending it drew to the city. Of its 7.5 million visitors over two summers, it was speculated that one- to two-thirds came from out of town. Estimates of the money thus left in Cleveland from outside ranged from $25 million (by Dudley Blossom) to $42 million (by Mark Egan of the Cleveland Convention and Visitors Bureau). Blossom provided a somewhat more statistical measure of the exposition's monetary impact by pointing out that deposits in Cleveland's four largest banks from January 1, 1936, to September 1, 1937, increased by nearly $90 million.

Undoubtedly the exposition accomplished one of its main purposes, that of alleviating some of the hardships of the Depression. It provided employment for up to ten thousand workers, the majority of them Clevelanders. Exhibitors and concessionaires had paid out an estimated $4.2 million in wages over the two summers. It was nowhere near the scope of the WPA, which maintained a payroll in Greater Cleveland of from twenty to eighty thousand workers in 1937–38. Nonetheless, it was an appreciable supplement to the budgets of thousands of area families.

In 1937, as after the previous year, observers pointed out the intangible benefits of the enterprise. "There was a time not very long ago when Cleveland was known to the rest of the country at large as a town which had gone sour," Roelif Loveland wrote shortly before the expo's closing. "This impression has been corrected . . . in no small degree by publicity emanating from Cleveland. Cleveland finally gave 'em something to talk about besides municipal woe." William Ganson Rose, Cleveland historian and publicity counselor to the exposition, delivered his matured assessment a decade later. "This exposition did more than advertise Cleveland and stimulate business and employment during these critical years," he wrote in 1950, "it fostered enthusiasm and pointed the way to district recovery."

Legacies aren't measured solely in concrete or in monetary returns, however; they may also take form in cultural inspiration. Among the cultural legacies of the Great Lakes Exposition may be counted three Cleveland museums. Dunham Tavern, an early stagecoach stop and hostelry on Euclid Avenue, was nearly a century old and threatened by the encroachment of neighboring blight at the time of the expo in 1936. Landscape architect A. Donald Gray had campaigned for its preservation and included a model of the historic structure in the Horticultural Gardens he designed for the exposition. A group of like-minded citizens joined Gray to organize the Dunham Tavern Corporation that year, which restored the former inn as an example and museum of Cleveland's pioneer period.

The Cleveland Health Museum was also inspired at least in part by the exposition. It might be said to have come out of the health section of the Making of a Nation theme exhibit in the 1937 expo. Much of that display, including the Camp Transparent Woman, had been pulled together by the Cleveland Academy of Medicine, which had led in the incorporation of a Cleveland Health Museum the previous December. When the museum acquired and opened its own home on Euclid Avenue in the 1940s, one of its major exhibits was a transparent woman dubbed Juno. Though it ceased to operate as an independent institution early in the twenty-first century, many of the Health Museum's exhibits and activities were to be continued under the aegis of the Cleveland Museum of Natural History.

As the Great Lakes Exposition was being dismantled in 1937, Cleveland industrialist Frederick C. Crawford decided to buy a used car from the Varied Industries Building. It was a vintage 1910 Duryea, and Crawford purchased it as the premier exhibit for the automobile museum he had dreamed of establishing under the sponsorship of his company, the automotive parts manufacturer Thompson Products (later TRW). By the time the Thompson Auto Album opened on Chester Avenue in 1943,

Industrialist Frederick C. Crawford (center) cut a ribbon to mark the opening of the Crawford Auto-Aviation Museum of the Western Reserve Historical Society in 1965. Flanking him were society trustees Fred Wise and Herman Vail. They were grouped around a 1901 Toledo Steamer, but the genesis of the collection was a 1910 Duryea which Crawford had purchased from an exhibitor at the Great Lakes Exposition. *Cleveland Press* Collection.

Crawford had amassed a collection of close to thirty historic vehicles. "It is entirely conceivable that the Thompson Museum some day will be part of a much greater institution that preserves the history of Cleveland's achievements as a whole," read an early promotional brochure. That happened in 1965, when the Frederick C. Crawford Auto-Aviation Museum, one of the nation's largest automotive museums, reopened as part of the Western Reserve Historical Society in University Circle.

The cultural legacy of the Great Lakes Exposition eventually spread far beyond Cleveland. Billy Rose's Aquacade had an afterlife of its own. Of necessity, he left behind the unwieldy floating stage he had had constructed in Cleveland, where it served for a summer of light opera in 1938. *Rio Rita, Gay Divorce,* and *Show Boat* were among the productions seen on the former aquastage. Meanwhile Rose, with the assistance of Lincoln Dickey, Peg Humphrey, and Floyd Zimmerman from the Great Lakes expo, prepared a revival of Aquacade for the New York World's Fair in 1939. As it had in Cleveland, it became the hit of the New York fair and also of the San Francisco expo in 1940. For once, however, Clevelanders could affect boredom and say they'd been there, done that.

Perhaps the most unlikely cultural legacy of the Great Lakes Exposition was its reproduction of Shakespeare's Globe Theatre. Although it failed to survive beyond the first season, the Great Lakes version of the Old Globe made several lasting contributions to the American and British stages. John Kennedy, who had gained the plaudits of Cleveland critics, achieved success on Broadway under the name of Arthur Kennedy. Wayne McKeekan became even more renowned on stage and screen as David Wayne.

It was Sam Wanamaker, however, who was most deeply affected by his season in Cleveland's Old Globe. He collected acting and directing credits on both sides of the Atlantic but established residence in London in the 1950s. Finding Shakespeare's Old Globe long gone, Wanamaker became obsessed with the idea of reconstructing it on or near its original site on the south bank of the Thames. For a quarter-century he campaigned to raise funds and support for the project, which finally came to fruition three years after his death in 1993. When questioned about the motivation behind his quixotic pursuit, Wanamaker invariably would reminisce about his season of Shakespearean rep at the Great Lakes Exposition.

■

One intended legacy of the exposition was soon neglected, forgotten, and nearly lost. "For decades we have struggled with the problem of what to do about our lakefront," wrote Cleveland printer and civic promoter William Feather in his house organ on the eve of the expo's opening. "The solution seemed decades away, but suddenly we were given the answer. With this fine start there will be no halt now. What has been a shambles will be a place of permanent beauty." Many shared this resolution. "From now on Cleveland is going to have a downtown waterfront in which the people can take permanent pride and pleasure," editorialized the *Cleveland Press*. "Clevelanders will never let it go back again to wasteland."

Building on the lakefront development initiated by the Great Lakes Exposition became a general refrain over the next few years. At the end of the first season, the Come-to-Cleveland Committee released a plan to "carry forward the tremendous civic momentum of 1936." Foremost among its proposals were such lakefront projects as a municipal park and downtown airport on the expo site, improved beach and bathing facilities, and completion of a lakefront highway. "This committee feels the greatest single factor in the development of Cleveland within the next two years must be the lake front project," read its report. "The interest of Clevelanders is now centered on the possibilities of our lake front."

A year later, the *Cleveland News* sponsored a contest for the best proposal for lakefront development. Civic gadfly Peter Witt boldly called for a park extending from West 3rd Street all the way eastward to Gordon Park. "Let the people have the lakefront for themselves," he wrote. "Here's a city with 17 miles of lakefront and no place to get at it." One of the last survivors from the administration of the populist mayor Tom L. Johnson, Witt asseverated that the city should simply appropriate the lakefront, letting those "who claim riparian rights take their claims to court and see how far they get." A more conservative proposal from a recent graduate of Western Reserve University's Flora Stone Mather College was awarded the $100 prize by the *News*. Ruth Marie Benes's winning plan included a public park from Municipal Stadium to East 9th Street and a downtown airport in the former expo amusement area.

Earlier the *News* had summarized the proposals as falling into two general classifications: "A—Development of the lakefront area into a downtown park. B—Development into a huge terminal for marine transportation." Before long it was evident that the real winner was choice B. While the area east of 9th Street, including the expo's Goodyear blimp field, was developed after World War II into Burke Lakefront Airport, the land from 9th Street westward was dominated by port development.

Between the stadium and East 9th Street, where once fluttered pennants over the Hall of Progress and the Automotive Building, was merely a graveled lot, which provided parking for baseball and football games. Perhaps Winsor French had that empty space in mind when he wrote in 1952, "But for once we had some big-time stuff flourishing along the lakefront. There is also the possibility it could happen again and there is no use in pouring too much salt into old wounds." It didn't happen again in Winsor's time, and a bleak midwinter night scene on the East Ninth pier in the 1984 film *Stranger Than Paradise* seemed a metaphor for urban isolation and desolation.

Yet visions of lakefront development for the city's people never died completely. "The immense success of the Great Lakes Exposition of 1936–37 had made that point so well that even though many self-serving proposals were made in the intervening years, the saving of the land for the people had become increasingly a leitmotif of the city's planning," wrote Evan H. Turner, director of the Cleveland Museum of Art, on the eve of a lakefront renaissance in 1985.* The stadium parking lot was about to be excavated for an inner North Coast Harbor, bordered by greenery and museums. There were even a couple of incidental tie-ins

---

*Evan H. Turner, postscript to Holly M. Rarick, *Progressive Vision: The Planning of Downtown Cleveland, 1903–1930* (Cleveland: Cleveland Museum of Art, 1986), 87.

with the exposition of half a century earlier. The iron-ore carrier *William G. Mather*, represented by a scale model in the Cleveland-Cliffs Iron Company's expo exhibit, was now berthed there in its 618-foot entirety as a floating museum of the Great Lakes iron and steel heritage. Over in the Coast Guard basin, where the S-49 had offered expo-goers a look inside a submarine, the USS *Cod*, a World War II sub, was similarly open for inspection.

■

There are even bigger plans and wider visions waiting in the wings. "I'm a Burnham disciple as it relates to his vision to promote waterfront access as far as this city is concerned," says Chris Ronayne, a former Cleveland city planning director. "For the first hundred years, people were trying to get away from waterfront conditions, both for reasons of health and because of industrial development. Not intentionally, we walled ourselves off from the waterfront, a condition that continued all through the twentieth century."

As planning director, Ronayne promoted a waterfront district plan, "Connecting Cleveland," intended to breach the wall separating the city from its lakefront. Encompassing the entire shoreline from Edgewater Park to Gordon Park, the plan calls for moving the Port of Cleveland, to free up the downtown waterfront for recreational and residential development. The West Shoreway would be downscaled to a boulevard, allowing easier access to the lake. Landfill on the east side would provide increased space for parks and marinas. "The vision is multiple: recreational, residential, commercial/industrial. There's a place for all of it," says Ronayne. "It's the first comprehensive waterfront district plan."

People are also thinking again of the Great Lakes in regional terms. Although no longer the world's steelmaking center, the Great Lakes contain the region's greatest reservoir of fresh water, which may soon be more valuable than steel. A Great Lakes–St. Lawrence River Basin Water Resources Compact has been drafted by eight American states and two Canadian provinces to guard against the diversion of that resource to less-favored regions. Another potential resource in the Great Lakes is energy, not in the mold of Dr. Abbott's solar energy engine of 1937 but as wind power. "The best wind in the Midwest is out of the Great Lakes," said David H. Matthiesen, associate professor of materials science and engineering at Case Western Reserve University, where a Great Lakes Institute for Energy Innovation is exploring energy sources of the future. A single modern wind turbine now gyrating in front of the Great Lakes Science Center may be the harbinger of things to come. It happens to be standing near the intersection of Marine Plaza and Blossom Way on the old exposition grounds.

One intended legacy of the Great Lakes Exposition that was nearly forgotten over the years was the development of the downtown lakefront into a recreational area. For two summers, at least, visitors in Streets of the World had been able to promenade right along the shore of Lake Erie. With the creation of North Coast Harbor and Voinovich Park in the 1980s, the dream was partially revived. Author's Collection.

Cleveland has a history of conceiving and implementing big ideas—plans that in their time may have appeared beyond the city's resources. At a time when it was the nation's fifth-largest city, it erected an oversized auditorium and stadium and proceeded to fill them, time and again. In the 1920s, the Van Sweringen Brothers raised the country's tallest skyscraper outside of New York as the centerpiece of a Terminal Group that rivaled Rockefeller Center. After World War II, Clevelanders developed an art museum and symphony orchestra that are each ranked among the world's best. At the end of the twentieth century, the Gateway project proved that civic vision had not disappeared.

Perhaps it stems from the influence of Daniel H. Burnham, author of the city's 1903 Group Plan. "Make no little plans," Burnham had famously enjoined. "They have no magic to stir men's blood, and probably themselves will not be realized. Make big plans, aim high in hope and work, remembering that a noble and logical diagram once recorded will be a living thing, asserting itself with ever growing insistency." On the hundredth anniversary of the Group Plan in 2003, officials fittingly recognized its author by references to the "Burnham Mall." It is more important, however, that Cleveland keep his advice in mind.

The Great Lakes Exposition was a big plan, bold enough to claim its place alongside the city's grandest and best. It may not have left as visible a legacy as the others, but the memory of its enterprise and bravado remains as a beacon for the future.

■

Three-quarters of a century after the event, those who can still remember the Great Lakes Exposition had to have seen it at an early age. They are the memories of youth and even childhood, such as Fred Schuld's awe over the bulletproof glass in Dillinger's car. The expo was part of their rites of passage, and its lessons weren't always easy or pleasant. John Straka learned the value of a Depression dime when he squandered it on a deceptively ballyhooed sideshow; Bob Andree endured even harsher instruction when his pocket was picked at the Old Globe Theatre.

Most of the memories were pleasant ones. Straka got better value for his money at the orange sherbet concession of the Florida exhibit. "That was something new at the time—man, was that tasty," he says. Andree had better memories of the Aquacade the year after his Old Globe experience. "I had never seen precision swimming before. I was just eleven—it was hard to believe."

Working as a young sound technician in 1937, William L. Murtough was assigned to engineer remote broadcasts from the dance bands at Aquacade over the Mutual radio network. "My announcer was a college drop-out named Robert E. Lee," he wrote from retirement in Florida. (A native of Elyria, Lee would soon abandon radio to coauthor such stage hits as *Inherit the Wind* with Cleveland-born Jerome Lawrence.) Murtough found the exposition's "fair-like atmosphere" so exciting he didn't mind the eighteen-mile commute between the lakefront and his day job at Geauga Lake. "One day I was leaning over plugging microphones in when Johnny [Weissmuller] walked by and gave me a big slap on the pants with his wet hands," he recalls. "Funny what you can remember when you're 90 years old."

Dick Panek attended several times each summer on a student pass from Cleveland's Wilbur Wright Junior High School. The "carnival-type things" of the midway held less attraction for him than some of the exhibits in the Hall of Progress, where he was chosen to make one of the free long-distance telephone calls from the Ohio Bell booth. "That was a pretty big thing back then," he remembers. "I called my grandfather and grandmother in Massillon. They were shocked to hear from me." Panek also was allowed to pull the switch that lit the fifty-thousand-watt bulb in the General Electric exhibit.

Only nine years old in 1937, Cynthia Reese motored with her family to the expo from their home in Hudson. "But that was a very memorable trip for a child," she recalls. "I'll never forget the exposition." It was the Florida spread, with its Tara-like plantation house, that remains most vividly in her memory. "When we walked past . . . they would spray you with perfume—orange blossom perfume. They stood outside the exhibit; they had atomizers," she explains. "And oh, how I loved that orange blossom scent, and I wanted some—but it was still the tail end of the Depression, and just coming in from Hudson was expensive enough. We didn't spend money like that." Though she never was to get any orange blossom perfume for herself, the scent is still stored in her memory bank. "Oh, it was just heavenly."

Despite his losses in the second season, even Herman Pirchner had largely positive memories of the exposition. "It was a good thing for Cleveland. People came from all over America," he stated. "There was always some celebrity coming—every week." He gave Cleveland's exposition an edge over even the much larger New York World's Fair, which he visited a couple of years later. "It was too spread out—the people were too spread out," he said of the later event. "People like the energy of thousands."

For Bob Andree, who never attended any of the other world's fairs, Cleveland's show remained "an eye-popper for me. The fact that two miles were built along the lakeshore was just incredible." He doubts that anything like it could be done again, in Cleveland or anywhere else for that matter. "That kind of show kind of passed away," he says. "I was asked once what it would cost today, and I said probably twenty times what it cost then, which was $25 million."

■

Nothing remains on-site and little enough elsewhere. Four trees from either the Horticultural Gardens or the Florida exhibit were transplanted to the Cleveland Greenhouse in Rockefeller Park. Fred Crawford's 1910 Duryea is still on view at the Western Reserve Historical Society. Perhaps the most substantial remnant of the Great Lakes Exposition is a seven-ton block of Georgian marble fashioned into the sculpture of a semi-nude seated female, her head cradled in an uplifted arm (*pace*, Almon Shaffer).

It is William McVey's *Awakening*, lent by the Cleveland Museum of Art in 1936 to the expo's Horticultural Gardens. Never reclaimed by the museum, it remained in the Donald Gray Gardens long after the exposition. This was the "big statue of a woman" on which the Franko children would pose for family snapshots. Located originally at the western edge of the gardens, it was transposed to the opposite end at some point, probably

Some of the longest lingering memories of the Great Lakes Exposition were provided by the expansive and expensive Florida exhibit, seen wrapping itself around the Higbee Tower. Among its singular experiences were a Tara-like plantation house, orange sherbet, and orange blossom perfume. Apart from the Ohio Building, it was the only stand-alone state exhibit on the grounds. Author's Collection.

Tickets to the Great Lakes Exposition were sold in a variety of forms, including special passes for high school and middle school students. Dick Panek, a student at Cleveland's Wilbur Wright Junior High, purchased student passes for both seasons of the expo. For $2.50, he received twenty general admission tickets. "I would just go down on my own," he recalls. Even after twelve to fifteen visits a summer, he still had unused tickets left in both books. Courtesy of Dick Panek.

when the gardens were downsized. Despite serious deterioration from weather, pollution, and vandals, it was salvaged when the gardens were bulldozed to make way for a new stadium.

In 2001, *Awakening* found a compatible resting place in the Woodland Gardens of the Cleveland Botanical Gardens in University Circle. Those who come upon it in that sylvan setting may, for a fleeting moment, experience a sense of the otherworldly wonder awakened in Clevelanders by the Great Lakes Exposition.

....

SOUVENIRS! EXPO SOUVENIRS HERE!

Hearing that his cousin was working on a history of the Great Lakes Exposition, Avon Lake resident Dale Hall immediately thought of an ashtray handed down to him by his mother. Made of brightly colored enamel on steel, it came from the Porcelain Enamel Building on Marine Plaza, where artist Edward Winter was firing them on-site in a demonstration of the enameling process.

Some of them bore the standard exposition logo featuring an outline of the Great Lakes. For a quarter, visitors could personalize them with their own messages, one of the more whimsical being "Sweetums, put your ashes here. Save lots of work for wifey dear." With an eye to posterity, Mrs. Hall simply had hers engraved with the name of her infant son: "Dale Ritchey Hall, 1936."

Buildings might burn, participants die, and memories fade, but souvenirs have a life of their own. Even after the original owners have departed, their children and heirs will preserve them—even if only to put them on eBay.

Reflecting the event's smaller size and attendance, Great Lakes Exposition souvenirs aren't nearly as ubiquitous as those from Chicago's Century of Progress or New York's World of Tomorrow. Making the rounds of estate sales, flea markets, and now Web sites, however, it's surprising how many Great Lakes items eventually make their appearance.

Most of them fall into fairly common souvenir categories, such as pennants and pillows. One Great Lakes pennant features the expo's logo in white against a deep blue field; another shows some of the main buildings in burnt orange on a dark brown background, as if to harbinger the coming of the Cleveland Browns. A garish pillow displays the pylons of the main entrance and the artificial aurora borealis in flaming red in a black nighttime sky.

There are glass tumblers printed with scenes in expo blue and red; a brass ashtray/coaster with the Court of the Presidents raised in relief;

a heavy brass thermometer in the shape of a large key with the expo logo on its handle; a hot pad insulated with aluminum paper depicting expo sights; oval glass paperweights with views of the main entrance or the Automotive Building; die-cut copper bookmarks and letter openers picturing the ill-fated Horticultural Building in pink or baby blue.

One of the most treasured mementos seems to be a cast-iron model of a Greyhound expo tour bus, like the ones used on the grounds. Each bus, close to a foot in length, including cab and passenger van, was painted blue and white, like the originals. People will bring them for show-and-tell to programs on the exposition. Others will bring wooden canes with the Great Lakes imprint, awarded as prizes by weight-guessers on the midway.

Postcards constitute a double-duty collectible, having appeal for both exposition and postcard buffs. Great Lakes expo examples come in color as well as black and white. Some of the color scenes appear also in accordion-pleated folders containing nine double-sided cards. At least three souvenir booklets of expo views were also available.

Even the U.S. government got into the souvenir business, when it issued a commemorative half dollar in observance of the Cleveland centennial, featuring Moses Cleaveland's profile on the obverse and the Great Lakes Exposition logo on the reverse. Fifty thousand of them were minted and placed on sale at expo entrances for $1.50 apiece. Over the course of seven decades they proved to be worth the initial premium, for their value rose steadily to upwards of $35.

Flattened copper pennies now bear raised images of the main entrance, the expo logo, the Automotive Building, or the East 9th subway on their slightly curved oval surfaces. Possibly they were stamped in a concession on the Court of the Presidents or on the midway, or both. Whether the sacrifice of the original coin was borne by the concessionaire or by the customer is a matter of conjecture.

Souvenir good-luck pieces of brass, the size of a half dollar, with a horseshoe and four-leaf clover on one side and Great Lakes expo on the other, were handed out to those who visited Standard Drug's store on the grounds on Standard Drug Day. Mementos of the Grasselli Chemical Corporation exhibit in the Lakeside Exhibition Hall come in the form of a nearly two-by-three-inch metal plate bearing the profile of Moses Cleaveland on top and listing various Grasselli products and services on the other side. A hole is drilled near one edge, but it makes a better paperweight than pendant.

And the catalog goes on: a bottle opener with spoon; potpourri in a small straw basket; a red felt overseas cap; a cigarette lighter with a picture of the Terminal Tower; a penguin standing on a shell, probably from Byrd's South Pole ship; a pin box with cushioned lid. . . .

Amid such a cornucopia of eye-catching keepsakes, one in particular grabs the passerby and shouts, "Look at me!" Stored in the attic of the Western Reserve Historical Society, it's a large conch shell set in a plaster base, the whole about a foot in height. Three smaller shells are embedded in the corners of its triangular base. An electrical wire issuing from the bottom suggests that the main shell was lit from inside.

Printed on the base is the legend "1937 Great Lakes Exposition." A tropical scene on the conch with palm trees, sea gulls, and sunset suggests that it almost certainly was sold at the Florida exhibit. John Grabowski, research director at the Historical Society, has bestowed on it the distinction of "ugliest lamp in the world."

He may be right. If the expo lamp has any serious competition, it would probably be the infamous "leg lamp" from the movie *The Christmas Story*. With the recent opening of the *Christmas Story* museum house in Tremont, however, Cleveland may rest assured that, whichever merits the title, it has both of them.

Great Lakes Expo— By the Numbers

Dates: June 27, 1936–October 12, 1936   108 days
        May 29, 1937–September 26, 1937   121 days
        TWO-YEAR TOTAL   229 DAYS

Size: Grounds   125–35 acres, overall
                    Streets of the World: 10 acres
                    Horticultural Gardens: 3½ acres

        Buildings   201 (by one estimate)
                    Midway: Approximately 50
                    Streets of the World: More than 100

        Seating Capacities
                    Sherwin-Williams Plaza (1936)—4,000
                    Parade of the Years (1936)—4,000
                    Alpine Village (1936 and 1937)—1,000
                        (inside and outside)
                    Old Globe Theatre (1936)—600
                    Aquacade (1937)—5,000
                    Winterland (1937)—3,000
                    Town Hall (*The Drunkard,* 1937)—1,400

Construction: Time—80 days
                Workers (exclusive of WPA)—2,844

Initial Investment: 1936: $1.115 million

                      1937: $0.5 million

Estimated Value of Plant: $25 million to $30 million

Nationalities Represented in Streets of the World:
                      1936:   38
                      1937:   39

Yearly Attendance: 1936:3,979,229
                      1937:   3,518,740
          Two-year total: 7,497,969

Highest Daily Attendance:
                      1936:   125,192 (September 6, 1936)
                      1937:   105,819 (August 14, 1937)

A Day at the Expo

WEDNESDAY, SEPT. 6, 1936*

This is Daughters of Eastern Star Day
    Berea Day
    Cleveland Real Estate Board Day
    White Shrine of Jerusalem Day

9 A.M.
  Gates open

9 A.M. to 10 P.M.
  Great Lakes Exposition Art Exhibit, Cleveland Museum of Art, University Circle

10 A.M. to 10 P.M.
  U.S. Government Exhibits, Hall of Progress

10 A.M. to 10 P.M.
  Ohio Building, display of relics of Zoar Village, Ohio's first communal settlement

10 A.M. to 10 P.M.
  Westinghouse Exhibit, playlet, "Leisure for Living," in air-conditioned theatre, Hall of Progress

---

*From mimeographed "Program of Events," probably distributed at gates.

10 A.M. to 10 P.M.
Ohio Bell Telephone Exhibit demonstration, "Hear Your Own Voice," Hall of Progress

10 A.M. to 10 P.M.
General Electric Exhibit, lighting largest incandescent lamp in the world, Hall of Progress

11 A.M. to 11 P.M.
Firestone Exhibit, Marionette Show and Motion Pictures

11:40 A.M. and hourly until 8:40 P.M.
Electrical League Exhibit, Puppet Show, "Comedy in the Kitchen," Hall of Progress

12:30 to 4:30 P.M.
Hall of the Great Lakes, dancing, modeling, art craft playlets by City Recreation Division

2 P.M.
Concert by Orange Blossom Quartet, Florida Exhibit. Others at 3:30, 5:30, 7 and 8:30 P.M.

2 P.M.
"As You Like It," Old Globe Theatre, Amusement Zone

2:15 P.M.
Parade of the Years, Drama of America's Development in Terms of Transport, Blossom Way

2:30 P.M.
Style Revue of the May Company, Marine Theatre

2:30 P.M.
Hall of the Great Lakes, Home Hygiene and Care of the Sick demonstration by American Red Cross Nurses. Also at 7 P.M.

3 P.M.
Streets of the World, International Revue with German Band and Belgian Wooden Shoe Dancers

3 P.M.

Play-by-play Baseball Scores, Sherwin-Williams Plaza

3 P.M.

"Taming of the Shrew," Old Globe Theatre, Amusement Zone

3 P.M.

Hall of the Great Lakes, Red Cross First Aid demonstration. Also at 7:30 P.M.

3 to 5 P.M.

Prof. Gower and his strolling Band, Amusement Zone

3 to 5 P.M.

Pottery-making demonstrations, Horticultural Building

3 P.M.

Hall of the Great Lakes, Berea Day special demonstration. Also at 7 P.M.

3 to 3:45 P.M.

Radioland in Sherwin-Williams Plaza, all-star radio show with the Oleanders Quartet, Mary Lou Moore and Freddie Weper's Radioland Orchestra

3:30 P.M.

U.S. Coast Guard demonstration in boat-capsizing, Lake Erie off Marine Theatre

3:30 P.M.

Hall of the Great Lakes, Rescue Work by Cleveland Fire Department. Also at 8 P.M.

4 P.M.

Spectacular Water Show with Pee Jay Ringens in a 125-foot dive, Marine Theatre

4 P.M.

"A Midsummer Night's Dream," Old Globe Theatre, Amusement Zone

4:15 P.M.

Parade of the Years, Drama of America's Development in Terms of Transport, Blossom Way

4:45 to 5:30 P.M.
   Marine Theatre, Concert by Berea Band

5 P.M.
   Retreat Parade by Company "I," 11th U.S. Infantry, U.S. Army Camp

5 P.M.
   Streets of the World, International Revue with German Band and
   Belgian Wooden Shoe Dancers

5 P.M.
   "Julius Caesar," Old Globe Theatre, Amusement Zone

6 P.M.
   Horticultural Building, Cleveland Real Estate Board dinner

6:15 P.M.
   Lowering of colors with military ceremonies, Sherwin-Williams
   Plaza

6:30 P.M.
   French Cafe, Streets of the World, Folies de Nuit, with shows at intervals until 2 A.M.

7 to 7:45 p.m.
   Sherwin-Williams Plaza, Berea program with band

7:15 P.M.
   Parade of the Years, Drama of America's Development in Terms of Trans-
   port, Blossom Way

7:30 P.M.
   Spectacular Water Show with Pee Jay Ringens in a 125-foot dive, Marine
   Theatre

7:30 P.M.
   "Taming of the Shrew," Old Globe Theatre, Amusement Zone

7:30 to 10:30 P.M.
   Prof. Gower and his strolling Band, Amusement Zone

8 P.M.

Streets of the World, International Revue with German Band, Belgian Wooden Shoe Dancers, Russian dancers and Polish dancers

8 to 9 P.M.

Radioland in Sherwin-Williams Plaza, all-star radio show with the Oleanders Quartet and Radioland Orchestra, led by Freddie Weper

8:30 P.M.

Style Revue of the May Company, Marine Theatre

8:30 P.M. to midnight

Firestone Exhibit, Concert by Singing Color Fountains

8:30 P.M.

"A Comedy of Errors," Old Globe Theatre, Amusement Zone

9:15 P.M.

Parade of the Years, Drama of America's Development in Terms of Transport, Blossom Way

9:30 P.M.

Streets of the World, International Revue by German Band, Belgian Wooden Shoe Dancers, Russian dancers and Polish dancers

9:30 P.M.

"King Henry VIII," Old Globe Theatre, Amusement Zone

10 P.M.

Exhibit Buildings close

10:30 P.M.

Streets of the World, complete revue by Belgian Wooden Shoe Dancers

Midnight

Amusements and rides close

2 A.M.

French Cafe, Streets of the World, last performance of Folies de Nuit

(NOTE—The Art Exhibit at the Cleveland Museum of Art, University Circle, includes 385 of the world's most famous masterpieces. Lecture by Margaret Fairbanks on, "Spanish Paintings in the Exhibition," Gallery VIII, 11 A.M. Radio Talk, WGAR, by Milton S. Fox on "Twentieth Anniversary Exhibition," 2:45 P.M. Lecture on "Florentine Painting," by William M. Milliken, Gallery V, 3:30 P.M. Lecture on "General Tour of the Exhibit," by Ann V. Horton, Gallery V, 8 P.M.)

(NOTE—Western Reserve University Exhibit—This is Cleveland College Week.)

(NOTE—Horticulture Building—Zinnia Show, Artistic Arrangements and Table Decorations.)

(NOTE—Old Globe Theatre—Punch and Judy Show; Scotch Bagpipe Band and Scotch Girl Dancer; Pageant on Village Green, all half hour before each performance.)

A Word on Sources

Those interested in researching the Great Lakes Exposition may count themselves fortunate that the event took place between the years 1933 and 1938. That's when the Ohio Writers' Project of the Works Progress Administration (WPA), among other endeavors, prepared news indexes for the *Cleveland Plain Dealer*. There are half a dozen pages of listings for stories on the expo, arranged chronologically, in the 1936 volume and four more pages in that for 1937. They were published under the title *Annals of Cleveland*. Unlike the volumes for the nineteenth century, these do not contain any excerpts or summaries, only headlines.

There are two other rewarding collections of raw data. Many, if not most, of the *Plain Dealer* articles, as well as those from the *Cleveland Press, Cleveland News,* and sundry publications from across the entire country, were mounted in scrapbooks by the exposition's public relations firm, Miskell & Sutton. Those scrapbooks have been reproduced on eighty-eight sheets of microfiche available for viewing in the Science and Technology Division of the Cleveland Public Library's Main Branch. In the same branch's Microform Center may be found microfilm copies of the *Great Lakes Expo-nent,* the official four-page weekly published out of the exposition headquarters. It was issued from December 23, 1935, to June 10, 1936, then revived from December 5, 1936, to April 21, 1937. It was the ur-source of many of the newspaper accounts that later found their way into the Miskell & Sutton scrapbooks.

One contemporary publication that merits special mention was an "Exposition Number" of the bimonthly magazine published by the Greyhound bus lines, *The Highway Traveler* 8, no. 3 (June–July 1936).This contains detailed advance coverage of the Texas Centennial, the Great Lakes

Exposition, and the second season of San Diego's Pacific International Exposition. Its thorough preview of the respective attractions of each affords a unique basis for comparison.

A variety of programs came out of Cleveland's exposition, including two official guidebooks (*Great Lakes Exposition Official Souvenir Guide*), one for each of the two summers. Approximately sixty pages in length, they are spiral-bound and profusely illustrated. The *Book of the Pageant* is a souvenir program from the 1936 transportation spectacle, *Parade of the Years*. Billy Rose's Aquacade and Winterland issued souvenir programs in 1937. The Old Globe Theatre provided weekly playbills listing repertory and casts for its tabloid Shakespearean productions. An impressive *Catalogue of the Twentieth Anniversary Exhibition of the Cleveland Museum of Art: The Official Art Exhibit of the Great Lakes Exposition* was issued by CMA in 1936, followed by a more modest *Catalogue of an Exhibition of American Painting from 1860 until Today at the Cleveland Museum of Art* in 1937.

At least three photograph booklets were published containing scenes of the grounds in black and white. The *Official Great Lakes View Book,* published by Sutcliffe Studios in 1936, is the most impressive and durable. There were also a *Souvenir of the 1936 Great Lakes Exposition* published by Harry H. Hamm and *The 1937 Great Lakes Exposition* souvenir book issued by the Ben Wheatman's News Company. All may be found at the Western Reserve Historical Society, which also has undoubtedly the most extensive collection of original exposition photographs. Among the latter are groups belonging originally to Mayor Harold H. Burton and landscape architect A. Donald Gray. The Burton and Gray papers are also among the society's holdings. Photograph holdings may also be found in the Cleveland Public Library Main Branch and the *Cleveland Press* Collection at Cleveland State University.

Several books contain material relevant to the Great Lakes Exposition. It receives authoritative, if necessarily brief, coverage in William Ganson Rose's magisterial chronicle *Cleveland: The Making of a City* (Cleveland: World, 1950), written by the expo's promotion counsel. Holly M. Rarick's *Progressive Vision: The Planning of Downtown Cleveland, 1903–1930* (Cleveland: Cleveland Museum of Art, 1986) provides useful background on how the exposition fit into the history of its lakefront location. Billy Rose and the Aquacade have prominent roles in several volumes. Stephen Nelson's *Only a Paper Moon: The Theatre of Billy Rose* (Ann Arbor, Michigan: UMI Research Press, 1987) offers the most complete account of Aquacade's genesis and its place in the history of American entertainment. Colorful material on Aquacade's producer may be found in Billy Rose, *Wine, Women and Words* (New York: Simon and Schuster, 1948), and

Polly Rose Gottleib, *The Nine Lives of Billy Rose* (New York: Crown, 1968). Providing an understandably different perspective on the erstwhile "Mr. Brice" is Herbert G. Goldman's *Fanny Brice: The Original Funny Girl* (New York: Oxford University Press, 1992).

Notice should also be taken of some of the retrospective looks at the exposition in various newspapers and periodicals, often on quinquennial anniversaries of the event. Winsor French recalled its sights and personalities in a seven-part weekly series in the *Cleveland Press,* appearing every Saturday from July 26 to September 6, 1952. Richard Widman reviewed the event twice in the *Friday* magazine of the *Cleveland Plain Dealer* for May 21, 1982, and June 27, 1986. Rory O'Connor saw it in the context of "That Rousing Summer" in *Cleveland Magazine* 15, no. 6 (June 1986). Debbie Snook contributed an article on the expo to the *Plain Dealer Magazine* of June 2, 1991. John Vacha's "Biggest Bash" appeared, lavishly illustrated, in *Timeline* 13, no. 2 (March–April 1996). One of the most recent observances was "Sex, Celebrity, and Carnival Charm" by Erick Trickey in *Cleveland Magazine* 35, no. 8 (July 2008).

Case histories cited in "Hard Times on the Cuyahoga" may be found in the proceedings of the *United States Senate, Seventy-second Congress, Second Session* (Washington: GPO, 1933), 507–9. The stories on the Nowosielski family were written by John Johnston and appeared in the *Cleveland Press,* March 6, 7, and 9, 1936.

Index

Toto Leverne (in *Folies de Nuit*), 146; Madeline Gardner as, 137; Trudye Mae Davidson as, 133–37, *136*
tourism: Cleveland seeking, 13–15, 75; Florida exhibit increasing, 69, 157
Tower of Light, Higbee's, 68
Town Hall, *The Drunkard* in, 182–83
Townsend, Francis E., 77, *78*, 79
Townsend Old Age Revolving Pension movement, 77, 79, 83
trailer camp, 153
trains, in *Parade of the Years* pageant, 66–67, *67*, 82
transportation: into Cleveland, 15–16; within exposition grounds, 12, 15, 32, 50; as theme of *Parade of the Years* pageant, 66–67
Trickey, Erick, 196
Turner, Evan H., 202
Turnfest, 85
Twentieth Anniversary Exhibition, of Cleveland Museum of Art, 93–96
Twinsburg, Gypsy encampment in, 117

unemployment, in Cleveland, 22–23, 74
Union Pacific Railroad trains in *Parade of the Years,* 67
Union Terminal, 2, 15
Upshaw, William D., 136–37
U.S. Coast Guard Station, 104
U.S. government exhibit, in Hall of Progress, 61, 156, 160
U.S. Steel, 6, 12, 41

Vadnal, Frank, 198
Vallee, Rudy, 36, 83, 91, 138
Van Buren, Martin, 52
Van Sweringen, Mantis, 7
Van Sweringen, Oris P., 7
Van Sweringen Brothers', 2, 204
Vandenberg, Arthur, 83
Varga, H. E., 56
Varied Industries Building: Automotive Building renamed, 149, 156; Crawford buying old car from, 199–200; not demolished immediately, 194; "Television City" in, 156
Velez, Lupe, 179–80, 198
views: from Court of the Great Lakes, 44–45; from Goodyear blimp, 113; of grounds, 50; from Horticultural Building, 55; of Streets of the World, 122
"villages," in Century of Progress, 119

visitors: to art exhibit associated with expo, 95–96; celebrating landmark numbers of, 83–84; celebrity, 83, 159–60, *160,* 206; failure to reach four-millionth, 138–39; memories of, 205–6; numbers for second season, 154, 162–63, 187, 188; numbers of, 90, 147; picking up with improved weather, 187; September surge in, 90, 92; to Shakespeare performances, 102–4; for special days for ethnic communities, 129
Von Seitz, Alexander, 32–33
von Suboff, Ralph, 146
Vrombaut, John 126, 138

Wade Park Manor, 13
Waldorf Special Great Lakes Exposition Lager, 20
Walker, Frank, 7
Wallace, Henry A., 83
Walsh, Jim, 128
Walter, Bruno, 143
Wanamaker, Sam, 102, 201
Warfel, Jack, 187–88; on expo midway, 98; at Newspaper Headquarters, 54; on Shakespeare performances, 101, 104; on television exhibit, 156
Warner & Swasey: initial contribution for Exposition, 6; Observatory in East Cleveland, 46
water shows: at Marine Theater, 58. *See also* Aquacade
Watson, Frank, 22
Wayne, David, 201
weather: in 1936 season, 79–80; in 1937 season, 159, 162–63, 179, 184, 187–88; rainy, 162–63, 178
wedding, in Streets of the World, 129
Weeks, Bernice, 115, *116*
weight-guessers, 114–15, 209
Weismuller, Johnny, *191,* 198, 205; in Aquacade, 170, 173, 175–76, 178–80; Velez and, 179–80
Western Reserve Historical Society, 144; exhibit of, 37; Frederick C. Crawford Auto-Aviation Museum and, *200,* 206; souvenir light at, 210
Western Reserve University Building, 53–55; lie detector exhibit in, 156; new gas discovered at, 90
Westinghouse, special lighting effects by, 47